THE NATIONAL TRUST BOOK

Adam Nicolson was born in 1957. He graduated from
Magdalene College, Cambridge, where he read English,
in 1979. He has been keenly interested in walking since
the age of thirteen; his other interests include maps, the
Hebrides and literature. He is the son of Nigel
Nicolson, author of numerous books.

Charlie Waite was born in 1949. After ten years of
acting, both in the theatre and on television, he became a
professional photographer in 1974. Landscape
photography is his speciality. He is married to an actress
and they have a daughter.

frontispiece *The Ridgeway near Streatley*

below *On Offa's Dyke at Gospel Pass*

Adam Nicolson

Photographs
by Charlie Waite

THE NATIONAL TRUST BOOK OF
Long Walks

THE NATIONAL TRUST   Pan Books London and Sydney

Copyright © Adam Nicolson 1981

Photographs © Charlie Waite 1981

Designed by Martin Richards for
The National Trust
42 Queen Anne's Gate   London SW1
and
George Weidenfeld and Nicolson Limited

This edition published 1984 by Pan Books Ltd,
Cavaye Place, London SW10 9PG
9 8 7 6 5 4 3 2

Maps by Line and Line

ISBN 0 330 28211 5

Colour separations by Newsele Litho Ltd
Filmset by Keyspools Ltd, Golborne, Lancs
Printed in Spain by
Mateu Cromo Artes Graficas, SA,
Madrid

Author's acknowledgments

I would like to thank all those who have walked with me, especially Tony Beck, Bridget Bourke, Kildare and Jake Bourke-Borrowes, Olivia Fane, James Magan, and Rebecca Nicolson.

I would also like to thank the following for their generous hospitality: William and Belinda Bell, Mrs C. de Bosdari, Mr and Mrs Timothy Edwards, James and Alvilde Lees-Milne, and my mother, Philippa McAlpine.

At Weidenfeld and Nicolson Colin Webb and Anne Dobell have both shown enormous patience and understanding, for which I am more than grateful.

Above all I would like to thank my father for his constant enthusiasm, encouragement and advice, from all of which this book has benefited greatly.

Photographer's acknowledgments

I would like to thank the following for allowing me to take photographs: the Dean and Chapter of Canterbury Cathedral, Lady Ashcombe at Wadfield and the Right Honourable Lord Geoffrey-Lloyd at Leeds Castle.

To Adam Nicolson my most grateful thanks, and to J.W. for her constant encouragement and invaluable support.

Contents

SCOTLAND

NORTH SEA

Fort William

WEST HIGHLAND
WAY

Glasgow

Edinburgh

Kirk Yetholm

St Bee's
Head

Robin Hood's Bay

IRISH SEA

COAST TO COAST
WALK

PENNINE WAY

Manchester

Prestatyn

Edale

ENGLAND

OFFA'S
DYKE
PATH

WALES

Birmingham

Chipping
Campden

COTSWOLD
WAY

St Dogmael's

Ivinghoe

PEMBROKESHIRE
COAST PATH

Amroth

RIDGEWAY

Chepstow

London

Cardiff

Bath

Avebury

Canterbury

Minehead

Winchester

PILGRIMS
WAY

Poole

Eastbourne

SOUTH
DOWNS
WAY

SOUTH WEST PENINSULA
COAST PATH

Introduction

This book is a preamble, an introduction to a handful of long walks across Britain. All of them are over eighty miles from end to end, and the longest is over five hundred. They are only a selection of the many possible long distance paths across Britain – the Ramblers' Association acknowledge over fifty – but they are fairly spread over the extraordinarily various landscapes to be found in this country. Two of them, the Pembrokeshire and South-West Peninsula Coast Paths, follow the notched western coastline of the island. The Coast to Coast Walk, which is the best, starts on the Yorkshire coast at Robin Hood's Bay and crosses the breadth of England to the west coast of Cumbria. In the south there are three walks along the fingers of down that spread out from the central palm of chalk in Hampshire and Salisbury Plain – the Ridgeway along the Berkshire Downs and the Chilterns; the Pilgrims' Way on the North Downs; and the South Downs Way across the width of Sussex. The Cotswold Way, from Bath to Chipping Campden, is the fourth of the walks along the steeply scarped hills of southern England. Offa's Dyke Path roughly follows the border between England and Wales, for much of the time on or beside the eighth-century earthwork built by Offa, King of Mercia, against the Welsh. The Pennine Way is the hardest and the dirtiest. It is the only walk in this book which is worth doing once and once only. At the end of every other the satisfaction of having finished is more equally balanced by the regret that it is over. The tenth is the West Highland Way, the only one in Scotland, passing through the Highlands from Glasgow to Fort William.

Six of these walks are along routes laid out by the Countryside Commission, and one is the work of the Countryside Commission for Scotland. The Pilgrims' Way has in parts been used as the basis for a North Downs Way. The Cotswold Way is the creation of Gloucestershire County Council. Only the Coast to Coast Walk, the idea of A. Wainwright, the doyen of all Cumbrian walkers, is not an official route.

For the walker following such a route means no more than the occasional signpost with an acorn symbol embossed on it, or in Scotland a yellow thistle. In all except a very few places these signposts have been provided with the utmost tact and economy, appearing exactly where you need them, and only rarely emphasising a choice of route which would

have been obvious anyway. Oddly, they are more welcome in wilder places, where they can be a marvellous indication, when half-lost or in mist, that you are on the right track; in farmland a sudden cluster of them seems like nannying. Otherwise, being on a Countryside Commission path means only that there are stiles and footbridges which in other places would have disappeared years ago. These are things which you would notice only if they were not there.

Many people might think that it would be better to have no organisation at all, but the number of town-dwellers who have taken to walking means that this is impossible. A fifth of the British population now go for a walk of several miles at least once a week. The Countryside Commission's job is to prepare us for the countryside and it for us. Their delicate task is to deal with the ignorance and misunderstanding with which the relationship between town- and country-dweller is fraught. They perform it admirably. Only once in all the walking this book has involved have I been thrown off anybody's land. This incident (in the Yorkshire Wolds) was the single exception to the hundreds of friendly meetings I have had across Britain. For the general acceptance of strangers on paths across private land the diplomacy and carefulness of the Countryside Commission must be thanked.

Their work is mostly invisible. Despite the acorns and arrows each of these walks becomes a personal adventure, full of personal discovery. That is the pleasure of walking: the abandonment of all vehicles and the dropping of any kind of barrier between you and the landscape. You are on your own and the geology, geography and history of this island all become tangible; you get to know them through the soles of your feet. The differences between limestone and gritstone – one producing endless carpets of turf, the other peaty mud, which in Lancashire is called 'slutch'; between beaches made of the liquid sand of sedimentary rocks and of the large-grained gritty sand of igneous rocks; between the level backs of chalk downs and the deeply dissected nature of hills made of less pervious rock; between the unenclosed heights of Welsh mountains and the carefully divided slopes of all but the highest Pennines; between the settlement patterns of the Celtic and the Saxon lands – all these deep geographical and historical structures have an effect on such ordinary aspects of the walker's life as how dirty he gets, how quickly he can walk, how bored he will be, how many stiles he must cross, how likely he is to find a café in the next few miles. To go for a long walk is to enter into and subject oneself to the physical conditions and processes which have dictated the lives and actions of men in various parts of Britain. There is no better way of getting a sense both of the degree to which human beings have moulded our landscape and at the same time of how superficial and temporary that apparently massive contribution is. It is an elaboration merely of a surface which is shaped by two giant forces – the weather above, and the deep slow movements of volcanic and mountain-making energies below. At any one moment the look of the earth is the product of those two powers, one reducing, one elevating, each acting on the other.

Such a global perspective can be reductive. Since we are between Ice Ages, you might say, what could it matter, for example, that Glasgow City Centre has been half-destroyed by its new urban motorways? But such a view is not the prevalent one. In Britain we automatically regret the substitution of the present for the past. One of the most potent of our myths is that a perfect Britain once existed, but is now almost completely lost. Strangely, this golden age does not occupy one static position in the past, but advances just one step behind the present. In the eighteenth century Oliver Goldsmith looked back about twenty years, to the time before villages became deserted at the whim of landowners. Crabbe thought he was witnessing the destruction of rural England when he saw the landscape being divided up by the Enclosure Commissioners. Cobbett looked back about forty years to an England of beauty and fairness, while Hardy set his novels about the same distance into the past. Perhaps Laurie Lee's Gloucestershire of the 1930s constitutes our present dream of a lost England. But there is no need to bewail the disappearance of the landscape. As this book and the photographs in it show, it is still there, as beautiful as it ever was, if not exactly the same. After doing these walks I have come to realise that the best way in which to appreciate the landscapes of this country is not purely in an aesthetic, visual way, but in terms of the processes, both physical and historical, which have made and continue to make them. Those landscapes which retain their suppleness, their ability to change, that is to distinguish between change and destruction, are better places in which to live and work than those which are preserved, where insistence on a perfect, stilled external appearance denies any vibrancy in the life of the inhabitants. That is the difference between

preservation and conservation: one forbids change, the other controls it; one is suitable for works of art, such as great houses or great landscape parks, the other for villages, towns, working places. Conservation is the more difficult and subtler task. It involves allowing silos to be built next to sixteenth-century barns, and buses to park in the middle of old market towns. It involves the admission that if you are to have cars you need oil refineries, and if you are to have gravel drives you need gravel pits. For preservation the guiding spirit is the word 'No'. But preserving a village often kills it, as has happened in some places in Sussex and the Cotswolds. It is important to realise that the landscape is a process, whose beauty consists in its being written, rubbed out and written again, never in quite the same way.

When starting on a walk the first consideration is where you will spend your nights. Camping means carrying a great deal, but the modern backpacking technology is so good that you can easily fit tent, sleeping bag, stove, food, maps and spare clothes into a rucksack weighing twenty pounds or less. But this equipment is expensive, and there is something rather contradictory in going out to enjoy the natural life with a sack full of the highest technology. Besides, even twenty pounds can become too much to carry at the end of a long day.

The alternatives are Youth Hostels, whose dormitories and jolly atmosphere you either enjoy or not, and which can get booked up as much as a year in advance; or Bed and Breakfasts, which can become expensive over a ten-day walk. There is no doubt, though, that Bed and Breakfasts are the best if you can afford them. They allow you to walk unencumbered and sleep undisturbed, to start the day with food inside you and to meet some of the nicest people you could think of. Inevitably, though, such luxury will not always be available, and you will have to camp. There are enormous pleasures in this too, in being able to end the day wherever and whenever you want, and in the morning to walk a few miles to the next village for a breakfast of hot bread and bars of chocolate.

The arguments over equipment range from the virtues of woolly hats against balaclavas to framed or frameless rucksacks, thigh- or knee-length cagoules, wearing several thin jerseys or just one thick one. Most of this can be settled only by the individual. There are two things to remember. Nothing is worse than having too much to carry – the weight is felt less on the shoulders than on the soles of your feet; and in mountains the equation to bear in mind is 'Wet + Cold = Dead'. As you are bound to get cold you must not get wet. It is basically a question of being appropriate. To get dressed for the Pennine Way on the South Downs is as ridiculous as wearing stiletto heels in Snowdonia.

Not surprisingly, the greatest controversy of all settles on the feet. Most walkers wear elephantine boots. These gross, lumbering things become, for many, the seal of authenticity: with them you are a walker, without them you are not. I believe there is a good deal of Emperor's Clothes about these boots. They may be exactly what is needed for the roughest mountain walking, but for downland tracks and coast paths they are certainly not necessary. Reinhold Messner, who climbed Everest alone and without oxygen in August 1980, wore jogging shoes for at least the first half of the climb. In the light of this, wearing 5 lb walking boots on the Cotswold Way or even in Cumbria seems rather pretentious. It must be said, though, that there is real pleasure to be gained in rolling down a country lane in big boots, with the tread creaking down on to the tarmac like the tyres of a truck; but apart from that they are only more luggage. With something a little lighter on your feet walking is a much gentler experience.

It is said that a man must walk like a horse and a woman like a cow. Both of them amble, and that, I'm sure, is the way to do it, in a relaxed rather than an aggressive style, with the feeling that you are rolling the landscape easily under you, rather than making heavy progress through it. There is no reason why you should only lope along all the time. Why not run now and then or even dance? (There is the example of Will Kemp, the Shakespearean clown, who in February 1600 jigged the hundred miles from London to Norwich for a bet.)

Whichever way you do it there is physical pleasure to be had from walking – in your body's efficiency, in

> Making the kicked clover and buttercups
> Hiss with the edges of our shoes,

in the contempt you learn for distances, in the soaking you get on a summer day from wet grasses on the pathside. All this is the point of walking. It is not a way of getting fit. Walking (slowly) burns only 115 calories an hour, and besides, as Hilaire Belloc said, 'The detestable habit of walking for exercise warps the soul'.

A long walk is good for the combination of pure bodily enjoyment and the constantly changing mental stimulation. At the end of a walk I am left with the odd mixture of feeling intimately acquainted with the narrow strip of country that I have walked through and overwhelmingly ignorant and curious about everything outside it. Of course you can almost always see far beyond the immediate surroundings of the path, but all the same the main characteristic of a long walk, apart from its length, is its thinness. At times you might come to regard anything even three or four miles off-route as too much of a detour, involving half a day wasted, but it would be wrong to let your sense of final destination get so tyrannical a grip. Digressions, detours, diversions – these are the best part of a walk, as they are of a book. But however much you stray, the walk, if a little more serpentine, stays just as thin. Walking a long walk makes you realise how much you have *not* seen, and how much you have yet to learn.

It is neither all pleasure nor all comfort. It is exhausting, and in steep country difficult. It can often be boring and, when map reading becomes difficult, desperately frustrating. In bad weather on the higher hills it can be dangerous. My two most frightening moments were in the Pennines, when I fell waist-deep into a peat bog, and in Wales, when I thought three sheepdogs were going to attack simultaneously. These dogs, especially on the remoter farms, are the walker's bane. The most terrifying time is approaching the farm before the dog has emerged from hiding. You will try to sneak through unnoticed, but will invariably get caught. The thing to remember is that they are as frightened of you as you are of them. I am told that the best tactic in getting past one – although this can be embarrassing if the farmer finds you doing it – is to get down on all fours and bark back. So disconcerting is this to the dog, in theory, that it withdraws and leaves the way free through the farmyard.

A less extravagant but probably more effective way of dealing with dogs is to take one of your own: at best it frightens them off, at worst it acts as a decoy. But apart from that you must take a dog with you because it can show you how to walk. In 'Overland to the Islands' the American poet Denise Levertov suggests:

> Let's go – much as that dog goes,
> intently haphazard. . . .
>   Under his feet
> rocks and mud, his imagination, sniffing,
> engaged in its perceptions – dancing
> edgeways, there's nothing
> the dog disdains on his way,
> nevertheless he
> keeps moving, changing
> pace and approach but
> not direction – 'every step an arrival'.

That is just the way to walk a walk; give everything a sniff.

St Dogmael's to Amroth
170 miles

Pembrokeshire, as George Owen described it in 1603, is 'neither perfect square, nor long, nor round, but shaped with divers corners ... in some places concave, in some convex, but in most ... bending inwards as doth the Moon in her decreasing'. It is this sinuous line that the Pembrokeshire Coast Path follows for over 170 miles from St Dogmael's near Cardigan to Amroth on the old border with Carmarthenshire.

If you want your walking to show as an impressive distance on the map, this path, which never follows a straight line anywhere, is not for you. After 160 hard miles around the coast you will arrive at Tenby to find a signpost there that points back to the start saying 'Cardigan 28'. Pembrokeshire is a peninsula of peninsulas, and almost certainly the path that follows the coast will not be the shortest way to your destination. It is the purest kind of walking, in which you cannot pretend to be making for anywhere in particular, but must be content with your miles for their own sake.

This is not difficult since the essence of Pembrokeshire is found on its coast. A dramatic and unsuspected geological past is revealed there; and because so much of the county is in touch with the sea, marine communications have dictated its history and have left on the coast remains from every period.

Geology

Many of the rocks of Pembrokeshire are very old. On the coast opposite Ramsey Island are some of the oldest in Britain, made up of the lava and compressed ash of volcanoes that erupted at least 600 million years ago. Since then a continuous series of sedimentary rocks has been laid down in conditions varying from deep seas to forest swamps. The process of deposition has not been smooth. Pembrokeshire has twice been violently disturbed by collisions between the mobile continental plates of which the earth's surface is made up. The first of these upheavals, called the Caledonian Orogeny, raised the mountains of Scotland and North Wales, and in North Pembrokeshire twisted, folded and broke into

The Green Bridge of Wales on the unrivalled limestone coast of the Castlemartin Peninsula. Nothing could be clearer than the basic flatness of Pembrokeshire.

great mountain ranges the horizontal rock layers that had been quietly thickening for 200 million years.

In the next period only South Wales was covered by sea, to the bottom of which the eroded material from the north sank to become the Old Red Sandstone. As the floor of the sea began to rise the Carboniferous Limestone was deposited, then the Millstone Grit (when the sea had become quite shallow), to be followed finally by the Coal Measures, the product of forest swamps. 250 million years ago this accumulation was also interrupted by the second great mountain-building period, the Armorican Orogeny, which folded South Pembrokeshire into a series of regular waves, buckling and complicating the older, northern folds still more.

There is now almost no hint that once there were mountains here as great as the Alps. About 17 million years ago, the sea, when it was 200 feet higher than it is now, cut the mountains away and left the basic appearance of Pembrokeshire as a level plain. It may seem strange that waves can demolish mountains, but the same forces that planed off the '200-foot platform' can be seen at work today as the sea gradually eats into the modern Pembrokeshire coast, levelling it just as the earlier, higher sea levelled a previous landscape.

Rocks differ in their ability to withstand the demolition of the sea. It is generally true that older and igneous rocks are harder than those whose origin is in the sediment of sea-floors. The sea leaves these harder rocks as promontories and islands while exploiting the weakness of the sedimentary or fractured rocks between them to excavate bays and coves. This principle is at work on every scale from a section of coast a few yards long to the overall shape of Wales itself. Cardigan Bay, for example, has been formed in the relatively unresisting Silurian and Ordovician strata between the hard volcanics of the Lleyn peninsula in the north and the old rocks of Pembrokeshire in the south. The great cavity of St Bride's Bay has been made in the fractured Coal Measures between the resistant rocks of St David's to its north and the volcanic basalts of Skomer at the southern end.

But there is more to the Pembrokeshire coast than the interest of how it has come to look the way it does. Its appearance is strangely disturbing. Most of the country has a relaxed pastoral atmosphere which, even though exposed and a little harsh, is never violent or unwelcoming. The level sheet of green fields, with farms here and there and lanes between them, is interrupted only by a few small hills, called monadnocks, which resisted the action of the waves, and by the Preselis, which are locally called mountains,

but are really no more than hills. This agricultural Pembrokeshire extends to the cliff edge, where there is an immediate and shocking change. The sea of course is incessantly noisy and even on the stillest day never still, but more than the movement of the sea it is the rocks themselves which present an image of violence. Bands of black or plum red or orange stone, millions of tons of solid rock, have been manipulated and played with and crumpled at will into jagged graphs of past catastrophes, or into easy curves and whorls that are sheared off in mid-course. The coast of Pembrokeshire is never expansive enough to be 'magnificent scenery'. It is curiously contained and mean, even bitter in its tight, nearly ugly forms. It is this strong tightness that some of Graham Sutherland's Pembrokeshire paintings convey.

Arrivals by Sea

The first men to affect the appearance of Pembrokeshire came by sea, probably in about 5000 BC, bringing the ability to sow crops and a tradition of communal burial in Megalithic tombs. The path comes across only one of these dolmens or cromlechau (The King's Quoit near Manorbier), but many are easily within detour distance of it. They are all now denuded of the earth which once covered the stones, and so seem rather fantastic constructions, their enormous capstones teetering on the points of anything up to seven uprights. Strangely there is no evidence of the Neolithic people building stone houses for themselves, but only for their dead. It may be that their semi-nomadic life meant permanent homes were necessary only after death.

The Iron Age, in contrast, has left a great deal of evidence of its life-style. It was a militaristic era, and the many cliffed headlands of Pembrokeshire provided natural fortresses that only needed a bank and a ditch on their landward side to make them secure. These forts – you will pass over fifty of them, often dramatically cut into by cliff erosion – must have been the most horrible places in which to live, since few have a nearby water-supply and none are sheltered from the gales that blow at least thirty days a year on to this coast. Even though people did not spend all the time in these promontory forts, the fact that exposure to such hardship was ever preferable to the threatened treatment at the hands of other human beings tells us a good deal about Iron Age civilisation.

Roman rule hardly reached into Pembrokeshire and life may have changed little here while the Romans were in the rest of Britain. As Roman rule began to collapse the Celtic church – individualist, ascetic and puritan – began to grow. While communication in the

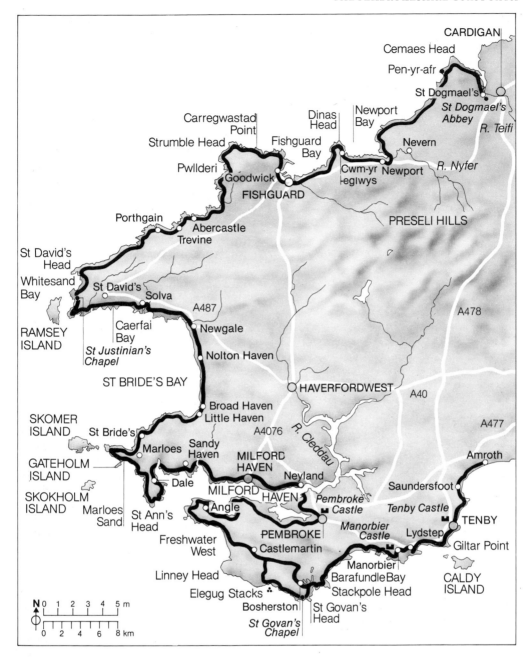

east was made more difficult by raiders from the north, the sea-routes in the west, linking with Brittany and Northern Spain, Ireland, the Isle of Man, Cornwall and Pembrokeshire, were open for the free passage of monks and hermits.

Christianity had been revitalised in the fourth century, and the new eremitic movement struck a familiar chord in Celtic culture. Before their conversion to Christianity the Celts had had a nature religion, whose solitary gods lived underground or on islands on the far side of the Ocean, and whose sanctuaries were in forests or by springs. The remains of Celtic Christianity that the path comes across show the strong continuity from the earlier religion to the Celtic church. The chapels of the saints are often not the nucleus of a village, but are hidden away in a cleft in a rock, like St Govan's near Bosherston, or sit alone on a bay where the saint may first have landed in this desert corner of the world. Thirty-three chapels in Pembrokeshire are, like the pre-Christian sanctuaries, built next to holy springs or wells, all of which were thought until recently to have healing properties.

The Vikings have a kind of ghost presence in Pembrokeshire. They were almost illiterate themselves, and so the only written evidence of their activities here is the plainly one-sided accounts of their victims – of their sacking St David's four times between 982 and 989, killing the Bishop Abraham in 1080, and eleven years later rampaging through the place

13

again. But they must have been here more permanently than this implies since there are seventeen identifiably Norse place-names in Pembrokeshire, almost all on the coast. What the Welsh had called Ynys Pyr, the Norsemen renamed Caldy; Aberdaugleddau became Milford (Milfjord) Haven; Skokholm, Grassholm and Gateholm all contain the root word *holmen*, a small island; Ramsey, Dale, Angle, Skomer and Goodwick are all Viking names, given by people who were, apparently, as much settlers and traders as rapists, and who did good business from this coast in horses, honey, malt, wheat and slaves. There is, however, no evidence at all of Viking settlement patterns in Pembrokeshire.

No other people altered the country as radically as the Normans. In 1090 Arnulph of Montgomery advanced via Cardiganshire to arrive at Pembroke. He brought with him a centralised feudal system that was quite alien to the native land-patterns of separate farms and very few villages. The difference between the imported and the indigenous styles is still visible, since the Normans, respecting the sanctity of the lands attached to the see of St David's, never moved into North Pembrokeshire. In the south they encouraged the settlement of English and Flemish immigrants. They introduced open-field systems, nucleated villages, castles and market-towns and turned the south into a model English county. There is a line, once sharp but now blurred, that separates the Welsh and English communities. This line, called the Land-scar or Landsker, reaches the coast in the north at Newgale, where the castle on the skyline at Roch protected it, and in the south at Amroth, where the eighteenth-century 'castle' stands on a Norman site. To the north of the line villages and towns have Welsh names and are more dispersed. The churches are of the plain Celtic type, with a simple belfry on one gable and no tower. In the south churches have disproportionately high battlemented towers, which served both as symbols of authority and as watch-towers and last defences. In south

St Govan's Chapel: a thirteenth-century building on a much older site. Remoteness and austerity were at the heart of Celtic christianity.

Pembrokeshire no-one can speak Welsh; villages have English names like Ambleston, Walton East, Rosemarket and Milton, and on the bi-lingual signposts it has been known for the Welsh name to be spray-painted out.

The sea was as important to the Normans as to any previous intruder into Pembrokeshire. Their defences were based very largely on the sea: the castles of Pembroke, Carew, Haverfordwest, Cardigan, Manorbier and Tenby all have access to salt water. This dependence on the sea continued until this century, so that the road-pattern is strangely lopsided: roads which are apparently important are cut off short at the coast, while villages of a good size like Trevine, between St David's and Fishguard, seem inadequately served by their roads. The reason for this is that the coastal villages communicated with each other more by sea than by land. Until the coming of the railways and improved roads, a small but vital trade in necessities was carried on between each of these villages, which were more in touch with each other than with their own hinterlands. All along the path are the now defunct remains of quays and warehouses that were used in this trade. In addition the high-quality anthracite coal that was mined in a wide outcrop bridging Pembrokeshire from St Bride's Bay, to Carmarthen Bay north of Tenby, as well as limestone from many places in the south of the county, were transported and sold up and down the coast. In almost every accessible inlet you will find the ruins of kilns – or kills as they are called locally – where limestone, off-loaded at high-tide, was burnt and the crumbly alkaline powder then taken in carts to be spread over the neighbouring fields.

Milford Haven

In the past twenty years Milford Haven has seen a more massive and concentrated development of Pembrokeshire's seaboard than at any time in its history. The Haven, originally a river valley drowned by the rising sea at the end of the last Ice Age, has long been known as Britain's best harbour. Defoe reported: 'some say a thousand sail of ships may ride in it, and not the topmast of one be seen from another'. Nelson, perhaps rather showing off his cosmopolitan knowledge, said that only Trincomalee in Ceylon could rank with it as a natural harbour. Despite this, it was not until the late 1950s that the full potential was realised – or needed – of a harbour that had a deepwater channel of 50 feet at all states of the tide. The new supertankers, weighing 100,000 tons and more, needed such a draught, and the oil companies moved in. Texaco, Esso, Gulf and Amoco all built refineries here, and BP built an ocean terminal from which it pumps oil to its refinery at Llandarcy near Swansea. By 1974 Milford Haven had become Britain's largest port in terms both of tonnage of shipping and of cargo handled. In that year 59,192,994 tons of cargo, over 99 per cent of it oil, were carried to and from the port. The four refineries can together process 8,575,000,000 gallons of oil a year, while BP pumps another 1,225,000,000 gallons to Llandarcy. The power station on the southern shores of the Haven at full load burns 17,000 gallons of oil a minute. The oil all comes, and much of it leaves, by sea, in tankers that have grown relentlessly larger, so that 250,000 tonners are now not rare, while several of over 300,000 tons have berthed here.

It takes two days to walk around Milford Haven, and the sight of these monstrous ships being edged slowly to their berths on the long pier-heads, of the spiky and foreign appearance of the refineries and of the unchanged look of the Pembrokeshire fields around and between them makes this one of the most fascinating landscapes in Britain.

***

St Dogmael's to Fishguard 28 miles

The start is at St Dogmael's, about two miles from Cardigan on the banks of the Teifi. Here is the ruin of a Norman abbey, founded in the twelfth century in an aggressively Welsh part of Pembrokeshire. In 1191, before completion, it was badly damaged in a Welsh revolt and subsequently repaired, only to suffer again a century later during the troubles connected with the Edwardian conquest of Wales. The remains still show the patching needed after both these partial destructions. (The Welshness of St Dogmael's has not changed: on the sign-board at the entrance to the village 'St Dogmael's' has been painted out to leave only 'Llandudoch' legible below it.)

The path leaves the small town along the banks of the River Teifi just as it starts to widen into an estuary. This is the mouth of the best salmon river in Wales, which may have influenced the siting of the Norman abbey. A good supply of fish was vital for the monks' diet and they secured exclusive rights to the salmon here, which are in season all year round. The garrulous Pembrokeshire Elizabethan, George Owen, enthused at length about these fish: 'In winter, when in most places they are found kipper, lean and unwholesome, here they are new fresh, fat and cruddy.' The monks got them at their plumpest: 'This fish is best in season at his first coming from the sea, where he goes to wash himself, and returneth into the river, most bright and shining, fat and delicate.'

The estuary is filled with the wide Poppit Sands, and at the edge by mud-flats on which small boats sit askew at low tide between drainage channels fringed with mats of Sea Purslane. Two miles from St Dogmael's you enter the Pembrokeshire Coast National Park and climb up from the sands in a deep lane on the banks of which even in December an occasional gorse is in flower. At Cemaes Head the path emerges from the protection of the estuary onto the sea-coast itself for the first time. The neat green fields are surrounded by slopes of orange bracken that come down to the cliff edge. From here to Pen-yr-afr, about a mile away, are some of the best rock shapes on the path. The Ordovician strata of alternating grits and shales were here subjected to strong but gradual geological pressures. The result was that without being broken or faulted the layers were bent in a relatively gentle rippling into successive waves and troughs of rock.

You do not follow this undulating line. Two processes have intervened between that crumpling of the rocks and the modern appearance of Pembrokeshire. The Pliocene sea cut the level 200-foot platform 17 million

A still pool near Pen-yr-afr, within a few miles of the beginning of the Coast Path.

years ago, but before the sea reached its present level it sank several hundred feet lower. The streams that ran off the surface of Pembrokeshire to this low sea fell steeply, etching sharp valleys into the earlier smoothed surface. The result is that now the walker on the coast path, far from enjoying an easy level ride 200 feet above the sea, is always climbing up and down into the steep little valleys of the many streams that cross the path. This is exhausting at first, but as the climb back up is always 200 feet you will develop a set rhythm to deal with it, in which, without either hurry or rest, you swing back up to the top again.

This pattern of severe ups and downs, revealing around corners fantastic geological twistings, continues steadily repeating itself for headland after headland, so that oddly there is no sense of progress overall. Only in detail does the landscape change. At times the path seems to be paved with long narrow paving stones, arranged as tightly as in any garden, but these are in fact the ends of rock layers

The houses of Llanstadwell and Hazelbeach and the chimneys of the refinery at Milford Haven.

stretching down into the earth, once deposited horizontally and later simply up-ended. If you look over the edge here the cliff is a single vertical plane of rock. In other places, the path is ridged with saw-tooth corrugations, or made up of broad, slightly inclined flags, both the basic product of the rock's varying angles of dip.

You will see wrens and fulmars on this coast, as well as choughs, which are rare in other parts of the country but quite common here. Jets from the RAF station at Brawdy near Solva play over the cliffs all day, making bombing runs from low out at sea and often performing an impressive cross-over manoeuvre designed to shake off tailing missiles.

Inland the Preselis come into view above Newport. The extent to which green fields have crept up their sides shows that they are hardly mountains, but it is true that their knobbly crests do have something of a moorland look to them. The hills are most

famous as the source of the Blue Stones of Stonehenge. A few years ago the elaborate reconstructions of the Neolithic haulage of the stones from here to Wiltshire were put in doubt, and it was suggested that a glacier was responsible for carrying them there. This claim is now equally suspect because of the lack of other evidence for the supposed glacier, and there for the moment the question stands.

About twelve miles from St Dogmael's, soon after passing an intensely black cove called Godir-rhûg, you round a corner into Newport Bay, on the far side of which is Newport, a collection of grey and white houses, the first since Poppit Sands. As the strong smell of coal-smoke comes across the bay the path crosses a golf-course on the dunes and in about three-quarters of a mile reaches Newport. Here is Carreg Coetan Arthur – a Neolithic burial chamber – a good café and some Bed and Breakfasts.

From Newport the path is along the southern bank of the Nevern estuary, which is choked with sand, through the attractive village of Parrog, then up on to the sea cliffs again. It passes Cat Rock, which is threaded

17

through with snaking lines of white quartz, and then a series of bays in which at low tide the rock platform cut by the modern sea is particularly clear.

Four miles from Newport you arrive at Cwm-yr-eglwys, where there is the broken end of a small chapel, smashed during a storm in 1859, and beside it a few tilting tombstones in what was once the churchyard. The village is at the base of a peninsula called Dinas Island, and it is possible to cut off the promontory by going along the now marshy valley at its base, originally made by melt-water from a glacier. But the walk around Dinas Head is one of the highlights of the walk so far and should not be missed. As you walk out to the Head, guillemots, razorbills and greater black backs can all be seen on Needle Rock on the east side of the 'Island'. The arrival at the trig point on the Head is good. To the north you will see back to Cemaes Head and Pen-yr-afr, while ships at the ferry terminal in Fishguard Harbour to the south can easily be seen. But far more exciting is the sight, if it is a clear day, of

A yew in Nevern churchyard: a look as ancient and twisted as the rocks themselves.

the Mountains of Wicklow, faint bumps on the far side of the Irish Sea. Pembrokeshire has always been closely bound up with Wicklow – in pre-history because those mountains were one of the few known sources of gold; in the Dark Ages because over there was the spiritual centre of the Celtic church; and in the Middle Ages because many of the conquerors of Ireland were Pembrokeshire men, and it was from St David's that Henry II's expedition set out.

From Dinas it is four miles to Fishguard. The fracture of the coast is great and the path dives down and up time and again. The hill to the south, Dinas Mountain, ends in the west at Mynydd Llanllawer, also, according to the Pembrokeshire antiquarian Richard Fenton, 'called the Maiden's Brest from no other similitude to that lovely hemisphere but its roundness'. The going here is rough and often brambly, but the thorns on either side never grow higher than a few inches off the ground because the acid salt-laden winds burn off any exposed buds. You pass through a caravan site and in two miles, as you turn around Castle Point, where there are three eighteenth-century cannons above a bright red cliff

All that was left of the chapel at Cwm-yr-eglwys after a storm in 1859.

capped with orange bracken, Fishguard Lower Town comes into view. From the old fishing port it is a steep climb up the road to the main part of the town, through which the path does not officially run, but whose cafés and Beds and Breakfasts will be needed by anyone who has walked from Newport.

Fishguard to St David's 32 miles

From Fishguard the first mile is along the beach at the head of the Harbour. At Goodwick on the far side was the terminus of the Great Western Railway, and for a while before the First World War there were great plans for the place. Vast new port installations were opened in 1906, and from 1909 until 1914 Cunard liners docked here, filling up with passengers from three or four special boat trains each. The war killed it, and although there is still a Cunard Café selling fish and chips in Goodwick the harbour's only business now is the ferry and small container traffic to Rosslare.

The path climbs high above the long quay and once it has left Harbour Village starts on the wildest part of the walk. It is six miles to Strumble Head, and from there another fourteen to the village of Trevine. In all this the sparse collection of houses at Abercastle is almost the only interruption to a bare and empty coast. Here you get the full strength of the weather coming from the west. As you walk you will see a long time ahead the heavy storms approaching from out at sea; when they arrive they will make your progress slow and exhausting, forcing you to take perhaps as much as three hours to cover the six miles to Strumble Head, at the end of which you will find your face burnt and your hair knotted together from the constant wind.

Three miles from Goodwick the valley of a small stream provides an escape from the gales. This is the place where the last military force to invade Britain landed in February 1797. About 1,400 ex-convicts from France under the command of the American 'Colonel' Tate were meant to land near Bristol or in Cardigan Bay and raise a peasants' revolt, all as a diversion from the main exercise, an invasion of Ireland by 15,000 regular troops. Tate mistakenly landed his men here; far from stirring sympathetic revolutionary fervour in the peasants of Pembrokeshire they antagonised them by taking their goods and provisions, amongst which were the remains of a cargo of wine from a Portuguese merchantman wrecked on this coast the month before. The French expeditionary force was soon irretrievably drunk. Meanwhile the defending army under the command of an amateur tactician, Lord Cawdor, got itself quickly organised, and after almost walking into an ambush withdrew again to Fishguard. Tate's officers, only twenty-four hours after landing, forced him to sign a note of surrender, and after less than two days on British soil the force marched down to Goodwick Sands to capitulate. The casualty list was eight Frenchmen drowned, twelve killed and one Welshwoman shot accidentally in a pub when a pistol went off as it was being loaded. Lord Cawdor was a hero.

You soon pass the site, on a narrow grassy platform next to the sea, of St Degan's Chapel, but there is nothing to see there now, and in about a mile and a half you reach Strumble Head, one of the decisive corners of the walk. Again you can look back to where you started, but for the first time St David's Head and the shapely monadnocks of that peninsula stand out to the south-west. On Strumble Head is a coastguard station and a lighthouse, now unmanned and controlled by radio from St Ann's Head. These stand high above the volcanic rocks of a kind called Pillow Lavas by geologists; they are formed when blobs of lava are squeezed out through the sea-bed and rolled up by water movements to the shore.

From Strumble to St David's Head the coast is a series of headlands and bays which reflect exactly the structure of the land: every headland is a volcanic intrusion and every small bay is cut in the broken Ordovician shales between. Pwllderi, about two and a half miles from Strumble Head, is one of the loveliest of these bays, celebrated in a poem by the Pembrokeshire poet Dewi Emrys, to whom there is a memorial here. Just to the south are the hamlet and farm of Trefasser, said to be the birthplace of Bishop Asser, the friend and biographer of Alfred the Great.

You sweep on, round Pen Bwchdy, coming in nearly four miles to the two beaches of Aberbach and Abermawr. After being well above the sea all day, you come down here to its level; but in a winter storm, when the waves come at you in a succession of grey walls, drowning all other sounds with the noise of their breaking, you get the impression, when standing on the grey sand, that you are well below the level of the sea. It seems that at any moment the breakers will roll on inland, submerging the beach and anything on it, since there is apparently nothing to contain this bulk of water at the edge of the land.

At the far side of the beach the path goes up past an old quarry and kiln, all over which the sea deposits great gobs of spume whipped up from the edge of the surf. You pass a spectacular fort on the Penmorfa peninsula and in about two and a half miles reach the tiny village of Abercastle, whose buildings are untidy and whose harbour entrance is a dramatic place in storms. Here is a fortress-like island of black rock, called Ynys-y-Castell, on whose flat top are some bumps in the earth, probably the remains of a particularly exposed

early Christian site, but called collectively the Grave of Sampson's Finger. Above Abercastle on the mainland is the best of the Pembrokeshire cromlechau, Carreg Sampson, whose massive capstone was lifted on to the points of the seven uprights (probably in about 3000 BC) by Sampson's little finger, which was later buried on the island opposite. From the dolmen it is about a mile to the village of Trevine, once the site of an episcopal palace. There are Bed and Breakfasts and a pub.

From here the coast, without losing any of the variety and drama of its geological formation, becomes more civilised. As you approach St David's the wild bare atmosphere of the coast further north is lost as the path comes across more and more evidence of long human habitation. Within two miles of Trevine is Porthgain, the most evocative ruin of industrial Pembrokeshire. The tiny harbour, protected on the seaward side by a stubby quay, is lined by banks of crushers, binns and shoots in which stone quarried from the cliffs west of here was broken up, graded and shovelled down to the ships waiting below. These brick buildings were last used in 1931, but have already acquired, perhaps because of their surroundings, an unexpectedly romantic air.

The path climbs from the harbour and for a while follows the old tramway along which the stone was brought from the quarry. You pass some of the best cliff scenery on this northern coast, around the bays of Porth-dwfn and Porth-egr, where you can look straight through a split in the rock slitting the small peninsula from side to side. In about a mile and a half you come to some beautiful slate quarries that were also connected to Porthgain by another tramway. When the quarry was closed down, a channel was blasted from the sea to the quarry floor, to create the harbour 'The Blue Lagoon'. It is a striking place: the deeply black walls are regularly notched where the slate has been cut in rectangular slices, while the pool in the bottom is for some chemical reason a Bahamas-sea blue. Beyond, a mile off shore, the sea sucks with spray and spittle over the three rocks of Llechuchaf, Llechganol and Llechisaf. You pass another Iron Age fort, heavily eroded, and, below the coasting circles of the fulmars, rocks that look like Easter Island heads.

The massive volcanic intrusions that have formed the high ground almost parallel to the coast all the way from Strumble Head now come up to the shore at Penbiri. The ground underfoot changes to moorland, covered in heather, with granite boulders sticking out through it. The culmination is in the great igneous thrust of St David's Head and, beyond it, the group of rocks called the Bishop and

Clerks who, according to George Owen, 'preach deadly doctrine to their winter audience, and are commendable in nothing but for their good residence ... Nor are they without some small choristers, who show themselves but at spring tides and calm seas'.

The tip of the head is made into an Iron Age fort by some large banks, while outside them the irregular pattern of stone-walled fields is Iron Age in origin. As Graham Sutherland has described it, each field has 'a spear of rock at its centre. It is as if the solid rock foundation of the earth had thrown up these spears to transfix and hold the scanty earth of the fields upon it'.

From the high ground of the point the path reaches in about half a mile the wide beach of Whitesand Bay, where the site of St Patrick's Chapel marks the main prehistoric point of departure for Ireland, and where surfers now ride in on the swell from Atlantic storms. From here you can walk two miles along the old road to the capital of Pembrokeshire and of the Church in Wales, the Cathedral City of St David's.

St David's to St Ann's Head
41 miles

In the Middle Ages two pilgrimages to St David's were the equivalent of one to Rome; some claimed that the Bishop here should be an Archbishop equal to and independent of Canterbury. Such grandeur hardly attaches to St David's now. Only the cathedral and the ruins of the Bishop's Palace, both in a hollow below the houses and shops, set St David's apart from countless small market towns in Wales. St David was born near here in about 520, the son of Non and Sant, Prince of Ceredigion. He was prepared for a saintly life at Ty Gwyn on Whitesand Bay, and first proved his extraordinary holiness when during a noisy Synod at Brefi in Cardiganshire the ground on which he was standing rose of its own accord to make a small hill from which he could command the attention of the understandably mesmerised crowd. After travelling

Aquamarine at Porthgain, and in the distance Strumble Head.

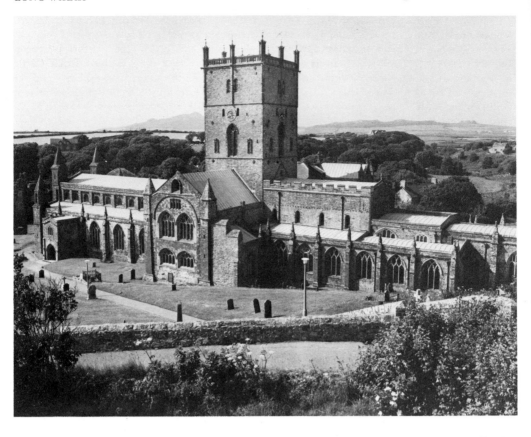

St David's Cathedral. Beyond it are the volcanic hills called monadnocks which stood out as islands in an earlier sea.

to Jerusalem and widely in Wales he returned to where he had spent his childhood and founded a monastery on the banks of the River Alun, where the cathedral and palace now stand. From the start things were hard. As Gerald of Wales later explained: 'St David's is in a remote corner of the county, looking out towards the Irish Sea. The soil is rocky and barren. It is exposed to winds and to extremely inclement weather. However these saintly men deliberately chose to establish the archbishopric there, for they wanted to live as far removed as possible from worldly upsets, preferring the hermit's to the pastoral existence, so that they might enjoy a spiritual life that no one could take away from them.' As it turned out even this was not easy. The local chieftain, Boia, who lived on a conspicuous monadnock west of St David's, resented the foundation of the monastery and used insidious tactics to try and get rid of it. He persuaded his wife to tell her maids 'to go where the monks can see you and with bodies bare play games and use lewd words'. The monks fell for this unfair temptation, but David alone stayed pure. Boia's wife went mad and murdered her stepdaughter; Boia himself, his household and camp were destroyed with a thunderbolt from heaven.

Nothing is now left of the buildings which St David knew. The present cathedral, built in the dusty purple and red sandstone from the cliffs at Caerfai just south of here, was constructed in the twelfth century under the bishopric of Peter de Leia. The exterior is relatively dull, but the inside of the building has one unique and dramatic feature. From the west end of the long nave the floor slopes appreciably up towards the high altar, so that when in the nave one's head is well below the floor level at the east end. So impressive an architectural image is this that one might imagine it had been deliberately incorporated into the design, but more likely it was imposed on the builders by the nature of the site.

Next to the cathedral on the other side of the little Alun is the lovely ruin of the Bishop's Palace. Although parts of it were built at many different times it was given its characteristic style in the mid-fourteenth century by the cultured, pleasure-loving Bishop Gower. He added an enormous Great Hall, with a rose window at one end and at the other an elegant entrance porch that was reached by a broad external flight of stairs arriving at a doorway framed by a deeply moulded ogee arch. Bishop Gower imported foreign masons for this work, whom he also used to add, around almost the whole building, a tall arcaded parapet, that served no useful function at all but gave the palace the Italian style the cosmopolitan Bishop liked.

From St David's you can walk back to Whitesand Bay, or take the small lane past Boia's stronghold to reach the coast opposite Ramsey Island at St Justinian's. This is where St Justinian landed after walking across Ramsey Sound with his head in his arms after it had been cut off by murderers on the island. There is a small roofless chapel to him here, filled with nettles.

As you walk south to reach the corner of St Bride's Bay, you can look across to Ramsey, where 20,000 saints lie buried, and see the few white houses pushed into lee-holes away from the gales. Beyond the island the low bump of Grassholm appears, twelve miles away, and beyond that, on a very clear day, the lighthouse on the Smalls. These rocks are the end of a volcanic ridge that stretches out to them from Skomer, through Grassholm, and two other groups of rocks called the Barrels and the Hats.

It is an impressive moment when you turn into St Bride's Bay. You see across to Skomer and the Marloes peninsula. Further east the

The size of the man fishing at the edge of the sea indicates the scale of the wave-cut platform revealed at low tide in St Bride's Bay.

narrow chimneys of the Milford Haven refineries poke above what looks like an absolutely level plain – the 200-foot platform. Almost due east the tower of Roch Castle marks the north-east corner of the bay and the beginning of English Pembrokeshire. Much of the coastline in view is owned by the National Trust.

You pass above, unseen, the place with the best name in Pembrokeshire – a cave called Ogof Mrs Morgan (who Mrs Morgan was no one knows). Equally strange perhaps is that this huge bay should be called after St Bride's, which is nothing but a cottage or two and a church on the bay's southern side. The figure of St Bride herself may explain it. Although there was an historical St Bride or Brigid of Kildare, her cult took much from Brig or Brigid, who was one of the most important of Celtic goddesses, the mistress of fire, the patron of poets and daughter of Dagda, the Lord of Knowledge and greatest of the Irish native gods. It may be this Brigid after whom the bay is named.

The path now weaves in and out of a series of little bays, one of which, Porth-clais, penetrates deeper than the rest and is the place where Elvis, Bishop of Munster, was landed

Cliffs at Marloes.

Stacked like slates in a builder's yard: rocks at Marloes Sands.

by divine intervention at the very moment when David needed to be baptised. Half a mile further on is the place where St David was born, in the middle of a great gale. It is marked by a small covered well and a modern statue of St Non, his mother.

Around the next headland in Caerfai Bay is the cliff quarry for the cathedral. The stone is a boring grey when dry, but when wet from the sea is the colour of a good plum jam. Some of the best rock formations since Pen-yr-afr are here. In Caerbwdi Bay the Cambrian sandstone has been rolled into an almost circular whorl, which has not only been sliced through so that its structure is revealed, but one whole side has been stripped off so that it presents a broad curved flank, about 60 yards long, as smooth and unbroken as the side of a whale.

It is good walking, through heather and patches of bracken, all along the northern side of St Bride's Bay. There are rabbits here and many wrens, which look quite out of place on a stormy cliff-top in winter. You pass an Iron

A sleek submarine roll in Caerbwdi Bay near St David's. Immense but extremely slow pressure produces the buckling of the crust.

Age camp whose ramparts are exposed in profile where a landslip has sheared through them. The jets which are a constant feature of the whole walk here become more insistent than ever, since their base, which they share with the large Air-Sea Rescue Sea-King helicopters, is only a mile inland at Brawdy.

Ten miles from St Justinian's – a wonderful ten miles – you will arrive at Solva, a pretty ex-fishing village that lies at the end of a narrow hooked harbour which is a drowned river valley submerged when the sea rose at the end of the last Ice Age. The cliff and rock scenery at its mouth is extravagantly black and broken, but the harbour itself, except in a southerly gale, is always a good one. The village may be rather self-conscious about its prettiness now, but its inhabitants were once known for ruthlessly hanging out false lights and taking whatever they could from the inevitable wrecks. (Just west of Solva is a cave called Ogof Tobacco, matching Brandy Bay and a bay near St Bride's called Dutch Gin.) The locals have not lost their acquisitive instinct. In the winter of 1979 a large cargo of timber, planks of Malaysian mahogany, worth £10 a foot, were washed up on the beaches of St

Bride's Bay. During the night an 'army' of local people descended on the beaches to remove the timber with whatever means possible. This operation continued for two or three days. The debate in every bar from the Cambrian Arms in Solva to the Lobster Pot in Marloes was whether it would be classed as flotsam or jetsam. If the captain of the ship had deliberately ordered it thrown overboard, to reduce weight in a storm, then it was jetsam, and finders would be keepers. If, however, the wood had been accidentally washed overboard it still belonged to the original owners, or their insurers, would be classed as flotsam and all that was found should be turned over to the Receiver. But the captain, to protect his interests when accused by the owners of losing a valuable cargo, might claim that what he had ordered to be thrown overboard had in fact been washed over.

Out of Solva the path at first climbs up past a particularly good clutch of limekilns, dips down to another drowned river valley and then continues on the cliff-tops for three miles until at Newgale a long level strand is reached, one of the best sweeps of sand in Pembrokeshire, backed by a tall shingle storm beach.

After heavy winter storms have removed a large part of the sand there appear here, as in several other places on this coast, the stumps and snapped-off trunks of a forest that was invaded by the rising sea in about 5000 BC.

The sand of the beach at low tide provides a delicious walking surface, with exactly the right combination of underlying hardness and surface give, but after only a mile you must leave it for the road at the site of yet another small chapel, this one dedicated to St Caradoc. Here you enter the western end of the Pembrokeshire coal field, which has been mined since the fifteenth century. Chimneys and old shafts mark the old workings. The very good coal that was extracted from here burnt without a flame and was in high demand, but was accessible only in thin, fractured beds. Even so, large quantities were exported from Newgale and Nolton Haven so that even in the seventeenth century George Owen was alarmed that so much exploitation of the mineral 'in time will wholly wear out the Coal and so leave

The sea excavates where folding has weakened the rock; a cave at the northern end of Newgale Sands.

A fort, built in 1868, on St Catherine's Island off Tenby. Catherine was the patron saint of spinners, an important trade in medieval Tenby.

the county destitute of fuel'. It was not finally exhausted, though, that finished off the Pembrokeshire mining industry, but the difficulty of getting at the seams and the relatively high cost of transport. Down this eastern side of St Bride's Bay and under the sea there are still, it is reckoned, 230 million tons of unworked reserves.

It is three miles from Newgale to Nolton Haven, which consists of no more than a pub, a house or two and a Nonconformist chapel, and from there another three of quieter and softer landscape to Broad Haven, which feels more like a temporary encampment than a village, and is quite different from Little Haven, a Cornish-type place just around the corner, where there are three pubs and several Bed and Breakfasts.

Half a mile beyond Little Haven, at Musselwick, you turn the third corner of St Bride's Bay, and now head straight into the west wind. The path threads through a small patch of hazel and oak wood, but the appalling exposure of the coast stunts and gnarls the trees. They are covered in grey lichen and look as brittle and frail as old men's limbs. Soon you cross into country underlain by the Old Red Sandstone; the cliffs are sharply stepped in profile and give a raw, bloody look to the coast. With this as the background it is extremely strange to arrive – here at this rough end of the world – at a stately home on the cliff tops, spread around with smart wide lawns. The incongruity is heightened when one learns that this was once the home of a Lord Kensington, was turned into a hospital, and has recently been bought to be developed into flats. Here too are the tiny hamlet and chapel of St Bride's, built from the red rock.

Beyond the hospital you return to the undiluted exposure of the cliffs, turning south and west again, around the pretty Musselwick Sands, along a path made horribly muddy by cows, until, just over three miles from St Bride's, you reach the tiny beach of Martin's Haven, littered about with rotting boats and winding gear. Here the Old Red Sandstone has given way to an igneous intrusion, making cliffs that are not stepped, but are visibly bubbly, preserving in stone the shapes of the magma that boiled up from inside the earth. In summer you can take a boat from here to Skomer.

Just beyond the Haven, after a lovely walk on short turf through Lord Kensington's Deer Park (there are no deer), you come to the end of the southern horn of St Bride's Bay. Opposite lies Skomer, covered with bracken and oddly foreshortened so that the tiny Midland Isle, in the channel between, seems as large. Here is another decisive corner, and you turn south, past a stream which, in trying to reach the sea as a waterfall down the cliff, is blown back all over the path. In two miles you come to Gateholm, an 'island' that is joined to the mainland except at high tide, and on to which you can climb to see the slight remains of some rectangular huts that may have been an early monastic settlement. Beyond stretches Marloes Sand, nearly a mile long and with groynes of harder rock sticking up through the beach like ribs. The sands are brought sharply to an end by a solid red cliff, half a mile beyond which you come to Westdale Bay, where you can look down to the charming gothic Dale Castle, in whose garden even the cypresses have been distorted into grotesqueries by the constant wind from the west.

As you walk the two miles to St Ann's Head you pass the remains of a large Iron Age fort on Great Castle Head and of coastal defences, much of which has been dismantled and many of whose buildings have simply been shovelled over the cliff in the sure knowledge that the sea will pulverise all it is given. The Dale peninsula ends in some spectacular folds and cuts in the rock. Above them are some neat white cottages, a vegetable garden, a lighthouse and the look-out station where the coast guards watch over Milford Haven.

St Ann's Head to Angle 38 miles

Across the mouth of Milford Haven, from St Ann's Head to Rat Island, the nearest point on the other side, is just over two miles. To walk there you must cover nearly forty, through the most beautiful industrial landscape you will have ever seen. There were of course great protests at the 'desecration' done by the oil companies on the shores of the Haven, but the landscape has not been destroyed. What wrecks the land is the transient, the badly-designed, the sloppy, the ill-maintained and the gimcrack. The power station and refineries that stand here are none of these things – they cannot afford to be so, since untidiness is inefficient and inefficiency expensive. One thing only threatens the effective visual impact of a refinery. For safety it must sprawl – the tanks must be well separated to stop the spread of fire. There is a danger that in spreading too wide the whole might lose coherence and break up into a mess. This has been brilliantly avoided all round the Haven. The vast low storage tanks – more like discs than cylinders – have been painted a variety of organic, tweedy colours so that they virtually disappear. The result is that from St Ann's Head you are left with a skyline of chimneys of all widths, above a rural landscape whose essential shape has not been mutilated and which performs the same agricultural function as before, unaffected by the citadels of high technology.

The first place one comes to in moving off from St Ann's Head has associations centuries away from all that you see around you. In Mill Bay, where there are now the remains of a relatively recent wreck, Henry Tudor landed with about 2,000 men on 7 August 1485. The beach is small and the landing must have been crowded, but Henry wanted to be out of sight of both Dale and Pembroke castles, which he guessed were occupied against him. From here he marched the 176 miles to Bosworth Field in fourteen days.

Past enormous concrete transit marks on Watwick Point, used to keep the ships in the deepwater channel, the path comes into a small belt of trees and continues to the base of Dale Point, where an Iron Age fort has recently been excavated to reveal the stone revetments of the banks. At the end of the point is a small fort, built in 1856 as part of a large scheme for the defence of the Haven, and now used as a Field Studies Centre.

Dale village has nothing much to offer, but beyond it the incongruities of Milford Haven start to sharpen up. Monk Haven, two miles from Dale, was a busy landing place in the Middle Ages, much used by pilgrims to St David's who wanted to avoid the journey around the dangerous western coasts. It is likely, though, that the road to St David's from here was in use much earlier as one of the through-routes taken both by Neolithic traders and Dark Age *peregrini*, linking on the other side of the Haven with the Pembrokeshire Ridgeway that runs through to the far coast at Penally near Tenby.

Our path continues around Great Castle Head, where a transit mark is built on top of an Iron Age fort, and comes to Sandy Haven, where Graham Sutherland found another, complementary side to Pembrokeshire, quite different from the hard openness of the St David's peninsula in the north: 'The left bank

Near St Ann's Head.

as we see it is all dark,' he wrote, 'an impenetrable damp green gloom of woods which come down to the edge of low brackish moss-covered cliffs – it is all dark save where the mossy lanes (two each side) which dive down to the opening admit the sun, hinged as it were to the top of the trees, from where its rays, precipitating new colours, turn the red cliffs of the right-hand bank to tones of fire. Do you remember the rocks in Blake's Newton drawing? The form and scale of the rocks here, and the minutiae on them, is very similar. The whole setting is one of exuberance – of darkness and light – of decay and life. Rarely have I been so conscious of the contrasting of these elements in so small a compass.'

Sandy Haven must be waded through, which is only possible for two hours each side of high tide. Beyond, you pass fields in which the ploughed earth is a warm dirty ochre while, offshore in the Haven, Stack Rock is nothing but rock and nineteenth-century gun emplacements. On the far side of the Rock the Esso jetty reaches 3,000 feet out into the deepwater channel, where its five-berth head stretches sideways for 4,200 feet. By now the refinery itself will be on you, revealing its insides like viscera, all pipes and connected organs.

Another two miles brings you to the town of Milford Haven itself. Extraordinarily, there was no port in this unparalleled natural harbour until 1800, when Charles Greville, Sir William Hamilton's nephew, sank all his capital in the new town and harbour and by encouraging immigrants from Nantucket turned it into a whaling port. It has kept its original grid-iron plan.

On the far side of Milford the walk declines. The flattish country inland is not interesting, and after the Gulf refinery you have to walk on the road to Neyland, a town destined for dereliction from its beginning in 1856 when I.K.Brunel chose it as the terminus for his Atlantic–Manchester railway. Liverpool was always a more practical way into the Midlands. Irish trade went to Fishguard in 1906 and at the same time the fishing fleet left for Milford. Neyland is not an uplifting place.

There is now no ferry to Pembroke Dock and you must make a one-and-a-half-mile detour to get to the high new road bridge over the Daugleddau. Pembroke Dock on the other side has been no luckier than Neyland. The naval dockyard was abruptly closed down in 1926, and as three out of four men in the town worked here this brought great hardship. During the last war the navy's oil storage tanks here were a prime target, and in 1940 and 1941 the town suffered terribly from incendiary raids.

You leave Pembroke Dock on its southern

side and come down a gravelly lane to another world, the muddy quiet estuary of the Pembroke River, with no real hint that the sea, let alone three depressed towns or a major oil port, is anywhere near. Now and then, through the trees that thickly fringe the path and the river's edge, you will get a glimpse of Pembroke Castle, just a pile of square silhouettes from here, until in about two miles the path arrives at Pembroke itself. Here, as you round a corner, the castle, already high on its rock, rises straight up above you, a single sheet of wall.

This is the natural headquarters of the county, or at least of the Englishry, since it is right in the middle and easily accessible by sea. Not surprisingly, the Norman Arnulph de Montgomery built his round-towered fortress here in 1090. It was replaced in the thirteenth century with the present curtain-wall design, which was both roomier inside and militarily more efficient. Apart from the castle Pembroke is essentially one long street of houses built up along the Tenby road, bulging slightly at one point to make room for a market.

This is not the way we take, though. As so often, the path sets out directly away from its final destination, and strikes west, at first along the road to Monkton, where the eleventh-century Benedictine priory contains an *art nouveau* choir, and then for three miles along very wet field-paths towards the giant power station on the banks of the Haven. In wet weather there is no pastoral quiet here. In the distance the station hums like a milking machine and overhead the high voltage power lines rattle.

When you finally reach the power station – and there may be some difficulty in finding the way – it is a very neat thing, just a tall chimney and a large box, from which the two lines of pylons move away up the hill like ski-lifts. From here you skirt the Texaco Refinery, which has 90 storage tanks, holding altogether 315 million gallons of oil. Past the Texaco jetty you come in about a mile to Popton Point on the corner of Angle Bay, where BP have incorporated an 1863 fort into their ocean terminal. It was at the jetty here that one of the biggest ships ever to visit Milford Haven, the 327,000-ton *Universe Kuwait*, berthed in October 1973.

The path is now along the low shores of Angle Bay, where the red sandstone is covered in oarweed and bladderwrack. You pass a derelict quay and some old hulls among the modern yachts, coming finally to Angle village, which comprises about one hundred houses and two forts, both overgrown and

St Ann's Head, Skomer in the distance.

The thirteenth-century castle on a branch of the sea at Pembroke: a natural headquarters in a maritime county.

ignored. The hillside to the north of the village is divided into strip fields, preserving a pattern of land distribution that was originally made in the Middle Ages. The walk on the coast around this hill is excellent. As you emerge from the protection of the Haven, things begin to roughen again. At the western end of the Angle peninsula you arrive high on the cliff opposite Thorn Island, whose top is entirely taken up with the most dramatic of the many nineteenth-century forts in the area. This impregnable fortress with sheer rock walls has now become a hotel. It is a good place to be at the end of the day. The radar and lighthouse on St Ann's Head will be silhouetted by the last light, and you will experience a strong if unidentifiable pleasure in being able to see so near to you a place which you know is two days' considerable effort away.

Angle to Amroth 36 miles

From West Angle Bay a rough and thorny walk along the south coast of the Angle peninsula for four and a half hard miles brings you to the long sands of Freshwater West, which is a good-looking beach, but dangerous for swimming. From here there follows a long road walk, well away from the coast and through a landscape that on a wet day in winter is enough to drain enthusiasm from even the strongest walker's heart. The army have taken over as a tank range all the land from Freshwater West to Bosherston. Not only is the coast of this area – the old Hundred of Castlemartin – some of the best limestone cliff scenery in the country, but the land itself, in George Owen's time at least, was known to yield 'the best and finest grain and in most abundance ... that maketh the bread fairer than any other wheat of the shire'. As you tramp along the dreary road to Castlemartin all you will see to your right among the derelict farms and observation towers are flocks of scraggy sheep that are brought down from the Preselis to winter here.

When firing is not taking place the army allows you to join the coast for the stretch from The Green Bridge of Wales to Bosherston. This offer is certainly worth taking up. Limestone is both porous and soluble so that weaknesses in it are easily exploited by water that can bore tunnels and rot away great cavities in the rock. This produces particularly

33

exciting shapes in the cliffs. The porousness also means that no water lies on the surface for long and that there are no streams to cut the sharp little valleys that are so exhausting a feature of other parts of the coast. On limestone, in theory at least, you can breeze along on the level dry surface, with the westerlies at last firmly behind you and, below, the deeply pierced cliffs and stacks that are the nesting places of shags and fulmars, kittiwakes, razorbills and guillemots.

As you arrive at this coast two enormous rocks called the Elegug Stacks greet you, one an unshapely black hunk, the other a wall. Just west of them is a high wide natural arch called The Green Bridge of Wales. Not far to the east

BELOW *Not long after the limestone in these cliffs near Bosherston was laid down on the sea floor, massive earth-movements, known as the Armorican Orogeny, upended the bedding planes. Such a vertical, or near-vertical, structure produces these sheer cliffs. They move rapidly inland. On the right, just above sea-level, the notch cut by the storm waves can clearly be seen. In time, the cliff above will collapse and the coast recede a few yards more.*

ABOVE *The Elegug Stacks, a few yards from The Green Bridge of Wales, are spotted with sea-birds and stained with their guano. Faulting and folding in the rock, and the consequent selective erosion by the sea, have brought about such spectacular cliffscapes.*

RIGHT *Near St Govan's Head.*

you come to Crickmail Down, under which the sea has excavated a kind of double cave, so that from above it looks like a flooded crypt, with heavy arches springing from great piers. All along, where the roof of a cave has been weakened by water coming down from above, a hole appears well back from the cliff edge, and at high tide and in heavy seas the swell can blow spray up through these. These blow-holes are alarming places, with the look of hell-mouths about them. Most thrilling of all these limestone features, though, only a hundred yards from a pink armoured car, is Huntsman's or Adam's Leap. Here a very narrow fault has been worked on by the sea so that a trench two hundred yards long, about one hundred feet deep, and in one place no more than six feet wide has been cut in from the cliff edge. It is difficult to resist the terrifying temptation to jump across.

All this makes up for the deadening Castlemartin road. The culmination of this stretch is the famous and wonderful St Govan's Chapel, a tiny stone cell filling a small cleft in the cliff; in its absolute lack of ornament and in the sense of drama of its position it says a great deal about the spirit of the Celtic church. There was probably a cell here in the fifth century, but the present building is no older than the thirteenth. Not even the sex of St Govan is known, or even if Govan was the saint's name. Some people believe that it is a corruption of Gawain, who after Arthur's death repented of his licentiousness and turned hermit.

From the chapel you can either continue round the coast to Broad Haven, or take the road inland to Bosherston, where there is a pub and a large boulder which was brought here by a glacier from the Hebrides. The village is on the edge of 2,000 acres of National Trust land, given to them in 1976 by Lord Cawdor, a descendant of the hero of 1797. If you go to the village the way back to the coast is through the prettiest part of this estate, around a three-fingered lake called the Bosherston Lily Ponds, which you cross by a series of low balks just wide enough for one person.

You come out on to the dunes above Broad Haven, and in about a mile and a half reach the most delicious bay in Pembrokeshire, Bara-fundle Bay, which at low tide is filled with rich yellow sand as if with cream. You must climb the sharp limestone on the far side, coming

soon to the cottages and curly rocks of
Stackpole Quay. Just beyond, the limestone
gives way again to Old Red Sandstone, the
path changes colour, and starts again to rise
and fall with the contours. At Greenala Point, a
mile from Stackpole Quay, in the deep ditches
of a promontory fort away from the wind, you
will find a lovely mattress of old long turf,
never cropped and never mown, a place for
half an hour's sleep.

Another mile brings you to the shacks and
chalets of Freshwater East, beyond which the
path moves out on to the promontory of West
Moor Cliff, then in around Swanlake Bay,
coming around the next headland, East Moor
Cliff, to Manorbier Bay. Not until you have
reached the head of the bay, however, do you
see the pretty and delicate castle of Manorbier,
a complete contrast to the masculine bulk of
the fortress at Pembroke, and understandably
the object of life-long affection for Gerald of
Wales, the most remarkable man to come from
Pembrokeshire, who was born here in 1145.

Gerald should have achieved more than he
did. He had all the attributes: noble birth,
good looks, great energy and courage, an
unshakeable moral passion, wide learning and

*The stump of a geological trough or syncline at Stackpole
Quay.*

a sense of humour. The seventeen books he
wrote show an unending curiosity in almost
everything and convey more than anything
else the unstoppable vitality of the man.
Through his grandmother, Princess Nest, he
was related to most of the native princes of
Wales, and by the end of his long life he had
come to know everyone: Pope Innocent III,
Henry II, Richard I and John, as well as the
Archbishops Baldwin, Hubert Walter and
Stephen Langton. How was it that this well-
connected, brilliant and deeply ambitious man
came to die in 1223 in relative obscurity in
Lincoln, having held no higher post than the
Archdeaconry of Brecon?

If Gerald was admirable, he was not a
likeable man, lacking any hint of modesty and
at times showing the intolerant bitterness of
the self-consciously and excessively virtuous.
These personal faults, though, rarely keep a
man back in public life, and the reasons lie
more in the peculiar political circumstances of
his time.

Gerald had a single ambition – to be Bishop

of St David's, which he claimed was by right a metropolitan see. But Henry II, whose final decision it was, saw uncomfortable parallels between the prospect of Gerald installed in St David's, pushing for the independence of the Welsh church, and the traumatic Becket experience of only a few years before. Gerald's blood-relationship with many of the most important political figures in Wales only increased the danger of insurrection following his appointment.

Despite these huge obstacles, Gerald's commitment to the struggle that consumed much of his life was characterised by an unsappable strength in the face of setbacks and an absolute refusal to compromise. Three times he went to plead his case in the Vatican, only to meet each time with frustrating delay. In 1203, twenty-seven years after he had first been passed over for the bishopric, Gerald suddenly gave up the fight, and devoted most of his remaining twenty years to his books. Of these perhaps the most accessible is *The Journey through Wales*. This is meant to be a description of Archbishop Baldwin's tour through Wales in 1188 to drum up support for the Third Crusade, but the author wanders off on the

most extravagant and fanciful diversions. He had great sensitivity to landscape, and produced beautiful descriptions of Llanthony, Snowdonia, and most famously of Manorbier, where 'from its nearness to Ireland heaven's breath smells so wooingly' and where below the fish-pond, the orchard and the grove of hazel trees you can stand on the rocky headland and see ships on their way to Ireland 'brave the ever changing violence of the winds and the blind fury of the waters'.

You continue around Manorbier Bay, on whose eastern rim is a Neolithic burial chamber, The King's Quoit; but after less than a mile the army have again prevented the passage of the coast path, and you must walk on the road for two miles to Lydstep. Here the map announces in gothic script *The Palace*, next to the Post Office, but all you will find is a plain grey medieval building sometimes said to have been Bishop Gower's hunting lodge. You come to the coast again south of Lydstep, where it is owned by the National Trust, and where the finely bedded limestone layers stand absolutely vertical. These rocks are the

Lydstep Haven.

Caldy Island, with the bright flash of Sandtop Bay in the middle of it. Above the island, in the far distance, the Gower Peninsula is faintly visible, twenty-one miles away.

shorn-off base of one of the series of steep folds into which south Pembrokeshire was pushed in the Armorican Orogeny.

Lydstep Haven, a favourite place of Edmund Gosse, is now full of caravans, but if you lean your back against one of these monsters you can still see what a good place it is. On either side the rocks dip towards each other, forming a deep trough or syncline that the sea has eroded to make Caldy Sound. The mouth of the Haven is almost filled by Caldy itself and on the north side the smooth sheets of rock stretch east to Giltar Point, spraying back in high plumes the swell that knocks against them. It was while walking along the

top of these limestone cliffs in 1904 soon after the death of her father that Virginia Woolf decided to devote her life to literature. It is a wonderful three miles to Giltar, regularly punctuated by blowholes, one of which when the conditions are right groans and wheezes asthmatically.

At Giltar you turn into Carmarthen Bay, and for the first time see beyond the end of the walk. It is about a mile and a half to Tenby along the beach that stretches north from here. It is a good one for pebbles – both limestone and red sandstone and a blotchy red and white conglomerate. From the beach Tenby is made up of vertical stripes of colour-washed houses pushed tightly together, with the fortified St Catherine's Island lying just off-shore. Tenby was adopted as a refined watering place in the late eighteenth century, and has stayed one ever since. The resort was grafted on to a town

From here to there the way is over the coal measures that have come across the county from St Bride's Bay. The map is now filled with contours, but the going is not too hard. These more sheltered east-facing coasts allow some hardy trees – small, lichen-covered oaks, spruces, pines and larches – to establish themselves. In amongst them you will find occasional holes that disappear steeply underground, from which in the days of small-scale mining the coal was extracted.

Saundersfoot, once a coal exporting harbour, is now used only by yachtsmen and has several pubs and cafés. It is possible to walk all the three miles from here to Amroth along the beach, scattering the flocks of waders as you go, but it is more fun to go through the tunnel that the official path takes, which was originally blasted for the tramway that connected the mines at Stepaside, two miles inland, with Saundersfoot. Whichever you choose the way is plain enough. Between the road and the sand is a large shingle bank, in which many of the heavy grey pebbles are beautifully marked with white crystalline rings. With only a few hundred yards to go you pass the eighteenth-century Amroth Castle ('on site of Fortress', the Ordnance Survey rather grandly says), but there is nothing to mark the end of the walk itself. Only when, looking back the way you have come, a thin slip of sky appears between the western end of Caldy Island and St Catherine's Island off Tenby, will you know you have arrived.

MAPS: OS 1:50,000 Numbers 145, 157, 158

GUIDES:
John Barrett, *Pembrokeshire Coast Path*, HMSO 1974
Patrick Stark, *Walking the Pembrokeshire Coast Path*, Five Arches Press, Tenby (no date)

BACKGROUND:
E. G. Bowen, *Saints, Seaways and Settlements*, University of Wales 1969
Gerald of Wales, *The Journey through Wales* and *The Description of Wales*, translated by Lewis Thorpe, Penguin 1978
Brian S. John, *Pembrokeshire*, David and Charles 1976
Milford Haven Conservancy Board, *The Port of Milford Haven*, 1974
George Owen, *Description of Pembrokeshire*, 1603
Graham Sutherland, *Sutherland in Wales*, Alistair McAlpine 1976

INFORMATION:
Information Officer,
Pembrokeshire Coast National Park Development,
County Offices, Haverfordwest,
Dyfed SA61 1Q2

which since the Middle Ages had been an important fish-market, and a harbour of strategic significance, leading in the twelfth century to the construction of the castle (now in ruins) and later of the great town wall, much of which still stands. The National Trust owns a fifteenth-century merchant's house in one of the small medieval streets. This combination of the cramped town plan of the Middle Ages with a bright holiday style has given Tenby its characteristic air, a kind of Lyme Regis and Hay-on-Wye in one.

From Tenby it is an easy afternoon's walk to the end. You must struggle through a bit of suburbia on the town's northern edge, but you soon come to a convincingly rural muddy path, as the rock below changes from limestone to the impermeable millstone grit. Two miles from Tenby you reach Monkstone Point and at last the end of the walk is clearly in sight.

The South-West Peninsula

Coast Path

The South-West Peninsula Coast Path is the longest footpath in Britain. It is nearly double the length of the Pennine Way and almost three times as long as the Pembrokeshire Coast Path. On a map the shape of it is very clear, down and up a blade of land sticking out of England into the Atlantic; the roughness and exposure increase as far as Land's End, where you turn and then slowly withdraw back into England. But this shape gets lost on the walk itself. You are sunk in the notched detail, in the sudden turns inland up estuaries, in the calf-grinding toil of the repeated dips in the coastline, and in the continual contrasts: the mining landscapes of St Agnes and St Just, and the china clay mountains near St Austell; the chalets and beach huts near Newquay and the string of Regency resorts in South Devon; the coarse-grained brightness of Penwith and the lushness of the inlets on the south coast. On the Pennine Way the uniformity and poverty of incident makes an introduction unnecessary. Here the abundance and variety of it make one impossible. Where the Pennine Way leaves one with a sense of continuity, the lasting impression of this walk is of interruption and turning sharp corners.

This peninsula, which was the Celtic kingdom of Dumnonia, is prehistorically richer than any other part of Britain except the Wessex chalkland. Stretching out into the western sea, like a net dropped into a flood tide, it was bound to catch a good deal of what was floating past. Oddly, there is much less evidence on the coast of what was left by the Neolithic, Bronze and Iron Age people than there is on the higher ground inland. There are of course some important remains on the seaside, such as Carn Gloose near Cape Cornwall, the many Iron Age cliff forts and the Bronze Age fields at Gwithian and Morvah, but unlike parts of Wiltshire or Dorset these coastal landscapes have only rarely been visibly shaped by prehistory.

The human contribution is almost all concentrated in the tight nodules of the fishing ports. Parts of these, and many miles of the coast in between, now belong to the National Trust. A great deal of this is due to Enterprise Neptune, the most ambitious conservation scheme ever launched in Britain. Over the country as a whole the Trust now protects

Channel breakers flood into Kimmeridge Bay, Isle of Purbeck.

41

more than 400 miles of coastline. In some places, such as Hartland Point in Devon, this coastal path would not have come into existence at all if the Trust had not acquired the land.

In others, where car parks have been provided, local inhabitants have sometimes complained that their previously unspoilt cove has been ruined by the publicity which Trust ownership brings. But the National Trust in these cases is only the scapegoat for the inevitable pressure put by an industrial country on one of its few unindustrialised corners. The whole of the West Country is affected by the desire we all feel to take a longing and rather blurred look at a way of life that is now beyond reach.

To accommodate the tourist, cream-teas and pasties are to be found everywhere; indeed for a month and a half there is no need to eat anything else. The pasties are notoriously revolting. It is an old story that the Devil dare not enter Cornwall in case he is put in one. You can only dream of

A pasty costly made,
Where quail and pigeon, lark and leveret lay
Like fossils of the rock, with golden yolk
Imbedded and injellied.

Minehead to Tintagel 109 miles

Nothing could be less monumental than the start of this monstrous walk. You slip between two limewashed cottages on the harbour in Minehead. Immediately the path begins a steep zigzag climb, until you are soon a long way above the sea, far higher than the Pembroke-shire Coast Path ever gets, and as much as half a mile inland. The way is on a gravel track over moorland, with rags of gorse on it, and with a

view northwards over the Bristol Channel to the coast of South Wales.

The first descent of many is to the comfortably thatched village of Bossington on the edge of Porlock Bay. It is part of the enormous Holnicote Estate owned by the National Trust. The bay itself is lined by a high shingle storm beach piled up on the very edge of green fields. There is no gradation from one to the other. Porlock Weir is at the far end of the bay under high and woody 'hog's-back' cliffs, which are not really cliffs at all, but hills arriving steeply at the sea. The village once traded across the Bristol Channel, sending timber from the woods behind it to be used as pit-props in the Welsh mines, and receiving coal in return.

Porlock Weir is eight miles from the beginning of the walk. Another five miles brings you to the border with Devon at County Gate. The way is by an ancient toll-gate at Worthy, where cars have to pay, but where walkers go free. Climbing for a mile through oakwood you come to Culbone church, which claims, like the one at Lullington in Sussex, to be the smallest in England. If it were not for the wooden prod of a spire (about eight foot high), you would think it was a stable. The path climbs again through oak and ash, with violets below them, out on to a green lane through sheep-filled pastures. It hardly seems like a coast walk at all.

At County Gate you reach the A39 and cross into Devon. To the south is a wonderful curving view down into the deep valley of the East Lyn. Above it is the dark mass of Exmoor which it drains. Here is the first taste of the quite extraordinary concentration of prehistoric objects in the South-West Peninsula. On the hill by County Gate is a cluster of Bronze Age barrows; just down the hill from them are the remains of some conical Iron Age houses

(less exciting than they first sound), and a little to the west, at a site called Old Barrow, what is left of a Roman signal station. There was another, ten miles west of here, near Martinhoe. Both were probably involved in co-ordinating the movements of the Roman fleet in the Bristol Channel, as well as providing advance warning if the Silures from South Wales, for a long time a problem for the Romans, were setting out to raid this coast.

The way leaves County Gate, and by a path half-way up a 950-foot drop into the sea, which is steep but by no means sheer, comes to the lighthouse on Foreland Point. A steep climb brings you to Countisbury, where for a time only the finials of the church tower are visible above the hill-edge. From there it is only two miles to Lynmouth, either along the coast, or more interestingly by Watersmeet (NT), a mile inland. Here the East Lyn, in a narrow gorge hung about with sessile oaks, and with a Victorian lodge (providing teas) on its banks, meets the Farley Water. Both then run down to Lynmouth in a valley that is no wider than before, channelling the water fiercely until it reaches the sea at Lynmouth. Just before it flows into the sea the East Lyn is joined by the West Lyn, and the resort is built at their junction. This topography produced the Lynmouth Flood Disaster of August 1952. Exmoor had been saturated by rain for a fortnight. On the evening of Friday the 15th there was a cloudburst and five inches of rain – one and a half month's average rainfall – fell in one hour. Another four inches fell during the following night and day. It is reckoned that the two rivers brought down 100,000 tons of rock and debris into the town. When the waters had gone down, ten- and fifteen-ton boulders were found where the streets had been. Thirty-four people were drowned. The foreshore was littered with crumpled and shredded cars and with the remains of buildings demolished and carried out to sea by the flood. New and wider beds have been built for the two rivers through Lynmouth, and no buildings now crowd the banks too closely. The place feels gutted.

From Lynmouth to Lynton on the hill above you can take the only lift on any long-distance footpath. This is the nineteenth-century cliff railway, which is operated by an ingenious system of hydraulics, and rises 900 feet at a gradient of four in seven. Lynton is still a Victorian resort, with respectable hotels and villas that have corner turrets to catch the sea-view. A tarmac walk takes you to the Valley of the Rocks, Devon's own version of Monument Valley, which has a famous Iron

Farley Water (on the right) meets the East Lyn River at Watersmeet.

Age hut circle in it. It may be a glacial meltwater channel.

The twelve miles from Lynton to Combe Martin are at first on a small road, past Lee Abbey, a marvellously sited Victorian mansion, around Woody Bay, and then continuing above the crudely serrated cliffline. You come to another of the great notches sliced into this coast by streams. In the graphic vernacular of North Devon these steep valleys are called cleaves, which exactly expresses the cleanness of the cut. The hill beyond it (NT) is as bare as a slag heap, all dirty grey scree. The way skirts the moorland of Holdstone Down, but climbs straight to the top of Great Hangman (NT), which rises blackly beyond Sherrycombe. It is a long labouring haul to the top, from where there is the biggest view so far. In the north, Wales is just visible, while along the coast you have just covered only the tops of three successive ridges can be seen. Inland are intersecting swoops of farmland, everywhere green, while in the west the coastline to come is lower and more broken. Combe Martin, a single-street village with a famous survival on the hill above it of strip fields, marks the end of Exmoor National Park. The four and a half

miles to Ilfracombe are bad, running close to the road, if not on it. The resort itself squeezes you for every penny you have got. In the summer there are regular trips to Lundy from here. This granite island, owned by the Trust, is twenty-five miles away, only a shadowy darkening in the sea-haze from the coast west of Ilfracombe.

Ilfracombe straggles westwards. You climb out of it on to the Torrs Walk (NT), rising to a lovely open grassy stretch as far as Lee, where there is a massive hotel and café. National Trust land continues the far side of Lee Bay. The way is on a primrose path above Damage Cliff, up and down into steep combes where the rock is finely and sharply bedded with a glisteny sheen on it. Around Bull and then Morte Point, where the turbulence from the tide race stretches as far out from the point as the point does from the coast, you drop to the length of Woolacombe Sand. All the previous small coves have been grey, but here the sandstone produces the first yellow beach on the walk. There is not a building on it for two and a half miles. The dunes at the back are

Clovelly and inhabitant.

At Hartland Point.

sown with marram grass to keep them stable. Round Baggy Point at the far end you turn into Barnstaple Bay, where the Taw and Torridge make their joint estuary. Below are the Braunton Burrows, four square miles of sand dune, built up layer by layer from seaward, some of it a Nature Reserve and some a firing range. The way does not venture on to the Burrows, but comes to Braunton, where the path breaks. You must get a bus round over the Taw at Barnstaple and over the Torridge at Bideford, before resuming the walk at West-ward Ho! on the far side of the estuary.

Westward Ho! is a purpose-built resort, laid out as a commercial speculation in the 1860s, and named after Charles Kingsley's novel. Even though a branch line was built to connect it with Bideford this would-be Deauville never took off. The rather stolid and sensible buildings sit beside the beach, faded and cold. Westward Ho! does not match its punctuation. It has become a place to retire to.

Clovelly soon appears on the far side of the bay, a white spill in the dark and woody cliffs. It is eleven miles to get there, most of it on a twisting and tiring path. Buck's Mills, about half-way there, is a tiny ex-fishing village which, as well as the usual pit-prop/coal barter, imported limestone from South Wales; this was burnt in a kiln down by the shore. About a mile beyond Buck's Mills you join the Hobby, a looping terraced road through large beeches

which was constructed in the nineteenth century by the owners of Clovelly Hall, possibly to provide employment during the slump after the Napoleonic wars. It arrives at the top of Clovelly's cobbled street, which drops sharply to the small quay and harbour at the bottom. This must be one of the prettiest villages in England; unlike Broadway in the Cotswolds, another claimant to that title, it has stayed immaculately tasteful and discreet. Even the name sounds like a cocktail of the word 'lovely' stirred in with clotted cream, and that is exactly the tone of the village.

Beyond Clovelly the path runs through National Trust land along the cliff edge to the sharp corner of Hartland Point, where you turn south. The coast changes from being woody and protected to bare and broken rocks facing the full impact of Atlantic storms. About a mile inland from Hartland Quay, just down the coast, is the church of St Nectan. It stands in the village of Stoke, but is the parish church of Hartland, a few miles to the east. Its tower is its glory, 128 feet high, a landmark to sailors, and of a soaring, bare austerity, rising dramatically out of the Devon landscape of thick hedges and warm red earth. Back on the coast again the cliffs at Speke Mill's Mouth are shaped into extravagant curls, with a waterfall sliding into the sea over a single slab of smooth rock. The tendency of streams is to cut their beds down to sea-level. Where a stream arrives at the coast still well above it and drops into the sea as a waterfall, it probably means that

Millook, near Bude.

erosion by the sea in that area is exceptionally rapid.

From here it is about six miles to Morwenstow church, all of it spectacular cliff scenery. Buzzards soar on the up-currents over the cliffs. The island of Lundy now is end-on to the north and narrower than before. The path is through masses of flowers – the inevitable thrift and sea-campion, birdsfoot trefoil and foxgloves. Morwenstow church tower and the telescope dishes above Duckpool stand out clearly to the south. Nearer at hand you pass an Iron Age fort on Embury Cliff, and fields with boundaries curved in a shallow S, a sure sign that these are groups of medieval furlongs which were later enclosed. The S-shape made it easier for the plough teams to turn at each end.

At Marsland Mouth you reach the Cornish border. There is nothing to mark it. The names do not even change from Saxon to Celtic. Cornwall survived as the Celtic kingdom of Dumnonia until the ninth century (the last syllable of Cornwall is the same word as Wales, the Saxon for foreign) and the old edge between Saxon and Celtic can be traced in a line – not quite as sharp as the Landsker in Pembrokeshire – going south-east from around Millook near Bude. It is from there that the Celtic prefix tre- or tref-, meaning a village, starts to predominate over -ton, the Saxon suffix.

This coast is corrugated, on a large scale, with one cleave after another, and with the twisted strata of the rocks themselves, most sharply in the isolated Gull Rock. You pass Morwenstow church, with a tower that is dumpy compared to St Nectan's. The chimneys of the vicarage next to it were themselves shaped into various church towers by the famous eccentric parson R.S.Hawker (1803–75) who wrote *The Song of Western Men* (with the refrain 'And shall Trelawny die?') as

well as other poems. He also insisted on burying drowned sailors with full Christian ritual after they had been washed up on the shores below. The custom was to inter them in unconsecrated ground on the sea-shore itself.

It is six miles from Morwenstow to Bude. You pass the two cream-coloured steel cradles of a satellite tracking station on Lower Sharpnose Point, with views down to the south-west of headlands on the coast – Cambeak, Tintagel and the very distant Trevose Head, each one greyer with the distance, and each one an inducement to make for Land's End. From the massively land-slipped Steeple Point you drop to Bude beach. At low tide it takes you all the way to Bude. The rocks in the cliffs have been exotically folded, in the same Armorican Orogeny that distorted much of Pembrokeshire. All the mouldings of the earth and the borings of the sea down these cliffs, especially in Warren Gutter, are too good to hurry past. You could dawdle an afternoon away here.

The other side of Bude is a slightly tedious stretch of road and hideous bungalows. The only interesting moment is when, looking over the cliff, you are faced with a whole sheet of petrified sand, tipped at an angle of about forty-five degrees, and preserving exactly the ripples on the bed of a geological sea. At Millook there is a particularly striking set of concertina-ed and up-ended striations, which have produced vertical zigzags in the face of the cliff. Beyond it are deeply cleaved pastures and landslipped cliffs. After reaching Crackington Haven (a pub and some houses) you climb through National Trust land to Cambeak and the sudden revelation of the coast to Tintagel. In the distance is the romantic outline of a castle, as you would expect, but this is the nineteenth-century hotel built to cater for the Arthurian boom. In the immediate foreground is the crumbling mass of High Cliff and below it the rocks called the Strangles. Thomas Hardy set the crisis scene of his novel *A Pair of Blue Eyes* on the top of High Cliff. The heroine's suitor, Knight, slips over the edge of the precipice, but manages to hold on to a piece of quartz on the very edge. While hanging like this he looks up from the chasm below: 'Opposite Knight's eyes was an imbedded fossil, standing forth in low relief from the rock. It was a creature with eyes. The eyes, dead and turned to stone, were even now regarding him. It was one of the early crustaceans called Trilobites. Separated by millions of years in their lives Knight and this underling seem to have met in their place of death ... Time closed up like a fan before him.' The cliffs between here and Boscastle, particularly Beeny Cliff, came to have a central place in Hardy's mind. In 1870 he came to St Juliot just inland of here as a young architect to restore the church. When there he met Emma Gifford, with whom he fell in love and who four years later became his wife. She died in November 1912 and in March the next year – the same month as his first visit to St Juliot – he came here again and wrote a flood of poems of remembered love, full of guilt at not having loved her enough when she was alive and of a bemused but unshakably honest sense of loss.

At Boscastle the rocks change, from the sandstones and shales further north, where earth movements have produced grand architectural distortions, to finely bedded slates, bent in much tighter, more intimate ways. Boscastle harbour entrance is difficult to get into, being narrow and curved, and is a strange place too, with the rocks around it dark and bitterly twisted. It is four and a half miles to Tintagel, and all the cliffs are as black as this. The field walls are beautifully built in black slate too, laid precisely in herring-bones and litchen-blotched. It is good preparation for

Rocky Valley near Tintagel, the haunt of St Nectan, a Cornish hermit, and according to Daphne du Maurier a place 'superbly dissociated from humankind'.

Tintagel, the most romantic castle site in England. The earliest connection made between Tintagel and King Arthur was by Geoffrey of Monmouth in the twelfth century, just as Reginald, Earl of Cornwall, was building the first castle here. The medieval builders almost certainly came across parts of the Celtic monastery which was founded on the island in about 500 by St Juliot. It was Tennyson who popularised the legend that Tintagel was the stronghold of Gorlois, Duke of Cornwall, where his wife Ygraine was kept for safety when Uther, King of the Britains, invaded the Duchy. After Merlin had disguised Uther as Gorlois, the King entered Tintagel and seduced Ygraine. Gorlois died and Arthur was born. The castle was repaired in 1852, and a new path made up into the ruins. Tintagel can be one of the most evocative places in England, as much for the incredible exposure of the Celtic monastery as for the Arthurian romance. During a storm is the time to be here, the most Arthurian time of all, when it is easy to imagine how

all day long the noise of battle rolled
Among the mountains by the winter sea.

Tintagel to Land's End 99 miles

It is a beautiful day's walking from Tintagel to Rock in the Camel estuary, eighteen miles away. You leave the village to arrive at the coast by the isolated church of St Materiana, exposed and alone on the cliff edge. The way continues past quarries from which great quantities of slate for walls and roofs have been cut. Much of it was shipped from Port William, to which you soon come, but nothing goes out from there now. Between here and Port Isaac, eight miles from Tintagel, there are eight combes, each about 200 feet deep. In the middle section there are four in a row. You will take the first in your stride; the second will wake you out of your probable reverie about Tintagel; at the top of the third you will have lost all delight in walking, and as you grind up the fourth life will seem to be some absurd parody of the myth of Sisyphus. You finally

Doyden Castle on the shore near Port Quin, a folly of about 1830 once used for banquets.

drop into Port Isaac for lunch. The slates from the famous Delabole quarry used to be exported from here, and there are still some working fishing boats in the harbour. Otherwise it is pasties and cream teas.

The path beyond Port Isaac follows inland farmtracks across the neck of a peninsula (going inland is a relief after 120 miles of bruising Atlantic coast) to Port Quin (NT). It is said that the entire male population of this tiny village was drowned in the eighteenth century

Waves break on the Doom Bar in the Camel estuary, North Cornwall. An easterly longshore drift brings tons of sand into the estuary every year, blocking it for all but the smallest boats.

when trying to escape from a press gang. Just the other side of it is a little castle on Doyden Point, a nineteenth-century folly in which, as in the Kymin above Monmouth, lunch parties were held. Only a few hundred yards beyond it is the wreck of the *Skopalos Sky*, a Greek freighter, with the stern torn off, but with the winches and other gear still on the deck. The pleasure of looking at wrecks is surely more than a simple revelling in someone else's disaster, or imagining the scene of the wreck itself. Perhaps it is the stark incongruity of something so strongly made being thrust up and made useless by rocks and the sea. The *Skopalos Sky* is firmly stuck and does not move with the waves. It seems to be bolted on.

You go on round Port Quin Bay to the pinnacles of Rumps Point, where there is an Iron Age cliff castle, and then on to Pentire Point, which is made of knobbly pillow lavas. The field walls here were built with lumps of this unstratified rock, which bubbled up as molten lava under the sea. The view along the coast is of the tall tower on Stepper Point which serves as a guide for shipping in the daytime, and beyond it the lighthouse on Trevose Head. But better than either of these is

the lovely Camel estuary, a receptive landscape into which the eye penetrates with a sense of relief, filled with yellow sand (the notorious Doom Bar on which ships going into Padstow get caught) and with the fields coming smoothly and unbrokenly down to the water edge. You can walk along the sand almost all the way in, past the church of St Enodoc, half-buried in the dunes, as far as Rock, where in summer there is a passenger ferry across to Padstow. In the evening flood tide men fish for salmon in the estuary.

Padstow is quite a robust place, more so than many beautified Cornish harbours. In the town is a church worth visiting for the font carved in the fifteenth century from the iron-blue Catacleuse stone which outcrops near Trevose Head. The church is dedicated to St Petroc, a wandering Celtic saint like St Nectan. Another church is dedicated to him in Pembrokeshire near Bosherston. From Padstow to Newquay is about twenty miles. Much of this is holiday coast, with beautiful

The Camel at Padstow. There has been a ferry here since at least the fourteenth century.

beaches and a great deal of shapeless holiday development. But there are high points. From the lighthouse on Trevose Head, if you are there on a clear night, you will see the beams from Hartland Point and Lundy in the north and from Godrevy and Pendeen in the south, illuminating in all about 120 miles of coast. Going south from here the rhythm is of beach after beach interrupted by dark strips of harder rock. Beyond Park Head (NT) you come to Bedruthan Steps (NT), which are isolated volcanic crags standing in the sand, once used by Bedruthan, a Cornish giant, as stepping stones. One of them was the scene in 1846 of the wreck of the *Samaritan*, which was carrying silks and cottons. The locals dressed in them for years afterwards, sardonically calling the wreck the *Good Samaritan*. From here it is six miles to Newquay, past an Iron Age fort on Griffin Point and, at the far end of the four-mile long Watergate Beach, another on Trevelgue Head. Judging by the elaboration

The fourteenth-century church of St Enodoc on the Camel Estuary: for hundreds of years buried beneath the encroaching sands, and even now half huddled in them.

of the entrance, with four parallel banks defending it, the people who lived here were probably the latest set of Celts to arrive from the continent, perhaps in the second century BC. (Some archaeologists do not hold with the theory that technical advance could only have come with an infusion of new blood from Europe. There is no reason, they suggest, why the Celts already here should not have thought of adding an extra bank or two themselves.)

Newquay is teeming with fun. There is nothing coy about it. Its open commercialism is rare in Cornish resorts; usually it is submerged in a slurry of cream teas. But Newquay is not Old Cornwall. To see a bit of that it is worth walking three miles inland to Trerice, an Elizabethan manor-house owned by the National Trust. Newquay's suburbs go on for a long time, but once out of them you are in deep lanes, passing some farm cottages covered in clematis, with a view eastwards of the mountains of white quartz waste from the china clay works near St Austell. The house is more tucked away than you could imagine. At the end of a lane where you would expect only barnfowl you find peacocks walking about in front of a house with a smooth ashlar face,

big, well-shaped gables and the enormous window of the Great Hall occupying a fifth of the main facade. The position of Trerice is self-effacing, but its interior is all display, with deeply moulded plaster ceilings and caryatids above the fireplaces.

For ten miles west of Newquay the coast of Cornwall is as piercingly beautiful as the Aegean, particularly in Holywell Bay and the black coves called zawns cut into Penhale Point beyond it. The view is over to the snub nose of St Agnes Head and the two rocks off it called Man and His man. Three miles along Perran Sands, backed by high sandhills that

Trerice, a few miles from Newquay, built by Sir John Arundell in the 1570s from a local limestone called Growan, which when first cut from the quarry is yellow, but silvers with age. No other house in Cornwall flaunts such extravagantly curled gables, and Sir John probably brought the fashion home with him from the Low Countries, where he had served with the English armies.

run into cliffs covered with fulmars, bring you to the small resort of Perranporth. Beyond it there is a sharp change. For about eight miles the path runs over moorland and between wide patches of spoil from the nineteenth-century tin and copper mines here. In places the cliffs are stained red from the one and green from the other. The valley running down to Trevellas Port is particularly harshly wrecked, with the ruins of engine houses standing in it, without even the blur of age to improve them. This for a few decades in the nineteenth century was the world's most productive source of copper. But the discovery of larger ore-bodies in Michigan, together with the fact that in many of the Cornish mines the copper was beginning to pinch out, brought a collapse in the 1860s. The work to be done mining tin was too small to fill the gap, and many Cornishmen left to work the new mines in America.

Beyond Trevaunance Cove, eight miles from Perranporth, it continues much the same. You round St Agnes Head, past Man and His man, and turning the corner you see the white

The engine house of Wheal Coates tin mine just south of St Agnes Head.

Penwith granite: cliffs near Treen, a few miles from Land's End.

tower of Godrevy Light and St Ives beyond it. The path is stony through black heather. Engine houses stand like village-less churches on the clifftops, reaching two-thirds the height of their granite and brick chimneys. From Portreath, seven miles from Trevaunance Cove, it is 18 miles to St Ives, over the Carvannel (NT) and Reskajeage Downs, through gorse and heather, round Navax and then Godrevy Point (all NT) to the long sands of St Ives Bay. The Godrevy Light is white on a barren rock a quarter of a mile off the point. It was the model for the lighthouse in Virginia Woolf's novel *To the Lighthouse*, remembered from childhood holidays in St Ives, but transported in the book to the Hebrides. In the novel the lighthouse is always seen from the far side of the bay, apart and symbolical: 'For the great plateful of blue water was before her; the hoary Lighthouse, distant, austere, in the midst; and on the right, as far as the eye could see, fading and falling in soft low pleats, the green sand dunes with the wild flowing grasses on them, which always seemed to be running away into some moon country ...'

The way to St Ives is across the shockingly cold and tin-stained Red River, and along the sand to Hayle. Grains of the lighter, yellower sand are blown over the grey body of it, but are caught in the sea-made ripples. Inland at Gwithian remains of ploughed Bronze Age fields have been found, with the plough- and spade-marks still visible. Hayle is an industrial town with a power station. It was once the site of iron foundries as well as big tin and copper smelters. It imported vast quantities of iron and coal from South Wales, and, as well as the products of the foundries and smelters, exported Cornwall's famous early vegetables. Early in 1858 30,000 dozen broccoli were sent out from Hayle harbour by steam packet in a single week. Major parts for Trevithick's steam carriage, which climbed Camborne Hill in 1801, were cast here. To get to St Ives you have to walk round the Hayle estuary to Lelant and then along the Porth Kidney sands.

Like every other port in Cornwall St Ives used to smell of salted pilchard, which was the mainstay of Cornish fishing for centuries. The fish were salted, packed in barrels, and sent off, many of them abroad. The fish would appear in great dark shoals which could be seen better from the cliff top than from a boat. The system described by Richard Carew in 1602 was used until the early years of this century: 'Three or four boats lie hovering off upon the coast directed by a Balker or Huer standing on the Cliffe side, who best discerneth the course of the Pilchard and cundeth the master of each boat by crying with a loud voice, and wheazing diversified and significant signes with a bush in his hand.' The most famous of the Huer's cries was the one he uttered on first sighting the dark shoal in the sea, when he would shout 'Hevra! Hevra! Hevra!' from the cliff-top to the men waiting in the harbour. The catch was enormous. In 1850 a lugger was built in Polperro big enough to carry seine nets one and a half miles long. In May 1905 a pilchard shoal arrived that was said to be 100 miles from end to end. But then, quite suddenly, this source of near infinite and very cheap food dried up. The last great shoal, of three million fish (which were worth only £4,500) appeared off Porthgwarra near Land's End in 1916. After that their numbers quickly diminished. The failure of the pilchard is one of the great Cornish mysteries. The reason for it is probably simply that they were over-fished.

St Ives is rightly famous. Palm trees grow in the gardens walled off from the streets; it is more a European than an English town. At low tide there are clean yellow beaches inside the harbour quays. It seems that the light has a peculiar clarity, and many artists have gathered here. Barbara Hepworth's studio and garden are now open to the public as a museum.

St Ives is at the root of the last great boss of granite with which Cornwall and England come to an end. It is called Penwith, and it is twenty miles along its sheared and rigid coastline to Land's End itself. The drama of its position, in every way a bastion against the Atlantic, together with the obstinacy of its unrounded edges, make these some of the most stimulating miles of walking on the whole way. The sea is a delicious aquamarine; inland the ground rises to the knobbly ridge which runs the length of the peninsula. It is slow going, with the land often boggy between the boulders, some of which have chips of glistening mica in them, and some of which are cut in strange smooth scoops. It might take all morning to go the five miles to the Tinner's Arms at Zennor. All along, as Hardy wrote in his notebook in 1872, 'The sea is full of motion internally, but still as a whole. Quiet and silent in the distance, noisy and restless close at hand'. Half a mile inland from the village is Zennor Quoit, a very late Megalithic tomb, built in about 1600 BC, and now partly collapsed. Some of the stones were taken to build a shed in the nineteenth century.

You continue past two Iron Age camps on Gurnard's Head and Bosigran Castle. A mile inland is the contemporary village of Porthmeor – all this in a landscape which is now spectacularly isolated and desolate. The question arises: why did primitive people choose to live in places of such discomfort, when Sussex was always available? The mineral ores must have been part of the answer; here were both copper and tin, the necessary ingredients for bronze, as well as iron, lead and a little silver.

Besides, much of prehistoric England was impenetrable under the primeval forest. But just as important is the fact that buildings or artefacts made of granite or the equally hard and finer Cornish greenstone are likely to last for millennia. It may be simply because more has survived here that it seems so prehistorically populous.

For several miles of the way to Pendeen Watch the way is through and beside one of the most remarkable pieces of landscape history in England. These are the so-called Celtic fields, many of which are garden-sized, some no more than five yards by ten. Various things point to their extreme age. The makers of, for example, the Zennor Quoit would certainly have ploughed for food, and would have had to clear land before they could plough. Where there was a very large boulder in the way the simplest thing was to plan the fields around it. A wall incorporating such a boulder was likely to stay there, and many of these walls contain them. These fields may well be the oldest human constructions still in use in England.

St Ives, its back to the Atlantic, and beaches inside the quays.

There is a stubby lighthouse at Pendeen, which was built here to fill a blackspot between Longships off Land's End and Godrevy. Ships used to mistake Gurnard's Head for Land's End and turning round it sail straight inshore. A single grapefruit-size bulb is used. Around it revolves a four-ton cradle carrying the magnifying lenses, the whole assembly floating on a ton of mercury. On clear nights the light can be seen in the Scillies, which even on exceptionally good days appear as no more than a dark pencil line on the horizon. Between Land's End and the Scillies stretched the legendary land of Lyonesse, 140 parishes of which were drowned in the Flood. Almost certainly this is a folk memory of the drowning of large parts of the Scillies, when the sea rose at the end of the Ice Age.

Pendeen Watch is on a corner and you turn now into a tract of Cornwall that was once the scene of intense mining activity. A single mine, Geevor, is still working, but the majority are cold and still, with columned chambers, tall empty halls and towers like stocky minarets. The red stain from the tin is everywhere, on the stones and in the streams that wash down through the site. There are two engine houses

Erme Mouth, South Devon.

BOTTOM LEFT *The landslip of soft red sandstone in South Devon called The Floors. At the far end of it is Budleigh Salterton.*

BELOW *Sidmouth: a visit by George III in 1791 ensured its prosperity and another by the Duke and Duchess of Kent with their infant Victoria in 1819 prolonged it.*

The only working tin mine in Cornwall, at Geevor near St Just: below it the sea is stained red.

down the cliff itself, and below them red scum on the sea. All this is set in among Celtic boulder walls, with horses on the green grass. The paths are stony between piles of waste 'dead'. As in Milford Haven, industry was introduced into a rural landscape here without producing a sense of rape.

From the mines around Botallack it is seven miles to Land's End, by Cape Cornwall, and the chambered cairn above it called Carn Gloose. This turns out to be uninteresting, little more than a pile of rubble with gaps in it, not very different from the tips of 'dead' around the mines at Botallack. Land's End appears, and this side of it a strip of sand in Whitesand Bay. The cliffside is riddled with adits, drains and shafts. If you walk barefoot on the beach in Whitesand Bay you will find the sand grainy between your toes. This granite sand would clog an egg-timer, and is quite different from the almost liquid, sedimentary sand which ran between your fingers in the Camel estuary.

You come to Land's End. It is a double point with the weirdly incongruous names of Dr Syntax's and Dr Johnson's Head. The lighthouse on Wolf Rock, nine miles away,

seems to stand unsupported in the sea. Nearer at hand is the Longships tower light. There will always be hundreds of people here, on the pilgrimage to the bottom of England. It is almost as if a form of geographical gravity were drawing us here.

Land's End to Fowey 104 miles

Land's End is exactly two-fifths of the way from Minehead to Poole Harbour. You turn the corner and set off for the 312 miles that remain, now with (in Eliot's words)

> Your shadow at morning striding behind you
> And your shadow at evening rising to meet you.

It is fourteen miles to Penzance, along the spectacular granite coast, which has weathered along shrinkage lines in the rock into stacks and caves and half-isolated pinnacles. There are many more villages down by the coves on this southern coast than on the northern. You pass Porthgwarra and St Levan, coming to Porthcurno, where the famous Minack Theatre is cut into the cliff in steps, and where the sand in the cove must be the whitest in England. On this tiny beach the telegraph cable from India, much of it laid by Brunel's

Great Eastern, was brought ashore in 1870, having come by way of Gibraltar, Malta, Alexandria and Suez from Bombay. The Lizard peninsula appears to the east, long and flat, like Pembrokeshire, a raised sea-bed. At Penberth (NT) small brightly painted inshore fishing boats are drawn up on the slip, with the old capstan and grey cottages above them. You pass Lamorna Cove, and, as you climb Carn Du, St Michael's Mount suddenly appears in the east. The style of a coast walk is to reveal things around corners. On moorland the transformation of the view is slow and growing, but here new sights are sudden and immediate. The Mount is one of the best, the most romantic silhouette in England, and rather un-English because of it. It is two miles to Mousehole, a grey and white harbour with excellent cafés, and another two along the road to Newlyn, which is Cornwall's only surviving fishing port of any size. Between it and Mousehole is the appreciable gap between the factory style of real fishing and the rather cleaner version served up for tourists and walkers.

Newlyn merges into Penzance. The best building here, in Chapel Street, is the extra-

St Michael's Mount, the most romantic silhouette in England, greatly enhanced by nineteenth-century additions on the seaward side.

ordinary Egyptian House, used as a National Trust shop. Its front is the kind of façade you might expect to find on a 1920s cinema, but this house was built in 1830. For some reason vertical lines are considered here to be un-Egyptian, and every one on its façade leans inwards.

It is about three miles along the Bay to St Michael's Mount. This small upsurge of granite, called Ictis in antiquity, was one of the places from which tin ingots were exported to the continent. The trade was under way by as early as the fifth century BC. Just north of here, at Halmanning near St Hilary, four Greek vases of that period have been found, while two Attic cups and a jug of a century later were discovered at Teignmouth in Devon. It is difficult to associate the sophistication of these objects and of the culture which produced them with the relatively crude constructions of contemporary Cornwall. Perhaps the tin trade should be seen as the exploitation by the advanced societies of an undeveloped Britain. Nothing of this period remains on the Mount. In 1044 Edward the Confessor established a chapel here dependent on the Benedictine Abbey at Mont St Michel in Normandy, and from then the Mount has been remoulded and added to at steady intervals, so that now the house is an extraordinary jumble of periods and styles. One of the best rooms is the

*Lyme Regis: the contradiction of
architectural delicacy on the edge of a
potentially violent sea.*

63

refectory of the medieval monastery. Around the walls is a seventeenth-century plaster frieze depicting in cartoon figures the Ballad of Chevy Chase, which is set near Otterburn on the Pennine Way. At the top of the Mount is a pale blue drawing-room and boudoir, re-modelled in 1744 out of the Lady Chapel. From the terraces outside all of Mount's Bay and the length of the Lizard can be seen.

It is ten miles to Porthleven, at first along the Golden Mile, where cauliflowers and other market garden produce are grown right on the edge of the sea, and then on through banks of wild flowers, campion and sea campion, bluebells, violets and wild garlic. In Prussia Cove you might see ravens and seals off the rocks where the most famous of Cornwall's smugglers, John Carter, landed his contraband from France. Cornwall is associated with smuggling and with heroic villains wearing black eye-patches, though in truth no more smuggling went on here than on any other coast. But walkers on the coast path have good reason to be interested in the history of smuggling, or at least in the way it ended. In 1856 the Coastguard Act was passed and smuggling was finished. From their houses on the coves and huts on the headlands the coastguards tramped out the path you now follow, or a good deal of it, not short-cutting from inlet to inlet, but painstakingly winding around every twist and up to every point. The aim was to leave no place hidden, since one unvisited spot would be all the smuggler would need.

You continue along Praa Sands and up the cliff on the far side of it, owned by the National Trust, where there is the ruin of another engine house, Wheal Prosper, which was closed in 1860 after the undersea workings began to leak. The pits and shafts are overgrown with the plants that thrive in the shelter of Mount's Bay, an entirely different atmosphere from the stony wrecks around St Just. Approaching Porthleven, below a memorial cross to drowned sailors, is a 50-ton boulder known as Giant's Rock. It is gneiss with garnets embedded in it, a rock not found anywhere else in Britain. It may have been brought here in an iceberg. Porthleven is a harsh and ugly granite place, satisfying grist to an eye jaded by too many fey harbours.

The twelve miles from Porthleven to the bottom of the Lizard Peninsula are marvellous walking. You start out on an undulating track above Porthleven Burrows (NT), which are grassy sandhills, and then pass on to the Loe Bar, a bank of what is either very fine shingle or very coarse sand. Dammed behind it is the Loe Pool, the two still, dark arms of which curve away inland, fringed by trees blow-dried into a curl away from the sea, and by fields

piped with neat hedges. Bodies of drowned sailors are buried here.

At the end of the beach you climb again past recent cliff falls round Halzephron (a corruption of the Cornish for Hell Cliff) and then down to Gunwalloe church. Its belfry is separate and attached to the rock. This is an archetypal Cornish place, with the golden sand smoothing out a small bay contained between black, sharp cliffs. The church is dedicated to St Winwalloe, a Cornish Breton, who never sat down in church, wore neither wool nor linen, but only goat hair, slept on birch bark with a stone for a pillow, drank water and occasionally crab apple cider, and ate only barley bread mixed with ashes. This was not particularly extraordinary among the wandering Celtic saints of the Dark Ages. A fifth of all the places in Britain named after saints are in Cornwall. Their connection with Wales, Brittany and Ireland brings a geographical realignment, in which being on the shores of the same sea becomes more important than mere terrestrial contiguity.

From Winwalloe's church to the bottom of the Lizard is about eight miles. You pass above Poldhu Point where there is a memorial to Marconi, the radio pioneer. The first trans-atlantic radio message was sent from here in December 1901. All this is National Trust. Past Mullion Cove and Mullion Island, covered in seabirds, the underlying rock changes from the Old Red Sandstone to a collection of hard old sterile rocks which form the tip of the Lizard peninsula. You move on to blasted heath. It is their hardness which has meant that the Lizard has resisted the erosion which has removed everything from around it, and turned it into a peninsula. The most famous of the rocks is serpentine. It comes in two forms – a dark, bloody red and a green the colour and appearance of sage stuffing. Some of the rocks in Kynance Cove are made of it, as are the foot-polished steps leading up on to the cliff from the cove. It is amusing to find that the Lizard is made principally from a rock called serpentine, but unfortunately there is no connection between the two. The rock's name refers to the snaking bands of lighter stone to be found in it, while Lizard is probably a corruption of the Cornish for 'rocky height'.

The tail of the Lizard is blunt, coming not to a point but a mile-wide stub. You pass the southernmost café in Britain, and shops selling serpentine ash-trays and four-foot-high light-houses. Lizard village is half a mile up the road. In the peak of summer, traffic can take three hours to get from the village to the café.

It is ten miles from the Lizard to Coverack, past the lighthouse, by Cadgwith, a thatched village, and in parts through lanes lined with thorn bushes. In spring they are thick with

white flowers, almost furry with them. A stinking piggery greets you on the edge of Coverack, which is well arranged around a curving bay, and is half-way round the South-West Peninsula Coast Path.

To the Helford River is eleven miles, a good deal of it inland where quarries are still working on the coast. You can go by St Keverne, where in the churchyard are the communal graves of those wrecked on the dangerous coast here. The Manacles, a mile off Porthoustock, claim a good tithe of the shipping into Falmouth. Worst of all were the wreck on the same night in 1809 of HMS *Dispatch* and HMS *Primrose*, both bringing troops home from the Peninsular War. Graves from both wrecks can be found at St Keverne.

Just short of the Helford River you have to wade Gillan Creek at low tide, and then in two miles make your way to Helford itself. By now you will be quite blasé about the pure prettiness of Cornish seaside villages, but Helford, with trees leading down to narrow creeks, and houses half hidden in them, stands out even after nearly 300 miles of coast path. Across the Helford River you take the first of a number of ferries which punctuate the walk

The Helford River at low tide. As at Milford Haven in Pembrokeshire, the lower reaches of the Helford were drowned by the rising sea at the end of the last Ice Age.

rather irregularly from here to Exmouth. All of them are over river valleys that were drowned at the end of the Ice Age. The ferries are delightful, a kind of necessary and inescapable joyride. This one is only a small fibreglass dinghy, and the continuous sound on the crossing is the hollow, and distinctly modern, knocking of halyards against aluminium masts. In all but easterlies the Helford is a good harbour.

A mile beyond Helford Passage, on the far side, is Durgan, a whitewashed hamlet owned by the National Trust, at the bottom of a woody valley whose top end has been turned into a garden full of rhododendrons and old trees. The azalea lushness of this garden, called Glendurgan, would have been impossible on the north coast. It is only five miles round Toll Point (NT) and Rosemullion Head (NT) into Falmouth.

Henry VIII had built Pendennis and St Mawes Castles, on either side of the Carrick

65

Fowey Harbour: the right combination of commercial port and yachting basin.

Roads, as part of his scheme to fortify the whole south coast in the 1540s, but until 1660 there was no deepwater quay at Falmouth. At that time a port was planned and built on the site of two villages, Smith Hike and Penny-Come-Quick. Carrick Roads is one of Britain's best harbours, and the first good refuge for ships coming in off the western approaches. The Falmouth Packets, small fast ships, started a regular service to America and the West Indies in 1668 and the port prospered. When the railway arrived it became a fashionable resort, while the harbour remained full and busy. Three quite large and separate places – Flushing, St Mawes and Falmouth itself – stand around the Roads, separated by water and joined by regular ferries. It has something, but only something, of a Venetian air.

The way continues on the far side at Place, opposite St Mawes. It is little more than a hotel and a very simple thirteenth-century church. Only in summer is there a regular ferry from Falmouth. It is about twenty-one miles up the coast of this neglected part of Cornwall to Mevagissey. Long stretches of it are owned by the National Trust. There are great cliffs on St Anthony's Head, with long views to Nare

Head and the pier-like length of Dodman Point beyond it. About a mile the other side of Portscatho, and a little inland, is the large earthwork of Dingerein Castle. The name means the castle of Geraint. In the Anglo-Saxon Chronicle a Geraint is mentioned as King of the Britons in the eighth century. If it is the same one, this would be remarkable evidence of an Iron Age life-style surviving into the historical period.

The highlight of the whole day's walk is Caerhays Castle, just west of Dodman Point. This carefree castellated house was designed by John Nash in 1808 against a background of tall, monumental trees, of a fullness rare in Cornwall. Below the house is an ornamental lake, overshadowed by the natural beauty of the Cove next to it.

You swing round Dodman Point, entirely owned by the National Trust, and five miles beyond it come to Mevagissey. Its double harbour is full of large fishing boats, most of them now with their decks full of creels for shell-fishing. The boats are all brightly painted, but with a thick layer of filth over the paint. Incongruously these working boats, whose decking and bulwarks are bruised and splintered, have angelic names like *Reine du Ciel* or *L'Alouette*. Mevagissey's whitewashed houses are stacked above the quays.

It is five miles to Charlestown, a lot of it along the road, and then round the corner into St Austell Bay, which looks as if it needs dusting. Over the sheds of the china clay works a fine white powder has settled. Inland north of here is a wide area of half rotten granite. This is the matrix of the china clay, which is quarried with high-pressure hoses. The process is extraordinarily wasteful. For every ton of china clay produced, eight tons of useless material are tipped out on the famous white tents that make the landscape north of here. The industry has grown and grown. The first deposits were discovered in about 1745 and by 1820 20,000 tons were being produced a year. Now 2,000,000 tons a year are produced, and the quarry to quay processes take eight hours as opposed to the eight months they used to take. As well as making porcelain the clay goes into rubber and plastic products, paint, ink and dyes. The gritty bits in toothpaste are particles of china clay.

Beyond Little Hell, on the far side of Par Sands, you emerge from the industrial. The way comes round to Polkerris, where a short quay encloses little more than a beach. It is four miles to Fowey, past the towering red and white daymark on Gribbin Head (NT), and then into the mouth of this, the prettiest of Cornish harbours. Polruan is poured over the opposite hillside, and beyond it a series of headlands disappear eastwards into the haze. The harbour itself is full of yachts, dredgers and tugs, with the occasional china clay ship making its way up the Fowey river to the railhead at Bodinnick. Woody creeks wind away round corners from the harbour.

Fowey to Brixham 94 miles

The thirty miles from Fowey to Plymouth can be encapsulated in a few words. As far as Looe, eleven miles from Fowey, the cliffs are as wild and unclipped as they have been on the way up from Land's End. Inserted into them, a crack in this harsh coast, is Polperro, the most famous of all the Cornish fishing villages, and as tightly packed and turned in on itself as a place could be. At Looe there is a change. Much of the way to Rame Head, thirteen miles away, is on the road, and some of it through a military firing range which closes the path from time to time. Here too are caravan deserts. Almost the only moment of interest is in Whitesand Bay (NT), where a rock chamber has been hollowed out of the cliff foot and the

Polperro: boats packed in the notch of a harbour as tightly as the houses are around it.

resulting hole called the Sharrow Grot. This was done in the late eighteenth century by a naval officer in search of a cure for his gout. The grot has verses carved all over it. The six miles from Rame Head to Plymouth are different, coming round from the openness of the Head to the steep shores of the most beautiful harbour in England. The red sandstone villages of Cawsand and Kingsand are tucked into a scoop in the coast of the Sound, and beyond them an easy level track brings you into the parkland around Mount Edgcumbe, which was the estate coveted by the Duke of Medina Sidonia when he came up-Channel with the Armada. Temples, a conservatory and ruins are carefully disposed around it now. It is an excellent way to arrive at Britain's biggest naval base. You come to the ferry at Cremyll, and beyond the pub here the sight greets you of the grey bulk of warships up the Hamoaze towards Devonport. You take the ferry across,

A folly in Edgcumbe Park above Plymouth Sound. The Duke of Medina Sidonia planned to live here after a successful Armada had installed Philip of Spain on the English throne.

The knotted metamorphic rocks on Bolt Head near Salcombe.

and leave Cornwall after following its coast for 268 miles.

Plymouth still has the air of a bombed city, with wide open spaces in the new centre, and still, occasionally, an empty lot. Sir Paul Reilly put the finger on Plymouth: 'There is in all city dwellers a built-in requirement for the three H's – higgledy-piggledy, huggermugger and hullabaloo. Anyone walking round the new city centre of Plymouth at nine o'clock at night will appreciate the gloomy absence of these qualities.' Much of the old part, by Sutton Harbour and in the Barbican, escaped destruction, and there are small streets here in which the atmosphere of old Plymouth, if rather smartened up, survives. Down here is the quay where in June 1620 the *Speedwell* berthed after springing a leak on the way down the Channel from London. Her passengers, the Pilgrim Fathers, transferred to the *Mayflower* and continued to America.

The Coast Path begins again in Turnchapel on the far side of the Plym. There is no ferry across to it, and you have to make a long walk round through the outskirts of Plymouth before you reach coast that is not built up. It is then nine miles to the estuary of the Yealm at Newton Ferrers. The way is through HMS *Cambridge*, a naval gunnery school, where trainees fire at a drogue pulled slowly over them by an aeroplane. Beyond it, islanded in National Trust land, is Wembury church, almost on the sea edge, and almost certainly built there to guide sailors. Offshore is the pyramid of the Great Mew Stone. The ferry over the Yealm is the best of them all. You come down to stone steps that continue underwater and, standing there, simply bellow 'ferry' at the opposite shore. It may seem a primitive thing to do, but sooner or later one will come across.

From the landing place on the far side, the next nineteen miles are a whole. The way is along the edge of the good agricultural land of south Devon, with small farms (on average about 100 acres), large fields, mostly of sheep, a little arable and some dairy land. It is dissected in two places by drowned river valleys, at Erme Mouth and at the estuary of the Avon. You must wade them both (if the Avon ferry is not working), one ankle- the other thigh-deep.

All the way along the rocks are good, but those on the western side of Erme Mouth are quite amazingly beautiful, in finely different shades of pink, like shot silk. Bigbury-on-Sea and the joint villages of Inner and Outer Hope below Bolt Tail are the only intrusions on this empty stretch. It has none of the fierceness of Penwith, and is plainly a Channel, not an Atlantic, Coast. At Thurlestone there is even a golf-course next to the sea. It is a withdrawal from exposure, a softening towards Dorset.

The four-and-a-half-mile stretch from Bolt Tail to Bolt Head is different. All of it is owned by the National Trust, and sticks out like a hammer-head into the Channel. Quartz prods through the grass in places like blocks of mint cake.

The way comes round off Bolt Head into the Salcombe estuary. J. A. Froude, the biographer of Carlyle, had a house here, where Tennyson quite regularly came to stay. At the mouth of the estuary is the Salcombe Bar, with many beacons marking it. This is said to be the inspiration for Tennyson's poem 'Crossing the Bar'. After visiting Froude in May 1889, he left Salcombe by yacht, and as the boat reached the harbour mouth he noticed how the waves 'gave forth a surfy, slow deep, mellow voice, and with a hollow moan crossed the bar'. The poem itself was written the following October. On the west side of the estuary is Sharpitor, a National Trust garden which benefits from the almost tropical air that this protected place enjoys. Another delightful ferry takes you across at Salcombe.

From Salcombe it is four miles, full of bluebells and fern, past the extraordinary collection of Ham Stone, Gammon Head and Pig's Nose (all NT) to Prawle Point. Beyond it is one of the clearest examples in England of a raised beach. It is quite obvious in the coast extending east from the point that there are two shorelines – the present one and another, a line of cliffs a few hundred yards back, which is stranded in the middle of fields. It is easy walking along them for the four miles to Start Point, where the coast turns north into the great bow of Lyme Bay, which you do not leave until Weymouth. This is more obvious on the map than on the ground, where it is Start Bay that is revealed, lined by yellow

The sands of another Blackpool, near Dartmouth.

beaches, and backed by a gently bumpy landscape into which the exactly fitting cloth of fields seems to have been pegged down.

You pass the deserted and half-destroyed village of Hallsands on the cliff edge. The ecology of the coast here was destroyed when too much shingle (half a million tons) was removed at the end of the nineteenth century for building in Plymouth Docks. It took until 1917 for the seaward side of the main street to be finally undermined and collapse. Beyond Limpet (where the rocks are as good as at Erme Mouth, but grey) you come on to Slapton Sands, where on the slithery shingle the Americans practised for the D-Day landings. It is twelve miles into Dartmouth, along the Sands, which dam behind them the lagoon called Slapton Ley, a nature reserve. You will see ducks and herons, and maybe the odd sight of a swan on the edge of the sea. At the far end of the beach you walk along the road for four miles (around Blackpool Sands), then you follow a high cliff walk through National Trust land to Dartmouth, arriving above the fifteenth-century castle, a protection against French raiders, and turn into the steep dark harbour. Tall town houses stand round the quays of Dartmouth's inner basin. It has been a substantial seaport since the twelfth century, when it imported claret. The Naval College on the hill above it is visibly tidy from Kingswear on the far side of the Dart, and gives the whole town a crisp veneer.

From Kingswear to Brixham is nine miles, again along a winding country road as far as Man Sands, where there are a couple of coastguard cottages and a limekiln. The change to limestone underfoot is very obvious as you approach Berry Head above Brixham. It has been quarried here for centuries. The head is the southern point of Tor Bay. You drop from it to the edge of Brixham, a fishing port which has become engulfed in the holiday conurbation of Torbay. Officially the path breaks off at Brixham, and except for a short stretch this side of Paignton does not resume until Meadfoot Beach at the far side of the Bay. In the summer there is a ferry across from the pretty Victorian harbour to Torquay.

Torbay has a resident population of over 100,000 people. It is a monument to the fashion for the seaside which began in the

At Watcombe, north of Torquay.

seventeenth century and has not stopped yet. By the end of the eighteenth century any seaside place, with or without a mineral spring, had become suitable for health purposes, and the combination in south Devon of good weather and accessibility brought a rapid expansion in Exmouth, Teignmouth, Dawlish, Sidmouth, Seaton, Budleigh Salterton, Paignton and Torquay. It soon became fashionable to go to the seaside whether you were ill or not. Nevertheless the medical aspect continued well into the nineteenth century. In the 1840s every room in Torquay was provided with a spittoon for consumptives. Keats and Elizabeth Barrett Browning both spent time here.

In the middle of the nineteenth century sea air became more important than sea water; those resorts with sandy beaches became more attractive, and expanded more quickly than those with shingle. The railway arrived at Torquay in 1848 and ensured the prosperity of what Ruskin called the Italy of England. Sidmouth and Budleigh Salterton were only linked to the life-giving network in 1874 and 1897 respectively, and as a result they have kept more intact their tone of the earlier, more patrician holiday-making.

Torquay to Poole Harbour 114 miles

The fifteen miles from Torquay to the estuary of the Exe at Starcross are not good walking. At first you are on an empty and broken coast, a tiring switchback path, which brings you to Shaldon on the Teign. There is a ferry across to the resort of Teignmouth, which still exports potter's clay from up the river, but otherwise is given over to holidays. It is on the main Paddington–Penzance line, engineered through here on the very edge of the sea by Brunel in 1846. With a short break on the main road you can follow the railway itself as far as Dawlish Warren, a sandspit into which the sea is eating. It is now half the width it was in the eighteenth century. The way to Starcross is partly on a green lane, where you brush through gorse, and partly on the road. At Starcross is a red Italianate tower of crumbling stone standing next to the railway. This is a pumping station for the Atmospheric Railway, an early scheme of Brunel's, by which trains would have been driven along by a piston in a continuous vacuum pipe. The pipes were always leaking and the whole scheme was a disaster.

The estuary of the Exe is not as attractive as the Dart; it is wider and the banks bare and shallow. The ferry across it is the tenth on the walk and the last until Poole Harbour. The twenty-six miles from Exmouth on the far side to Lyme Regis on the Dorset border are the

A stack of hard red sandstone in Ladram Bay. The rock was laid down on the seabed about two hundred million years ago.

best part of the south coast of Devon. You start off along the promenade past rows of cream-coloured hutches, and then climb up on to the red earthy cliff, through caravans, and with the wide wound of high red crumbled cliff ahead called the Floors. Far away in the east is the white dot of chalk in Beer Head. Chalk is an eastern rock in England. That whiteness is as clear a sign as there could be that you are making progress towards Poole. Six miles from Exmouth the path drops into Budleigh Salterton, which has a grey shingle beach that spills on to the path, and a good beachside café. Sir Walter Raleigh was born at Hayes Barton just west of here, and when Millais came to paint *The Boyhood of Raleigh* the setting he chose was Budleigh Salterton.

It is six miles to Sidmouth, at first inland on a causeway above sedgy fields, to a bridge over the Otter, and then through tidied fields along a red cliff edge. The rock is harder and sharper than the other side of Budleigh, and jagged in layers. At Ladram are six ruddy stacks of it standing off shore, the fiercest coastal scenery since Penwith. There are two steep climbs before you come down into Sidmouth, which is the best of all the Regency resorts on this coast. This lovely town at the mouth of the Sid, squeezed between two red cliffs, is full of pretty villas with fragile verandahs and canopied balconies. Grimy from hundreds of miles round the coast, Sidmouth makes you feel like a country cousin.

From Sidmouth to Lyme Regis is about 13 miles. You climb steeply from the end of the beach on red marl, with Sidmouth and Sidbury revealed like a maze below. At the top of Salcombe Hill are buttercup meadows, darkened by the seed heads of the hay. After them, in National Trust land, come two exhausting coombes. The rock changes from red sandstone to greensand and clays, the inevitable accompaniment of chalk. The strung-out thatched village of Branscombe is inland from here, with a Norman church and cherry trees in the graveyard, and a good pub, the Mason's Arms. At Branscombe Mouth the path runs just below a sixteenth-century farmhouse owned by the National Trust with the beautiful name of Great Seaside.

Beyond it is the first of the landslips between here and Chesil Beach. This one foundered in March 1790 when ten acres of the cliff collapsed, and the shoreline receded by two hundred yards. The path through it is surrounded by thick scrub, with fragments of white and orange cliff above it. When you emerge at the top it is a mile on chalk turf into Beer, and another into Seaton, a brasher resort than most, the only one on this coast that is ugly.

It is six miles to Lyme Regis, one of them on a high windy golf-course, and the others through the Dowlands Landslip, different parts of which have slipped at different times. The most spectacular was on Christmas Eve 1839, when twenty acres of the cliff subsided, taking fields and hedges with it. The structure of the earth is weak here. Highly porous chalk lies on a bed of gault that dips at five degrees towards the sea. After heavy rain the chalk gets waterlogged and then slides massively seawards as if off a shovel. The path is very up and down through the broken and jumbled rocks of the slip, which are now covered in profuse vegetation, much of it large ash-trees, some fallen and all untended, with trailers hanging down from them in places like door curtains. In summer bluebells and wild garlic grow beneath a shrub horizon of hazel, hawthorn, privet and ubiquitous brambles. It is tempting to say that this almost unique example in southern England of untreated nature is what the men of the New Stone Age coming from Spain or France would have found, but that would be wrong. The ash-tree, which is a light-seeking plant, did not appear in England until the Bronze Age, when the natural oak and alder cover had already been widely destroyed. But in the texture and density of the Dowlands Landslip there is evidence of the natural luxuriance of this country, a jungly thickness and variety of vegetable life which seems quite alien to England. It is cheering to find that this restrained and demure land is at heart so exuberant.

At the end of it you emerge – it is like a tunnel mouth – to a view of the Dorset coast beyond Lyme Regis, a series of hills arriving at the sea as cliffs. Each has a cap of the yellow Upper Greensand, which is harder than the Liassic clays below it. You arrive at the Cobb, the harbour of Lyme Regis, which is full of

dinghies and is the place where the Duke of Monmouth landed in 1685 to begin his disastrous rebellion. The front of Lyme is brightly colour-washed, with frail trellissed porches on the doors. In the town is an excellent fossil museum, full of great cartwheel ammonites from the Lias cliffs and with reconstructions of ichthyosaurs like spaceships.

After Charmouth, a pebble beach two miles from Lyme, is one of the best parts of the walk, on steeply smooth turf up to Golden Cap, with the coast stretching ahead in a shallow curve to the beginning of Chesil Beach. Inland are the receding hummocks of Dorset, with villages in the crevices between them. The scale in this landscape is exactly right: it is stimulating without being browbeating. There is no sense here – as there is in bigger hills – of people and what they do being small or insignificant. Where the Lake District, for example, is naturally the poet's landscape, this by nature is the novelist's. On top of Golden Cap and set well back from its sea-quarried face is a memorial, studded with fossils, to Lord Antrim, chairman of the National Trust from 1965 until 1976.

From Golden Cap it is six and a half miles to Burton Bradstock, by Seatown, where they pack pebbles into plastic bags for export, and West Bay at the mouth of the Brit. Burton Bradstock might almost be wrapped in thatch. Roses hang off the cottages and instead of graves the churchyard is full of buttercups and daisies. Like Bridport, inland from West Bay, Burton was a centre of rope-making. There is an old mill in the village where locally grown flax was spun into ropes and nets. In Bridport there is only one rope-maker left. The highest quality football nets are made there.

Burton is at the northern end of Chesil Beach, which in a gentle curve stretches seventeen miles from here to Chesil on the Isle of Portland. The beach is a geological oddity. The pebbles are almost all flint, which occurs only in chalk, even though the underlying rocks behind the beach are all the older Jurassic limestones and clays. They were probably dumped here at the end of the Ice Age. The bank gets higher and wider the nearer it gets to the Isle of Portland, and more strangely the pebbles grow very steadily in diameter, from pea-size at the northern end to fist-size at the southern. No one is quite sure why this happens. It is certain, at least, that this very efficient grading is the result of different kinds of wave arriving at the beach.

Seven miles from Burton Bradstock you turn inland, around a hill capped by St Catherine's Chapel and blue with flowers, to Abbotsbury. The whole village is built from the yellow-brown oolite and thatched with reeds that grow in the Fleet, a lagoon behind Chesil Beach. You can visit the chapel to St Catherine on top of the hill. It is weather-eaten away, but has a new stone vault made of stone from the Clipsham quarries in Leicestershire, which is paler and cooler than the local limestone. The best building in Abbotsbury, though, is the abbey's tithe barn, built in the fourteenth century like the chapel, and ninety yards long, with great slits for windows, and a thatched roof the length of it. The reeds for roofing the village are now kept inside and it is locked shut with rust-coloured doors.

Abbotsbury is a classic case of the pretty village being taken over by the rich and retired, who raise house prices and exclude the locals. The village has become a place where the people who live there are as much tourists as those who come for day trips, an exquisite shell.

It is eight miles from Abbotsbury to Weymouth. A lane deep in cow-parsley drops from the village to near the Fleet. The whole side of the hill to the right, on which the chapel stands, was cut into terraces by the monks of the Middle Ages. On the Fleet itself you will see the birds from the famous swannery, where 500 mute swans breed yearly. The way continues on a lane high above it, with the continuous lines of the open Dorset downs in the north, on one of which is the Hardy monument. This, ironically, is not to the novelist, but another Thomas Hardy, Nelson's flag-captain at Trafalgar, who lived at Portesham below it. All the time the mass of Portland rises ahead. The coast path does not follow it round, but it is one of the oddest landscapes in England, quite distinct from Dorset, and joined to it only by the root of Chesil Beach. There can scarcely be another such gathering of hardness – the quarries into England's purest building stone, the military installations, the oil depot, the borstal, the prison and the natural cliffs. No wonder this speck of grit sticks miles out into the Channel.

After Langton Herring, you drop to the side of the Fleet, where the intention is to build a nuclear power station. On the water you will see swans, waders, ducks, herons and maybe some little terns which have a protected breeding site here. The surface of the Fleet is broken by eel-grass on which the birds feed. Beyond it the back of Chesil Beach looks almost like a lorry-dumped bank of shingle. Around the shallow bays and promontories you come to East Fleet, all that remains of a village and church smashed in 1824 by storms that came over the beach. At about the same time a 500-ton ship was blown over and into the Fleet. It is only a couple of miles along the narrowing lagoon to Weymouth.

At the very middle of Weymouth is a statue of George III, gaudily painted and gilded, not at all solemn, a holiday version of the usual royal portrait. He made Weymouth fashionable between 1790 and 1810, when the now familiar terraces were built. Weymouth seems a little more solid and built with a little less whimsy than somewhere like Sidmouth. Ships and helicopters belonging to the navy are constantly coming and going in the Bay.

From Weymouth to Lulworth is twelve miles, at first along the road to Overcombe, but from there clear along the cliff tops, past the dull remains of a Roman Temple and a palace-like Pontin's Holiday Camp. Inland you get a sight of the only chalk-cut horse in England which has a rider. He wears a cocked hat and was cut in 1808 as a tribute to George III. After Osmington Mills (a pub on the path) you skirt the deserted village of Ringstead, which is said to have been destroyed by a combination of pirates and the Black Death, and is now no more than a farm and a few swellings in the turf. The five miles to Lulworth, after a climb on to the occasionally self-combusting shale on Burning Cliff, are all on high downland. This is the end of the stub of chalk that comes down from Salisbury Plain through Cranborne Chase and the Dorset Downs to arrive here at the sea in clean white cliffs. The hills have the rounded firmness of all downland, with deep combes sweeping in and out of them, the most anatomical shapes of which rock is capable. But the formation here is more complicated than at the Seven Sisters or Dover. Just seaward of the chalk there was once a continuous but rather narrow wall of the Portland Stone. The rock arch called Durdle Door, which sticks out beyond the line of the chalk cliffs, is a remnant of it. But in Stair Hole, and more famously in Lulworth Cove on the far side of it, something more dramatic has happened. The sea has pierced the Portland barrier, and, once beyond the narrow hole it has made, has begun to scoop out wide bays in the soft Wealden clays which outcrop here. In Lulworth Cove it is as though the earth is holding its finger to its thumb. The rock itself is striped and folded, like layers of a twisted licorice allsort. This is the work of the great Alpine earth movements, forty million years ago.

The last stage of this gargantuan walk is the twenty-six miles from Lulworth to Poole Harbour. The first six of them are through the military range used for tank practice. For a week in June, all of August, the first half of September, almost every week-end, for three weeks at Christmas and one at Easter the footpaths through the range are open. At other times you must detour round through Dorset, which is no bad alternative. Through the range there is a guide post every fifty yards to keep you on the right track. Inland there are rusty tank shells, and the ruined village of Tyneham. The army, through neglect, has fossilised the farming system here, where medieval fields can still be seen, which deep modern ploughing would certainly have destroyed. Inland too is the grey ruin of Lulworth Castle, a seventeenth-century building with decorative crenellations and enormous windows in its fat round towers, none of which were ever meant to be of any military use. On Ring's Hill above Warbarrow Bay is the Iron Age fort of Flower's Barrow, spectacularly sited on the lip of the cliff.

The end of the range is marked by a nodding pump over Britain's biggest inshore oil-well, producing 400 gallons of oil a day from the Kimmeridge shales below.

The only crack in the grey Purbeck landscape is the valley of Encombe which leads inland to the woods and garden of an eighteenth-century house. At Chapman's Pool recent landslips have entirely changed the previous landscape over many acres. Pick your way over the stony rubbish and climb steeply to St Aldhelm's Head, where there is a twelfth-century chapel with four-foot-thick walls, dark inside and with a single pier from which all

The ruined Clavel Tower on Kimmeridge bay, built in 1800 by the Reverend Clavel, who looked at the stars from the top.

vaults spring. The saint was Bishop of Sherborne in the eighth century. It is six miles to Swanage, a high and windy cliff walk on good turf with many flowers. At Winspit, in the middle of an area covered in ancient fields, the path comes to the fragmented remains of quarries and stone mines. The broken stone is Purbeck-Portland, very white and one of the purest forms of Oolitic Limestone. But this is not the most famous of Purbeck stones, the so-called marble, which is actually a shelly limestone. It enjoyed a great vogue in the Middle Ages and can be seen in Exeter, Salisbury, Winchester, Canterbury, West-minster, Ely, Lincoln, Beverley, York and Durham. The first quarries of it were under St Aldhelm's Head. When extracted it is grey, but it darkens to blackness when polished.

Past the beautifully named Dancing Ledge, a platform on the cliff, and above the old quarries called Tilly Whim Caves, you come round Durlston Head, where there is a café and a 40-ton model of the world in Portland stone. It is just over a mile into the middle of Swanage, the last resort, where Alfred beat the Danes in a sea-battle. There are only seven miles to the end, along the groyned and sandy beach, and then up on chalk to Ballard Cliff, the eastern end of a narrow band of down that comes overland from Lulworth Cove. Four-teen miles away to the east are the Needles at the tip of the Isle of Wight. Stretching out to

them from this side are the pair of stacks called Old Harry and His Wife, one fat and substantial, the other sharp. There was more to the Wife until 1862 when the top of it broke off. Looking north you can at last see the end, where the yellow beach in Studland Bay disappears round a corner. Beyond it is Bournemouth's almost Florida-like skyline. Here you can dance down through the wild cabbage to Studland, the last cream-tea village, with a fortress-like Norman church, before embarking on the four curving miles along the beach to South Haven Point. You accelerate on the firm sand. Not until round the corner into Shell Bay does the tortoise-backed ferry appear. It takes five minutes to reach it. Brownsea Island, owned by the National Trust, sits darkly in the middle of the harbour waters. This is the end. It does not feel much like the Styx as you take the ferry to Bournemouth. Though no-one else will be remotely interested, you will be glowing all over.

————

MAPS: OS 1:50,000 Numbers 180, 181, 190, 192, 193, 194, 195, 200, 201, 202, 203, 204

GUIDES:
Ken Ward and John Mason, *The South-west Peninsula Coast Path*, Letts 1977; Vol 1 Minehead to St Ives; Vol 2 St Ives to Plymouth; Vol 3 Plymouth to Poole
Brian Le Messurier, *South Devon Coast Path*, HMSO 1980
Brian Jackman, *Dorset Coast Path*, HMSO 1979
Edward C. Pyatt, *Cornwall Coast Path*, HMSO 1976

BACKGROUND:
W. G. V. Balchin, *Cornwall*, Hodder and Stoughton 1954
Richard Carew, *Survey of Cornwall*, 1603
E. R. Delderfield, *The Lynmouth Flood Disaster*, ERD publications 1953
A. Fox, *South-West England 3500 B.C. – A.D. 600*, Thames and Hudson 1973
Thomas Hardy, *A Pair of Blue Eyes* (1873), Macmillan 1975
Thomas Hardy, *The New Wessex Selection of T. H.'s Poetry*, Macmillan 1978
W. G. Hoskins, *Devon*, Collins 1954
J. A. R. Pimlott, *The Englishman's Holiday – A Social History*, Harvester Press 1947
John Seymour, *The Companion Guide to the Coast of South-West England*, Collins 1974
J. A. Steers, *The Coastline of England and Wales*, Cambridge 1969
A. C. Todd and Peter Laws, *The Industrial Archaeology of Cornwall*, David & Charles 1972
R. A. R. Tricker, *Bores, Breakers, Waves and Wakes*, Mills and Boon 1964

INFORMATION:
South West Way Association,
'Kynance',
Old Newton Road,
Kingskerswell,
Newton Abbot, Devon TQ12 5LB

The Ridgeway

Avebury to Ivinghoe Beacon 90 miles

The Countryside Commission's Ridgeway Path stretches about ninety miles from near Avebury in Wiltshire to Ivinghoe Beacon in Buckinghamshire. This is, in fact, a slice out of a much longer and much greater prehistoric way. South-east of Avebury the old line is still traceable across the Kennet, up over Milk Hill and down into the Vale of Pewsey. It then climbs on to Salisbury Plain, at Marden Cowbag or maybe Chirton Maggot, turns west almost to Warminster, then south to Shaftesbury and on to Cranborne Chase, where it bends south-west, via Cerne Abbas, finally reaching the coast somewhere near Lyme Regis.

In the north, equally, the abrupt termination at Ivinghoe is not the prehistoric end of the way, which continued via Dunstable and Baldock into East Anglia, turning north at the Little Ouse, to arrive at the Wash near Hunstanton.

This great way – over 250 miles long – from one corner of lowland Britain to the other made use of the natural advantages of good drainage and relative treelessness which the chalkland and, north of the Thames, the Upper Greensand offered. It provided access throughout prehistory to the middle of England for invaders and traders from Spain and southern France from one end, and from Germany and Scandinavia from the other. It was to be the vehicle of the first great meeting of cultures in this country, which resulted in the Great Stone Civilisation of Salisbury Plain and of Avebury.

This coast-to-coast highway must not be thought of as an isolated M1 in a land otherwise covered with impenetrable forest. The Ridgeway was not the only ridgeway, but the greatest member of a complicated and articulate network of green roads which was the communications system before the Romans arrived, and which, until this century, in the form of drove roads and possibly smugglers' routes, shadowed the more orthodox roads in the valleys below. Our Great Ridgeway is almost unique in its surviving completeness; the rest now linger, in Edward Thomas's words, 'in broken vertebrae of lane and footpath'.

With all this in mind it is impossible to start on the Ridgeway as recommended, from a café

Looking back up the Stone Avenue towards Avebury.

on the A4. There is, besides, a wonderful means of gradual immersion in this walk, which begins nearly ten miles away in Pewsey.

From Pewsey to Avebury 10 miles

Mountaineers who plan to climb a Himalaya are not dropped at the mountain's foot, but walk themselves in to get used to the thinner air. It is the same with the Ridgeway, but back to front. Around Avebury the air is so thick with the past that, as Richard Jefferies said, 'the place is alive with the dead'. The morning's journey from Pewsey gives you time to acclimatise.

The first two and a half miles are along small lanes on the floor of the Vale of Pewsey. At Wilcot you cross the Kennet and Avon canal, and the sage-green wall of the Downs soon appears to the north. To the left, above Alton Barnes, is Walker's Hill, with Adam's Grave, a long barrow, prominent on it. You leave the small road at a sharp corner, a mile and a half beyond Wilcot. The map shows the kind of transition you are making. To the south the country is well marked with railways, yellow and red roads, place-names in Roman type and all the evidence of a vital economic life. To the north the map is equally full, equally covered in place-names and in the evidence of human construction, but it is all grey and colourless, with the words in Gothic script and the lines not bright yellow roads but strings of faint notches labelled 'Ditch'. It is a kind of ghost cartography.

The path climbs from the road into this dead country by an overgrown lane going diagonally up the hill – in Wales it would be called a 'rhiw' – passing to the left of a Neolithic enclosure on Knap Hill, whose users were probably buried in Adam's Grave, on the far side of the road at the top.

From the point where you cross the road the Ridgeway itself strikes due north for East Kennett, but a better way is to continue northwest to the crest-line of this down. As you walk you notice that everywhere the earth has been shaped at some time in its history. To Edward Thomas these remains of past disturbances made 'the earth look old, like the top bar of a stile, carved by saunterers, bored by wasps, grooved and scratched and polished again, or like a schoolboy's desk that has blunted a hundred ingenious knives'.

At the top of the hill you reach the greatest of the grooves – the Wansdyke. Why is the Wansdyke not more famous? It is a ditch and bank fully fifty miles long, running roughly east-west from Inkpen, where Wiltshire meets

Hampshire and Berkshire, to near Portishead on the Bristol Channel. It is, admittedly, very broken, and there is even some doubt that the sections now disconnected were ever part of a single scheme. Nevertheless, where it survives in full, as it does where we cross it, it is a huge thing, with the bottom of the ditch forty feet from the top of the bank. But its chief beauty, as with all such earthworks, is the line it takes across country. Archaeologists call these defences 'running earth-works', and that phrase gives exactly the right idea of the Wansdyke's style, moving with the ease of a cross-country runner over the Downs.

It was built to stop people coming from the north, and its scale implies a high degree of organisation among its builders. Further west it is on top of a Roman road, which means the Dyke is the later. It is quite reasonable to guess from all this that the Wansdyke was built by Roman Britons against Saxon invaders coming from the north, almost surely along the Ridgeway, maybe in the fifth century. The imagination moves easily to King Arthur.

From the Wansdyke on Tan Hill the Avebury site is laid out before you. It is a shallow irregular bowl scooped from the surrounding Downs. The eastern rim is made by the Ridgeway, dropping to the Kennet, and continuing up northwards over Avebury Down. The eye then swings down to the left, to meet the slight rise of Windmill Hill (NT). In 1743 the antiquarian William Stukeley described this hill with absolute charm exactly as it looks today: 'There is a very delicate hill north of Abury of a round form, with an easy ascent quite round, it is called Windmill hill. The turf is as soft as velvet. 'Tis encompassed with a circular trench exceeding old.' This exceeding old trench turned out to be the most important Stone Age site in Britain. Coming west and south, the horizon dips and rises again to Cherhill Down, on top of which is a wood, a column to Lord Lansdown and an Iron Age fort, whose grass, Stukeley wrote, was 'softer to walk upon than a Turky carpet'.

Within these horizons the prehistoric monuments do not make much of a show. Avebury itself is a mass of trees; and the long barrow above West Kennett is just out of view. Only Silbury Hill would be noticed by a stranger ignorant that this universally green scene was once the centre of England. Even then, its flat top and pudding shape need to be picked out from the identically coloured background.

From the Wansdyke go down the chalky track, past barns and fields sown in November with winter wheat, almost to the banks of the Kennet, which is dry in winter. Here you must climb back up the hill slightly to reach the West Kennett Long Barrow. On the way down, the barrow at East Kennett, covered in

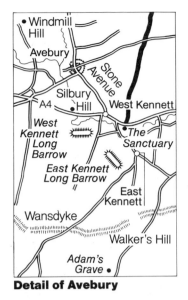

Detail of Avebury

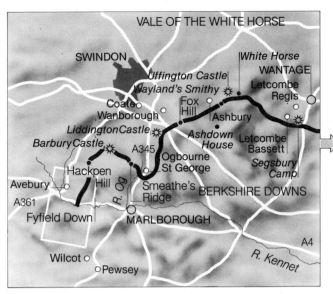

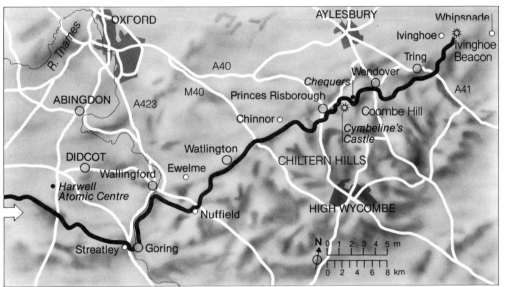

trees, is visible half a mile to the east. It has never been excavated.

The West Kennett barrow, by contrast, is bare and has been dug three times. A Dr Toope of Marlborough wrote to John Aubrey in 1685 to tell him that he had found some workmen digging bones from the barrow: 'I quickly perceived they were humane, and came next day and dugg for them, and stored myselfe with many bushells, of which I made a noble medicine that relieved many of my distressed neighbours.' Another dig into the barrow was done in 1859, but only in 1955 was a proper scientific excavation carried out. It was then established that the barrow was built in about 3250 BC by Neolithic people and was used as a collective tomb for about a thousand years. At least forty-six skeletons (there is some uncertainty because most were dismembered and jumbled together) were discovered here. Most showed evidence of arthritis, and some of spina bifida.

The tomb is large – 330 feet long – and its eastern façade of upright sarsens, closing off a small yard and the burial chambers themselves, is conceived on a grand scale and carefully made. Neolithic society was not hierarchical, and so it would be inappropriate to think of this as a royal mausoleum, but its scale implies that the people it contained were important. It may have been a centre for ancestor-worship.

The idea of the Long Barrow is easy to understand if one remembers that on Egyptian tomb-paintings, for example, the more important figures – pharaohs and other gods – are drawn larger than ordinary men. There is no distinction between 'great' in its metaphorical and its physical sense. In the same way a long barrow is a tomb big enough to hold important people. Later, people lost the sense of metaphor and assumed that an Adam, a Woden or another giant was stretched out inside these mounds. In fact, all those interred were in a clutch of five chambers at the east end

79

which only projects a seventh of the way into the total length of the barrow. It looks in plan like a swaddled papoose, whose face briefly protrudes from a long oval of body.

You can still walk into this burial place, which is wet and dark inside. In places the sarsens are worn smooth, apparently where the men who erected the barrow sharpened their axes, to cut not the stones, which are mostly single slabs, but the posts and poles by which they were manoeuvred into position. It is house-of-cards architecture – hardly architecture at all – where the stones, as well as being walls and roof, are religious objects in themselves.

From the West Kennett barrow the biggest thing in the landscape is Silbury Hill. To reach it you cross the Kennet and go a few hundred yards along the road, which is on the line of the Roman road from London to Bath. It was forced to bend by the massive presence of the artificial hill.

By the radio-carbon method, turf from the inner core of Silbury has been dated to 2660 BC. Like the pyramids, it was built up in a series of steps, each bonded with internal chalk walls. Only at the final stage was the hill given the

Silbury Hill, built from chalk in about 2660 BC and probably dedicated to the rites of the Earth Goddess. May Day dances were still held on the top in the eighteenth century.

regular profile it now has, and even then the last step, fifteen feet from the top, was not smoothed over and the resulting terrace can still be seen. The engineers did a remarkable job since in 4,500 years the hill has scarcely eroded at all.

Nobody knows what Silbury was for. It has been tunnelled twice and plumbed once, all three attempts driving straight to the centre and finding nothing. It may not have been a tomb. William Stukeley recorded that 'The country people have an anniversary meeting on the top of Silbury Hill, on every Palm Sunday, when they make merry with cakes, figs, sugar and water fetched from the swallow-head, or spring of the Kennet.' The scrubbing of the White Horse at Uffington was undoubtedly a survival from a prehistoric chore-cum-ceremony. It may be that Stukeley's spring-time dancing marked the same kind of continuity.

If it is a tomb, and Stukeley said he had 'no

scruple to affirm, 'tis the most magnificent mausoleum in the world, without excepting the Egyptian pyramids', it is surely likely that it was built with some knowledge of its Egyptian prototypes. Avebury had some contact with Egypt, however roundabout; in the West Kennett Long Barrow several Egyptian faience beads have been found. It may only be coincidence that the volume of chalk quarried for Silbury – 8¾ million cubic feet – is almost exactly the same as the volume of the smallest of the pyramids of Giza.

To reach Avebury village, you must retrace your steps along the A4 and take a footpath to the north along the tiny Kennet. Silbury Hill is on your left. If at first it seemed only a dull lump of earth, as you walk beside it it will grow on you. It is a beautifully settled thing, sitting like a fat squat Buddha in Wiltshire.

You come upon Avebury quietly. It seems at first nothing but a cul-de-sac village, prettier than most, provided with a church, a manor-house, a row of cottages and some barns. Only then do you notice that this unremarkable collection sticks out, like the handle of a frying pan, from a vast bank and ditch surrounding a circle of massive upright stones, within which are the remains of smaller circles and other patterns.

The relationship between shop, cottage and the unshaped stones seems easy, as though neither noticed the existence of the other. This is comparatively recent. There are houses and a pub inside the pagan circle now, but until the seventeenth century people built carefully outside, as the position of the church and the manor-house show. There were attempts in the Middle Ages to reduce the terror of the stones. The skeleton of a barber-surgeon, with his scissors and lance in a purse next to him, has been found crushed beneath one of them, which probably fell on him by accident in the fourteenth century when he was helping to bury it. With the decline of superstition in the seventeenth century the standing stones became not so much objects to be buried away and hidden as convenient quarries, nearer than the sarsens on Fyfield Down and a better building material than either chalk or flint.

Hand in hand with a lessening in superstition came a growth in the careful examination of antiquities. It is no coincidence that at the moment of Avebury's partial destruction by farmers it was first noticed and recorded by antiquaries. John Aubrey, apparently the first outsider to know that Avebury existed, gave Charles II a guided tour in 1663, but it was not until the next century that Avebury was first fully described, by William Stukeley, President of the Society of Antiquaries.

The devil for Stukeley was *Tom Robinson* (always italicised) who for petty gain destroyed tens of sarsens for building material. Stukeley carefully recorded the site of each destruction and, perhaps rather feebly, advised: 'The stone being a kind of marble, or rather granite, is always moist and dewy in winter, which proves damp and unwholesome and rots the furniture.' This persuaded nobody, and the example set in 1694, when the first stone was demolished 'to build the dining room end of the inn', was energetically followed throughout the eighteenth century so that barely a quarter of the original scheme now survives. Through a combination of modern archaeology and Stukeley's careful record we can know what it was.

The Cove at Avebury.

The standing stones at Avebury were erected between 2500 and 2200 BC. At the centre of the pattern stood two small circles, each about 350 feet across. In the middle of the northern one was a close group of three vast stones, known generally as The Cove, but which Stukeley referred to as 'this superb nich'. The middle of the other circle is fuller, with an unexplained series of stones called the Z feature.

Surrounding these was the great stone circle itself, 1,400 feet in diameter, and made up of about 100 sarsen stones brought from the Downs on which the Ridgeway runs, not far to the east. Twenty-two feet outside the ring of stones is a ditch and bank, still large, but once of enormous proportions – fifty feet from bank-top to ditch-bottom. It was useless for defence, since the ditch is inside, dug to mark off what was holy ground, and perhaps to provide a bank from which the ritual of the élite could be watched.

Characteristically, Stukeley imagined Avebury when it was complete as though it were a promenade at Tunbridge Wells or Bath: 'When this mighty colonnade of 100 of these stones was in perfection, there must have been a most agreeable circular walk, between them and the ditch.'

The bank, the ditch and the great circle are pierced in four places, roughly at the points of the compass. On either side of these entrances the flanking stones are larger, the ditch deeper and the bank still more massive. If design reflects ritual, the arrival at the circle must plainly have been of great importance. From the southern and western entrances avenues of menhirs – often in complementary pairs of a narrow upright and a more squat lozenge shape – curved away to the south-east and south-west so that 'The whole figure represented a snake transmitted through a circle'. Only the eastern avenue now survives, even then incompletely, but Stukeley saw the other leading to the village of Beckhampton about a mile away. Of this avenue two stones only are left, in the middle of an arable field; they are called Adam and Eve, or the Long Stones.

It is best to spend the night in Avebury and the next morning walk along the Stone Avenue to Overton Hill where the Ridgeway path begins. But before finishing the long day from Pewsey, you will want to see Windmill Hill. This small hill a mile north of Avebury is more famous than it deserves to be. There are a few lumps and blurred hollows, but you have seen enough of these today to last a lifetime. It is by chance that it is so well known. It was excavated in the 1920s, and as it was the first Neolithic causewayed camp to be found, it gave its name to the whole Neolithic culture of Southern England. The way from Pewsey passed another site exactly like it on Knap Hill, and the remains and finds here could be reproduced tens of times all over the chalk hills in the south of England.

As Stukeley guessed, it is 'exceeding old'. Evidence has been found for occupation of the hill as early as 3700 BC, and this is the modest nucleus from which the whole Avebury complex expanded. It was a farming community that kept animals and planted crops, although the scale of their sowing and reaping made it more like gardening than farming. In 3250 BC the 'causewayed camp' was built. In fact the 'causeways' over the three concentric 'ditches' are nothing but spaces between separate pits which provided the material for the continuous banks, the only functional part of what was, in effect, a stock enclosure.

There is no evidence of permanent settlement inside the banks, but material has been found in the ditches which shows that the area was generally in use until about 2000 BC. Alongside the pottery, bones, chalk figurines and phalli, a large number of crab apple pips and hazel nuts were found. These autumn fruits may indicate that the enclosures on Windmill Hill were deserted for most of the

A Neolithic tomb three miles east of Avebury called the Devil's Den. Strangely, it is far more like the cromlechau found in Pembrokeshire and the West Country than the tombs around Avebury itself.

Bronze Age round barrows on the down near Avebury.

year, but served as autumn corral of stock, in which the necessary slaughtering to preserve winter feed would be combined with a religious festival at the onset of winter. The enclosing banks, functional on Windmill Hill, may have been the originals behind the vast ceremonial earthworks surrounding the stone circle at Avebury.

The next morning, as you walk slowly towards West Kennett, you can comply with the advice of Henry David Thoreau to 'walk like a camel, which is said to be the only beast that ruminates when walking' and consider the nature of the religion and culture which made the circle you have just left and the long serpentine avenue now leading you south-east.

Archaeologists have called Avebury the metropolis of Neolithic England, as though a city equivalent to Ur or Sumer was once here. A city is necessary, they say, to assemble the manpower for the erection of such bulky monuments. It is assumed that they would have been built relatively quickly; the standard calculation for the construction of Silbury Hill, for example, involves 700 men for only ten years. This is unnecessarily quick. Cathedrals in the Middle Ages regularly took centuries to complete. Relatively few men were involved at any one time, and masons would spend their entire working lives on one part of one building. If this was the case with Avebury, we can dismiss the notion of a sizable band of professional monument builders. Even the idea of professionals may be wrong. Arable farming releases time previously spent on the search for food, and it may be that Neolithic society used the comparatively empty period between the sowing and the harvesting of crops to fetch and erect the sarsens. It has been calculated that to make the Stone Circle and the two avenues would have taken one and a half million man days. This apparently impossible figure can be broken down into fifty men spending thirty days a year on the job for one hundred years.

It seems quite possible that here was a small village, with its houses perhaps on the banks of the Kennet, and in the country around a collection of religious buildings which could match any in Europe at the time. What this leaves is a sense of great space, of a wide extent of earth and air shaped by a few vast human creations.

It is marvellously calculated. The Stone Circle at Avebury, Silbury Hill, the long barrows and the Sanctuary on Overton Hill are all parts of the same one place – but only just. The position of these elements in what must be called a religious landscape stretches one's conception of the unity of place exactly to the limit. Nothing is known of the religion at Avebury, but there is surely something in this which should appeal to walkers. Long avenues of upright stones; a strong emphasis on entrances and arrivals; the positioning of important places at random distances from each other, while still being part of one pattern; all this points at least in part to a ritual movement over the earth, to long processions from one temple or tomb to another. From no one point in the area is everything entirely visible, and this arrangement cannot be accidental. It must reflect the religious need for a ceremony in which the procession paid court to the earth simply by making a slow movement over it towards an end which (ritually at least) was unknown.

If the earth was one part of the religion at Avebury, the sky was the other. There is no need to indulge the extremes of astronomical speculation to see that it is sky-orientated. The fact that it was roofless is important, and to point unhewn masses of stone upwards is, in a way, to join earth and sky. That symbolic conjunction has a counterpart in the pre-history of Britain, which was a coming together of cultures in which the Ridgeway was the principal agent. The Neolithic farmers had come from the Mediterranean across southern Europe about 5000 BC, probably landing in Lyme Bay. From there the relatively bare chalk Ridgeway led them north to Salisbury Plain.

The agricultural way of life of these people made theirs a religion of the earth, to whose rhythms they were bound in life, and in which at death, in the long barrows, they were so elaborately enclosed. Almost certainly the Earth Mother was their goddess, the White Goddess to whom all the agricultural societies of the Mediterranean and Near East paid tribute.

In about 2400 BC a wave of quite different people came across from the Low Countries. There were not many of them, but they were warlike and above all had metal. These invaders are known as the Beaker folk, but it is a bad name for a strong marauding aristocratic race who placed moré emphasis on the warrior and the hunt than on the quiet domesticity of agriculture and the hearth. The religion of such a people will not be directed earthwards, but towards the sky-god, the masculine thunderer.

This powerful new force came fast down the Ridgeway from its northern end, or from the gap made in the chalk hills by the Thames at Goring. At Avebury the two peoples met, and the temple at Avebury can be seen as the product of the mixture of their earth and sky cultures. Around the base of the stones sherds of the late Neolithic and of the finer, harder Beakerware have been found side by side.

Certainly the Beaker folk dominated the new society, but Avebury, the sky and earth temple, shows that the process was one of mutual absorption. Agriculture continued almost unchanged; only at the top level did society change gear. For almost a thousand years a Wessex culture grew and flourished, based on the precious metals brought back from Cornwall, Wales and Ireland by war and trade. Of this culture, which was in touch with everywhere from Norway to Egypt, Avebury and Stonehenge were the twin ritual centres.

Overton Hill to Fox Hill 17 miles

At last you can begin on the Ridgeway. The way does not fit modern categories, since it is neither a footpath nor recognisable as a high road. It is a strip along the down, seventy foot broad, hedged or distinguished from the neighbouring field only by a slight darkening of the turf, or by the beginning of the ruts. The Ridgeway is not a construction, but only a habit of use. It is only a road because the hill here has been used as one for six millennia.

It is not clear, to begin with, that it is a ridgeway at all. Although you are walking along the eastern rim of the bowl in which Avebury lies, the land has no obvious direction. To your right is the broad bulk of Overton Down, covered in the sarsens from which both Avebury and Stonehenge were made. These are either glacial erratics or the remains of a sandstone layer which used to overlie the Downs, but most of which has been eroded away. They are said to look like flocks of sheep and are called Grey Wethers. You can walk in among them, and they become more interesting close to. They come in a small range of colours, edging from a slight red to marly blue or green, but never straying far from grey.

On this down there is also an experimental barrow, which was piled up in 1960 and left to weather, so that the speed at which its ditches filled up could be measured. This will provide archaeologists with a chronological key to the layers of accumulation in the ditches of prehistoric barrows.

The Ridgeway pushes on, making only one sharp kink to pass round a pond, presumably to water drove animals. The main movement of the way is a smooth swing round to the north-east. The ridge starts to establish itself as it emerges from the shelf of lower chalk on which Avebury stands. The first of the Iron Age camps, Barbury Castle, appears as a notch on the horizon as you move on to the sickle curve of Hackpen Hill, whose name means Hook Hill in Old English.

As you cross a road and pass above a modern white horse cut in the hill below, the western end of the Vale of the White Horse itself opens up, with beyond it the line of the Cotswolds. Much of the foreground is taken up by an airfield and the mass of Swindon, a town created by very rapid expansion after the arrival of the railways. All the area over which it now spreads was called by John Aubrey 'the fatting grounds, the garden of Wiltshire'. Aubrey came from south Wiltshire, and although he admired the productive qualities of the earth in the north, he reckoned it was deleterious to the moral and intellectual qualities of the inhabitants. They 'speake drawling', he wrote. 'They are phlegmatique, skins pale and livid, slow and dull, heavy of spirit; hereabout is but little tillage or hard labour, they only milk their cowes and make cheese; they feed chiefly on milke meates, which cooles their braines too much, and hurts their inventions. These circumstances make them melancholy, contemplative and malicious ... their persons are generally plump and feggy; gallipot eies, and some black.'

Barbury Castle is by now in the foreground. The approach to it is slightly downhill, on a line which is straight but in which, as Edward Thomas wrote, 'a curve is latent'. The fort is no longer in silhouette, and it appears slopped carelessly over its hill. But this is not carelessness. The main weapon used in the Iron Age was the sling. The advantage of a high-placed fort was the extra impetus gravity would give a stone slung downhill. What the designers of the fort had to prevent was the attackers being able to creep up unseen in 'dead ground' almost to the walls of the fort, where the advantage of gravity would be minimal. Barbury's slopped appearance is the result of its extension northwards to cover what would otherwise have been dead ground.

From Barbury the north-facing scarp of the Downs makes a sharp V southwards at the bottom point of which is the village of Ogbourne St George. The Ordnance Survey marks the Ridgeway as bypassing this indentation by descending the scarp at Barbury and making straight for the opposite scarp-foot below Liddington Hill. The Countryside Commission have wisely decided to follow the V round, avoiding two miles on the road, and including the most beautiful part of the whole walk, down Smeathe's Ridge.

The track goes straight through Barbury Castle and after a couple of fields branches right on to the clean back of Smeathe's Ridge. Another ancient track goes off to the right towards Marlborough and then you are on your own. To Ogbourne it is two miles, a gradual undulating descent, with the turf of the path just darker than the winter wheat on either side. The going is so easy, with the right mixture of softness and hardness underfoot, and the look of the way so inviting that it would make you run all the way to Ogbourne St George, if you weren't held back by the other pull, of wanting it to last for ever. On the right is a narrow dry valley, with the chalk showing in the ploughed earth, and holding in its bottom a small round bun of woodland. The other side is more open, with the Roman road to Mildenhall on the Kennet pushing straight through the flat valley, and beyond it Liddington Hill. Immediately below is the brick scatter of a military camp, with cows walking in and out between the deserted buildings.

This breezy walk ends quickly. You come down quite suddenly into a leafy lane which turns into Ogbourne's only street, in which every other house has been washed an ice-cream pink. The village has pubs and a café.

Officially the path crosses the tiny Og half a mile south of the village, but if you have gone up the street it is easy to rejoin the route by crossing the busy A345 and climbing past a rubbish-filled quarry back on to the Ridgeway. Now follows an admittedly dreary and frustrating two miles. There is even a danger that the euphoria blown into you by Smeathe's Ridge will be whittled away by the sliding and stumbling which is all the path now offers, enclosed between untransparent, scarcely translucent hedges. The puddles are deep and almost continuous. The conventional wisdom about ridgeway routes on chalk is that their good drainage kept them open in all weathers and all year round. But here, and in several other places on the Ridgeway, the overlying clay makes the going difficult even after slight rain. The answer must be that relative to the gluey, tree-blocked impasse of the low ground the Ridgeway was still easy going.

Eventually the path emerges from between its hedgerows and you breathe again. It is a mile to Liddington Castle. The approach is not as good as Barbury's, since the fort is hidden by the ridge until you are almost there. But Liddington was a place of great, even cosmic, meaning for Richard Jefferies, who was born in Coate, near the fish-shaped reservoir which can be seen from the fort, on the near side of Swindon. In his autobiography *The Story of My Heart* he describes how during the climb

The Manger at Uffington and the Vale of the White Horse beyond it. In this combe, visibly contoured by centuries of sheep, races used to be held after a cheese that was sent rolling down it.

Ashdown House, built in the seventeenth century by the Earl of Craven for his lonely and wifeless retirement.

'through rich pure air' up the steep slope from Liddington village, he would shake off 'the petty circumstances and the annoyances of existence', to arrive at the Iron Age fort on the crest. Here he reached a kind of Wordsworthian wholeness with the world: 'I was utterly alone with the sun and the earth. Lying down on the grass, I spoke in my soul to the earth, the sun, the air and the distant sea far beyond sight. I thought of the earth's firmness – I felt it bear me up; through the grassy couch there came an influence as if I could feel the great earth speaking to me.' And so he pours out the story of his heart for page after page, always to return to 'the firm, solid and sustaining earth of Liddington Hill'.

From the fort the path sinks to join with the Ridgeway proper again, then crosses the M4 to arrive in a quarter of a mile at the Shepherd's Rest at the bottom of Fox Hill and on the Ermine Way, the Roman road from Silchester to Cirencester and Gloucester.

Fox Hill to Wantage 14 miles

From Fox Hill to Wayland's Smithy is four and a half miles, all on a track closed off from the surrounding fields by solid hedgerows, full of Edward Thomas' 'dense, very old thorns, shapely or twisted in rigid agonies'. In November they are spotted with berries, ranging from an almost black purple to an unnatural electric pink, and covered in rosehips. The way is back from the edge of the downs, so that the effect is of being on a bleak plain, whose heavy-looking, wet soils and few woods give it an air of Cambridgeshire. All the open ground is under plough, and the Ridgeway itself is clayey and deeply puddled. The country has a puritan beauty, which Jefferies enjoyed for 'a hugeness of undivided surface' that he found up here.

Two miles from the Shepherd's Rest, just after passing into Oxfordshire, the Ridgeway crosses a track leading north and south. A mile and a half down it to the right is Ashdown House (NT), built of chalk in the seventeenth century by the first Earl of Craven. The pale, lonely, delicate house seems to embody the history of its pathetic builder. He was a courtier of Elizabeth, Queen of Bohemia, the sister of Charles I and mother of Prince Rupert of the Rhine. Desperately in love with his queen, he was never brave enough to tell her, spending his whole life, an object of ridicule for his contemporaries, silently and faithfully bailing out both Elizabeth and her children, with scant reward. He survived her by thirty-five years, but never married and died when over ninety, still a bachelor.

To reach the Ridgeway from Ashdown you must walk a mile up the Ashbury road, leaving it at Honeybunch Corner, to arrive within a few hundred yards of Wayland's Smithy, a long barrow of the same age and construction as the one at West Kennett. Wayland was the Saxon god of the forge, the owner of a white horse, who, as Scott made famous when he used the myth in *Kenilworth*, would either shoe your horse if you left it with a groat by the Smithy, or forge lumps of iron left there into horseshoes. When the barrow was excavated in 1919 some iron bars were found which were thought to be bits of Iron Age currency. They are now known to be hinges from a barn door left there hopefully, or perhaps experimentally, in the eighteenth century. They were not bent at all.

The mile from Wayland's Smithy to Uffington Castle and the White Horse (both NT) is classic Ridgeway walking, where the grassy track, lined by ruts which reach down to the chalk, is made significant by the age and fame of the monuments it joins, whose presence on the downs is entirely the product

The Ridgeway between Wayland's Smithy and Uffington Castle: not a road but a habit of use.

of the Ridgeway itself. Uffington Castle is another Iron Age fort, with a single bank and ditch, at one time revetted with sarsens, of which nothing is now to be seen. The fort crowns its slight spur, above the White Horse stretched out below, slightly to the east.

The White Horse seems to be the very centre of the Berkshire Downs, a point about which their whole line pivots, encapsulating the nature of the entire length. The horse is amazing first as a survival. It is extraordinary that the people of Uffington should have continued scouring this pagan earth-carving throughout centuries in which the official religion was expressly alien and hostile to its imagery. The horse's age is unknown, but most likely it was carved in the early Iron Age by people of the Atrebates, on whose coins appear equally disjointed representations of the horse, themselves eventually copied from the gold coins of Philip II of Macedon. If this is the right date, the White Horse has been the object of regular grooming for as good as 2,500 years.

It goes further than this. The horse is neither a naturalistic representation nor – unlike the Cerne Abbas giant – a grotesque whose only

appeal is its age and strangeness. The real beauty of the White Horse is that its form and its medium are exactly complementary. The slender, unhorse-like lines would be unsatisfying if drawn on paper, but tattooed as they are on to the solid muscle of the down there is no sense of weakness; it is a complete work of art.

Immediately below the horse is the flat-topped Dragon Hill (NT), which is either where St George slew the dragon, or perhaps a miniature Silbury, adapted from a natural hillock. To its left is a lovely combe called the Manger, into whose western side the hill sticks a whole hand of fat green fingers. At the scouring ceremonies they held, among other games, a race down the Manger after a cheese which was sent rolling into the combe; the first person to catch it kept it. Celia Fiennes came here in about 1687 and after observing that the horse was 'in perfect proportion, in broad wayes' made the charming mistake of assuming that the Manger was another name for the Vale of the White Horse as a whole, 'extending a vast way, a rich enclos'd country' as though such a great horse needed such a manger.

East from Uffington the Ridgeway makes you feel that there is nothing in the world to do but walk along the Ridgeway. The way is so plain and comfortable and wide. There is no need to look at a map for miles. The view to the north of the Thames valley, edged by the Cotswolds twenty-five miles away, confirms Edward Thomas's impression that 'the Ridgeway is like nothing so much as a battlement walk of superhuman majesty'. To the south the woods and windbreaks are disposed like regiments in an eighteenth-century battlefield print, their muskets in blocks like sections of a thickset hedge. All that is missing is the foreground general, baton in hand, on a white horse with one knee lifted.

Being able to see so much makes you breeze through the miles. Chalk-and-brick barns, furzy thickets and beech plantations all move effortlessly by. Into view, to the north-east, comes what at first seems a vast intrusion into the landscape – the six cooling towers and one high chimney of Didcot Power Station. It makes no compromise with the scale of its surroundings; it is the architecture of pure geometry in landscape. There is a tradition of this approach in English architecture to which no one objects – the great country house. A vast pile is dropped into the middle of fields, complete in itself, and making no attempt to 'fit in'. The strength derived from that refusal,

Crowhole Bottom near Wantage. Richard Jefferies loved 'the hugeness of undivided surface' on the Downs, but what he knew as uninterrupted sheepwalk has now almost all been turned over to arable.

Didcot Power Station focuses the landscape for forty miles along the Ridgeway.

combined with a good thoughtful design, does not wreck the landscape, but gives it a focus. Didcot Power Station does the same thing, but in a way far grander than even the grandest of country houses. Its towers attract the eye for forty miles, for two and a half days along the Ridgeway. Nor is it a static display. As your own position changes the towers will seem to move around each other, rearranging themselves as if in a very slow dance.

The way crosses the Wantage-Lambourn road and in a few hundred yards comes to the lip of a long winding combe called Crowhole Bottom. At the far end of this is the village of Letcombe Bassett, the Cresscombe of Thomas Hardy's *Jude the Obscure*, where Arabella first flirts with and then inveigles into marriage the naïve Jude. The village still has the cress-beds which were the source of Hardy's name for it. Jude himself lived at Fawley, called Marygreen in the novel, about three miles to the south, the other side of the Ridgeway. One of the most reverberative moments in the book is when the young Jude climbs up to the Ridgeway at

night to look for the lights of Christminster (Oxford), which has become in his mind the City of Revelation: 'What he saw was not the lamps in rows, as he had half expected. No individual light was visible, only a halo or glow-fog overarching the place against the black heavens behind it, making the light seem distant but a mile or so.' If you walk here at night – and the wide, uninterrupted grass of the Ridgeway might have been designed for night-walking – you will see that Oxford's sodium lights still glow in the same way.

The unlikely figure of Jonathan Swift spent the summer of 1714 in the rectory at Letcombe Bassett. The fatal split in the Tory party as Queen Anne was dying had appalled him so deeply that he had left London at the end of May – incidentally taking four days on the eighty-mile journey – to spend three months with the rector, a melancholy, thoughtful man who never said anything. Swift was badly out of his element, being forced to order claret from London and even to go for walks on the Downs to stave off the tedium. The joke in London was that he had gone to Wiltshire for his own accouchement, so inexplicable was his spending the summer in a country village. In

August he left for Ireland, only to return to England twelve years later.

If you are to spend the night in Wantage, you can walk down to Letcombe Bassett and along the chalk stream via Letcombe Regis into Wantage itself. This is a delicious walk, but to take it means you miss Segsbury camp, an Iron Age fort covering an enormous twenty-six acres, so wide and so arranged that it is impossible to see from one side to the other.

Wantage to Wallingford 21 miles

From Wantage, which has always been the market for the Downs, there are drove roads up to the Ridgeway beginning almost in the town itself. It is very satisfying to begin and continue a day's walking on these green roads, which were designed for long distance travel on foot. More than ordinary footpaths they give the sense that in walking great distances along them you are doing exactly what was meant to be done. This appropriateness gives an extra impetus, so that the fourteen miles from Wantage to the Miller of Mansfield in Goring can be covered without any push or hurry in a single morning, with time, distance and speed all fitting exactly the interval between breakfast and lunch.

South of Wantage the Ridgeway runs just above the insignificant remains of a Grim's Ditch, the name applied by the Saxons to almost any continuous earthwork that they found already in existence. Grim was another name for Woden or Odin, the father god of the Norse pantheon. The ditches may be north-facing Roman British defences or simply territorial boundary marks. On the other side of the Ridgeway and parallel to it a race-horse gallop is laid out. Its turf is lusher and greener than the rutted public track on which you must stay, however much tempted. At a week-end you will probably be joined by motorbikes. These are not offensive. To have a sacred 'no petrol engines' attitude to the Ridgeway would be precious. Part of its value is that it is not simply a footpath or bridleway. It is, besides, used by many people, including the Post Office, who deliver and collect at the farms it joins by van or lorry.

Your morning bowls on. You watch Didcot growing larger; notice how downwind the traffic on the Oxford-Newbury road booms at you, and upwind is strangely silent; feel how the tan put down for the racehorses is the most comfortable of all surfaces to walk on; pick out the line of the Thames by the willows lining its banks, or even in winter sun by the glint on the river itself; marvel at the narrowness of each slot in the practice starting-stalls beside the way, into which a horse and jockey are somehow crammed; see the ugly proliferation of building at the Harwell Atomic Energy Research Establishment, and compare it to the monumental simplicity of Didcot. You will find it strange that only now, above Harwell, are you crossing into Berkshire, despite having been on the Berkshire Downs for miles – this is the result of the 1974 county boundary changes. You can watch the jets flying into Heathrow exactly down the line of the Ridgeway; apparently the string of forts – Segsbury, Uffington, Liddington and Barbury – is quite clear from the air.

There is extraordinarily little building up here. The Agricultural Research Station at Compton has a bunch of silos that look like rocket launchers; there is a Roden Farm, the back of whose courtyard is turned against the west wind, but apart from that almost nothing. On Lowbury Hill, just north of the way, the map advertises a 'Romano-British Temple'. If you expect to see anything at all, let alone a Parthenon, it is disappointing. There is a swelling or two in the turf and a triangulation point, but nothing more. Nor is anything known about this temple or its cult. There is a remote possibility that it may have been a place of sanctuary for refugees on the tribal boundary between the Atrebates and the Catuvellauni.

A mile from the temple the Ridgeway, from being a turf and mud and water track, hardens underfoot and first as a gravel and chalk farm road and then as a metalled lane comes down in two and a half miles to the Thames at Streatley. It is like the end of a flight, so elevated was the morning's walk, so gradual the descent and so mundane the golf-club world you sink into at the bottom.

Streatley and Goring, known to facetious travellers on the Oxford train as Discreetly and Boring, are a pair of pretty brick-and-flint towns facing each other across the Thames. Until the Second World War Streatley was in effect the estate village of the Morrells, the brewers, who lived in the big house half-way down its street on the right (called The Big House). Every other house in the town was occupied by a member of their staff. Goring has since taken over the running with its streets being labelled in gold letters on green, and counting, allegedly, four millionaires among its inhabitants.

At Goring the Thames has cut down through what was once a continuous chalk ridge, now divided into the Berkshire Downs to the west, and the Chilterns to the east. The river marks the end of the Ridgeway proper. From Goring to Ivinghoe what is still called the Ridgeway Path follows either the Upper Icknield Way, below the wooded hills on a strip of Upper Greensand, or takes, where that

TOP LEFT *The chalky Ridgeway drops to the Thames at Streatley.*

ABOVE *Once over the Thames and into the Chilterns the Ridgeway Path begins to cross the grain of the land.*

LEFT *The flint chapel at Swyncombe in the Chilterns, dedicated to St Botolph, the patron saint of travellers.*

is now a metalled road, local field- and wood-paths. Route-finding begins at the Thames.

Out of Goring going north the path is squeezed between the railway line and the river, coming in two miles to South Stoke, a smart place now. Many of the houses on the bank have boat-houses attached, out of which protrude shiny motor launches that narrow to a sliver of varnished mahogany at the stern. There is an occasional sculler and some gawky smoke-blue herons, but as James Morris said, the river 'feels as though it long ago went into comfortable retirement'. Next to the grey tweed flint tower of South Stoke church is a granary on the short mushroom stilts – known as staddle-stones or dottles – which both allow air to circulate beneath the grain and stop rats getting in.

The path, right on the river bank in water meadows, crosses under Brunel's railway bridge, the bricks of whose arches are laid in bands of skew zig-zags, and comes to North Stoke, where Edward Thomas, walking the Icknield Way, dutifully 'turned aside to the church, but found what was better, a big range of tiled thatched sheds and barns extending on either side of my path, with a cattle yard in the midst full of dazzling straw and richly stinking cow-dung, and lying on it like a recumbent statue, a big black sow'.

Continuing north you come into the beautiful chestnut park of Mongewell House, occupied by the neat modern buildings of Carmel College, a public school. The Ridgeway Path turns east here along another Grim's Ditch, but Wallingford is only a mile to the north. You can stay at the George here, an old inn which has a room haunted by a weeping lady, and another where Dick Turpin used to stay.

Wallingford to Princes Risborough
20 miles

As you re-cross Wallingford's long bridge and retrace your steps for about a mile in the meadows opposite the Edwardian water-front, the Chilterns are dark and wooded to the east. They rise gently at this end of the Goring Gap, and have no sharp front to the north. Within sight of Carmel College, Grim's Ditch strikes

The flooded meadows of the Thames at Wallingford.

east, straight for four miles to Nuffield village. This ditch is probably a pre-Roman boundary between two estates separating two quite different settlement patterns. To the north the light soils were the first to be cleared, for cultivation and sheep-rearing. On the south side are later forest clearings, done by farmers whose main concern was swine and cattle. These different patterns may have been produced by two hostile Iron Age peoples so that the ditch could have had a military purpose too. It straddles the Icknield Way, here making for the smallest gap in the hills at Goring.

Nuffield village is 'unnucleated', that is the buildings are not gathered tightly in one clump, but relatively widely dispersed. This is the result of piecemeal clearing from the forest by individuals who built their houses in the patches they reclaimed. It is a pattern repeated all along the Chilterns. In the churchyard is a plain flagstone marking the grave of William Morris, Viscount Nuffield, the motor manufacturer and philanthropist.

The path turns north across the grain of the country, coming in two miles to one of the prettiest Chiltern combes, Swyncombe. The hill is curved in a wide Greek theatre of down, dotted all over with handfuls of beeches, that surround at the bottom the farm and tiny flint chapel of St Botolph, the patron saint of travellers.

On the other side of another ridge the path comes down the main Chiltern escarpment to join the Icknield Way for the first time, following it for the next eight miles. It is good to be back on a proper way again, on the plain with the Chilterns curving in and out to the right. It is a country of factory farms specialising in pigs. Field after muddy field is regularly patterned with the corrugated iron sties of these animals and their litters.

You pass Dame Lys Farm, which records the name of Dame Alice Chaucer, the grand-daughter of the poet and wife of William de le Pole, Duke of Suffolk. She is buried in Ewelme church, three miles' tramp from Swyncombe. The tomb has three layers: on top is an effigy of Alice, with a ducal coronet, the order of the Garter on her forearm and a mouth like a Public School matron; in the middle is a box containing her remains; below this, and to see it properly you must lie on the floor, is a shrivelled, ghastly, skin-and-bones carving of the proud duchess in death, an image of undiluted horror.

Watlington, a very small market town but uncompromisingly urban despite its size, is a mile to the north of the Way and can provide lunch. As you return to the path you will see cut into Watlington Hill (NT) an elongated triangle of white chalk, made in 1764 by an

The two representations of Alice, Duchess of Suffolk, on her tomb in Ewelme Church, near Wallingford: above, in the full pomp of her earthly state, with a coronet on her head, and the Order of the Garter on her forearm; below, in the strained and naked agony of death.

Edward Hone, who called it an obelisk. You now start on the best few miles east of the Thames. The Icknield Way is grassy but firm, occasionally going under a small wood, but more usually in the open below the hills which have acquired a much steeper scarp and on their crest a heavier, more solid cover of trees. The sense of direction which was the exhilaration of the Ridgeway is here re-established. The way crosses first another ancient track, the Ruggeway (which has been adopted for a long distance footpath from Bourton-on-the-Water to Henley-on-Thames), and then under the M40 by the Beacon Hill Nature Reserve. It is rare to find a long distance path *below* the hills it is following, and to be looking up at landscape as you walk is a new pleasure.

You will find a reminder of the beginning of the walk where about a mile beyond the motorway a sudden block of sarsen, absolutely

97

isolated and a surprising yellow, sits on the grassy side of the way. Soon the roar of the drags in the chalk quarries at Chinnor fills the air. Two vast pits open up on either side, leaving the Icknield Way as a balk between them. Over the chain-link fences above the cliff-edge on either side old man's beard has grown enormously and thickly. To the north the three tall chimneys and dusty white buildings of the cement works, built in the 1920s, do not look bad. Soon after the quarries, you pass, unnoticed, into Buckinghamshire.

If you are walking here in November the day will probably end before you reach Princes Risborough. This is not a disaster. There are advantages to night walking. The towns in the Vale of Aylesbury – Thame, Haddenham, Aylesbury itself, and nearer under the Chilterns, Princes Risborough and Chinnor – all have the same halo as Jude saw above Oxford. But you see less and less and other senses take over; your footsteps in a wood and the departure of a pigeon from a tree both sound too loud; in contrast, an owl will leave its branch in total economical silence. The layers of sodden leaves smell thicker than in the day, and you must literally feel your way carefully

Beeches in a wood above Princes Risborough called The Hangings.

over them and between the roots. To reach Princes Risborough you drop down to the dry valley at whose mouth it is, and follow the Icknield Way, here a metalled lane, to the edge of the town.

Princes Risborough to Ivinghoe Beacon 18 miles

Princes Risborough must once have had as coherent an urban character as Watlington, but it has been lobotomised by through-traffic. Hidden in a back-street is a seventeenth-century Manor House belonging to the National Trust, a solid piece of work by local joiners and plasterers, who knew enough to apply pilasters to the outside of the building, but not enough to see they looked silly if stopped short of the eaves.

The Ridgeway Path goes south of the town, to wander north on a switchback course along the front of the Chilterns. Coming down to a pub at Lower Cadsen, you climb up the narrowest path in southern England. You have to hunch your shoulders to fit, and reverse to a passing place if anyone comes the other way. It is best not to think about the fine level width of the Ridgeway. (This becomes romanticised the more you grind up and down the Chilterns. The awful clay and puddles near Upper Upham will be carpeted over in your memory with the ubiquitous green that actually only covered a couple of quarter-miles.)

The thin path ends and you emerge on to open down, pimpled with furze and juniper. There is a sudden rise in the level of neatness and in the number of 'Keep to the Path' notices. You have entered the Chequers estate. Chequers is a large sixteenth-century brick house, given by Lord Lee of Fareham in 1921 as a country home for the Prime Minister. The path is kept well away, down the end of the drive, where a slight rise obscures all but the roof.

From the metal kissing gate at the corner of Chequers park the path goes up into a widely spaced beech plantation in which a series of arrows lead a snaking path northwards to Coombe Hill above Wendover. The beech tree which contributes more than anything else to the Chiltern landscape is not indigenous to it. These woods have almost all been planted as an economic resource. It is not a good wood exposed to the weather, but its relative hardness and ability to take a polish make it good for furniture, tool handles and things like bobbins, brush backs and mangle rollers. At least since the eighteenth century Chiltern beech wood has been drawn by wagon to Marlow and from there shipped by barge to London.

As you kick your way north through piles of fallen leaves you can look across to the north-west to an Iron Age fort known as Cymbeline's Castle. This is not a purely fairy-story name. Cymbeline is probably a corruption of Cunobelinus, a historical figure, whose capital was in Colchester and who was chief of the Catuvellauni. He played a large part in resisting the first Roman invasions. Add to this that the name of the village on the spring-line below – Kimble – is derived from the Anglo-Saxon for royal residence, and it becomes less unlikely that the hill-fort was in fact Cymbeline's castle.

You come out of the woods on to Coombe Hill, a Site of Special Scientific Interest for its flowers and butterflies, owned by the National Trust. At 852 feet it is the highest Chiltern, and is topped by a monument to the dead of the Boer War which is in danger of collapse. Wendover is below to the east, at the mouth of a dry valley, characteristic of the Chilterns, which provides a communication corridor through the hills. These dry valleys were produced at the end of the last Ice Age, when, as the ice (which came up to but did not override the hills) began to melt, large lakes built up between the edge of the retreating ice sheet and the hill tops. The lakes rose until they lipped over the Chilterns' retaining wall. The little that spilt at first eroded the top away, allowing more water to come through, so cutting continuously deeper into the hill until the lake was drained and the dry valley, caused by a relatively temporary flow, was formed.

It is about eleven miles from Wendover to Ivinghoe Beacon and the end of the Ridgeway Path. This last stretch starts badly but gets better until the last miles are as good clean-heeled walking as any on the far side of the Thames. A mile from Wendover High Street a very bad two miles begins, a soggy path between scrubby undistinguished fir trees whose suffocating cover blots out the possibility of seeing anything. At last after interminable twistings you come to a five-bar gate and the end of it all. A proper Chiltern beech wood begins, with great grey muscular trunks, clear spaces between them, drifted with fallen leaves, and views down to the open fields below. The path cuts off a large peninsula of hill that pushes north into the plain, rejoining the edge at a TV mast, then making for the tiny hamlet of Hastoe and reaching at the far end of two miles of flinty farm road, Wigginton village. Defoe records 'an eminent contest' in the early eighteenth century here, when Mr Guy, of The Mansion, Tring, a mile to the north ('a most delicious house, built à la moderne, as the French call it'), set about 'enclosing part of the common to make him a park. Mr Guy presuming upon his power, set up pales, and took in a large parcel of open land, called Wigginton Common; the cottagers and farmers opposed it, by their complaints a great while; but finding he went on with his work, and resolved to do it, they rose upon him, pulled down his banks, and forced up his pales, and carried away the wood, or set it on a heap and burnt it; and this they did several times, till he was obliged to desist.' But Mr Guy won in the end. There is no Wigginton Common marked on modern maps, and the grey stipple of Tring Park spreads smoothly out almost to Wigginton Village itself.

The path now drops into yet another dry valley, crossing a lane called The Twist and then the A41 on the line of Akeman Street, the Roman road from St Albans to Bicester and Cirencester, the main east-west artery through the south of Roman Britain. Immediately beyond it the once large fields have been recently subdivided by post-and-rail fences into neat stock enclosures. The shock felt so

intensely in the eighteenth and nineteenth centuries at the enclosing of open land is understandable when you see here the sharpness with which the new pattern is imposed on the old. Road, railway and the Grand Union Canal all squeeze into this quite narrow dry valley and the path crosses them in quick succession. Tring railway station is here, a mile and a half from Tring because, according to Robert Louis Stevenson, 'the good people of Tring held the railway, of old days, in extreme apprehension, lest some day it should break loose in the town and work mischief.' There is a strangely grand Station Hotel here.

Again you climb up, almost due north, on to Aldbury Nowers, over the side of which the beeches disappear down towards Tring. The wood comes to an end and from here to the Beacon is open down. The vast Pitstone works below make Portland cement from the chalk and marl which are both quarried in the wide pits. You cross another lane, with only a mile and a half to the end, though it looks twice as far, then climb up and round Incombe Hole, a steep-sided combe cut by streams, like the Devil's Dyke in Sussex, when the water table was higher. At the top you must wind between

The works at Pitstone where chalk and marl, quarried nearby, are mixed to form the basis of Portland Cement.

furze to the Beacon, large ahead, catching glimpses, to the east, of the lion cut in the chalk above Whipsnade. To the west, between you and the Pitstone works, is a black post mill (NT) in the middle of a bright green field.

At last you come to the foot of the Beacon itself, now, as when Edward Thomas saw it, 'scored upon its flanks by many old descending trackways'. Its summit is the end of the Ridgeway Path, but it is really more of a semicolon than a full-stop; the Icknield Way goes on past Dunstable, past Hitchin, Letchworth and Royston, well out of view from the top of Ivinghoe Beacon, not stopping until it gets to the sea.

———

MAPS: OS 1:50,000 Numbers 165, 173, 174, 175

GUIDES:
J.R.L. Anderson and Fay Godwin, *The Oldest Road*, Wildwood 1975
Sean Jennett, *The Ridgeway Path*, HMSO 1976

The post mill at Pitstone owned by the National Trust; it is dated 1627.

BACKGROUND:

R. J. C. Atkinson, *Stonehenge and Avebury*, 2nd edition, HMSO 1971

John Aubrey, *The Natural History of Wiltshire*, edited by J. Britton 1846

Glyn Daniel, *The Megalith Builders of Western Europe*, Penguin 1962

Frank Emery, *The Oxfordshire Landscape*, Hodder and Stoughton 1974

Thomas Hardy, *Jude the Obscure* (1896), Macmillan 1974

Richard Jefferies, *The Story of My Heart*, 1883

Morris Marples, *White Horses and Other Hill Figures*, 1949

William Stukeley, *Abury* [sic], *a temple of the Druids described*, 1743

Edward Thomas, *Richard Jefferies* (1909), Faber 1978

Edward Thomas, *The Icknield Way*, Constable 1916

H. W. Timperley and Edith Brill, *Ancient Trackways of Wessex*, Dent 1965

INFORMATION:

H. D. Westacott, *A Practical Guide to Walking the Ridgeway Path*, Footpath Publications. Available from Ramblers' Association

Friends of the Ridgeway,
c/o Nigel Forward,
90 South Hill Park,
London NW3

The Pilgrims' Way

Winchester to Canterbury
116 miles

There are two ways for the walker on the North Downs today. One, the North Downs Way, is a footpath laid out by the Countryside Commission, which concentrates on good views south over the Weald and avoids metalled lanes. To achieve this it follows a carefully twisted course which involves a lot of map reading and a good deal of climbing. It begins at Farnham and ends at Dover. The other way, the Pilgrims' Way, sometimes coincides with the new footpath, but is quite different in aim and conception. It begins at Winchester and ends at Canterbury. For most of its length this old road keeps to the relatively well drained and sunny south-facing escarpment of the Downs, avoiding both the crest-line woods and the heavy clays of the Weald below. It has in places been surfaced for cars and in others simply erased where great landowners emparked their estates, but in the main it heads steadily eastwards, as natural to these downs as the ridgeways in Berkshire and Sussex are to theirs. This is the way to take.

The North Downs Ridgeway

Things are not, however, really that simple. The so-called Pilgrims' Way (there is no written evidence that a single pilgrim ever used it) is an idea cobbled together from various guesses and conjectures. The North Downs Ridgeway – a safer but less evocative name – was probably trampled out, like the other ridgeways, by herds of untended animals moving along lines of least resistance in search of food. Such a track would have ended up on Salisbury Plain. There is evidence that this animal track was adopted by Mesolithic people who arrived about ten thousand years ago. For unknown reasons they preferred tools made of chert, a kind of chalcedony found in Britain only in the Isle of Portland, to the more easily available flint. Chert axes have been found in three places in Surrey. Almost certainly they were brought up to Salisbury Plain and then along the North Downs Ridgeway.

The section of the Pilgrims' Way from Winchester to Farnham is a spur off the more important prehistoric through-route from Dover to Salisbury Plain. These first thirty

The Bargate stone and Horsham slab roof of Wotton Church near Dorking. Inside, John Evelyn, the diarist and first English landscape gardener, is buried beneath an unadorned coffin-shaped stone.

miles are not a naturally good cross-country line. The marshes of the Itchen valley and the heavy going up the River Wey would not have attracted the earliest travellers. The absence of an obvious route has important implications for a walker today. Over difficult ground, variations in season and in wetness, and in the knowledge and adventurousness of prehistoric men, would have led them to experiment with and eventually establish several parallel, linked tracks following a broad direction across the country. Any route the walker might now care to follow – except a patently bad one in an undrained and unmanaged landscape – is likely enough to have been used for millennia. Only when a ridge of hills strikes firmly, dryly and obviously in the required direction might the Way narrow to a single track, and not necessarily even then.

Pilgrimage

In prehistoric terms walking from Winchester to Canterbury was nothing very significant. To do so in the early Middle Ages, though, meant going from the capital of the kingdom to the centre of the church, from the secular to the ecclesiastical hub of power. After 1170 this journey would have been made as a pilgrimage to the shrine of Thomas à Becket.

Anyone walking the Pilgrims' Way is bound to ask themselves two questions about it. Why was Canterbury in particular the object of such huge numbers of pilgrims? And why did the people of the Middle Ages go on pilgrimage?

Thomas à Becket was thought of as a great saint, whose relics could work many and great miracles. But why was he such a great saint? Extraordinarily, his holiness was almost entirely expressed in a political way. By his martyrdom he guaranteed the political and

Part of the unrivalled stained glass in Canterbury Cathedral, paid for by the offerings of pilgrims such as these. The holiest walked barefoot.

legal independence of the church courts, an independence which lasted until the Reformation. There is no doubt that Becket intended to be martyred. Time after time in his long wrangles with Henry II he was given chances either to escape or to find a compromise, but he spurned these opportunities, not out of political incompetence, but with a kind of obstinate courage and a knowledge that his own death would be the seal on all that he was fighting for. When on 29 December 1170 he and those with him heard that four knights were coming armed to the cathedral, he stopped his men barring the doors, saying 'It is not fitting to make a fortress of the house of prayer. We came not to resist but to suffer'. Much of Becket is contained in the astute implications of that brave and apparently humble remark.

As for the pilgrimage itself, the cult of relics was at the centre of it. To the medieval mind the spiritual beauty of a saint's life did not desert his physical remains at death. The body of a dead saint was as holy as the man had been when alive, and possessed miraculous powers of healing. These powers, indeed, were the only proof after death of his holiness in life. To visit relics and be cured by them was almost invariably the aim of a pilgrimage. (There would be no distinction between physical and spiritual cure – medieval medical theory was psychosomatic through and through.)

But to reduce the pilgrimage phenomenon to this single cause would be wrong. The journey itself could be imposed as a penance. Tourism must have accounted for many so-called pilgrimages, while Jonathan Sumption suggests in his fascinating book *Pilgrimage* that the suffocating lack of privacy in any medieval community, where one's every action and motive were publicly scrutinised, would drive many to try to escape it. One of the only respectable means of doing so was to go on pilgrimage.

The style in which it was done could involve anything from the luxurious cortège of a penitent noble to the dependence of a single pilgrim on wayside charity. To go on foot was thought especially virtuous, and to go alone on foot even better. No shoes brought you still nearer sanctity, while for the extravagantly humble there was the example of some pilgrims who arrived at Limoges in the fourteenth century stark naked.

The Pilgrims' Way was first called that only in the eighteenth century, but because it was one of the main east-west routes in southern England and because Canterbury became one of the most popular shrines in Europe there can be little doubt that pilgrims used it. Almost certainly this was the route taken in July 1174 by Henry II when, after landing at South-

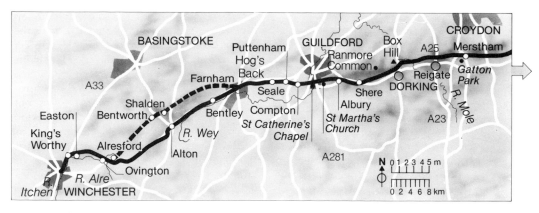

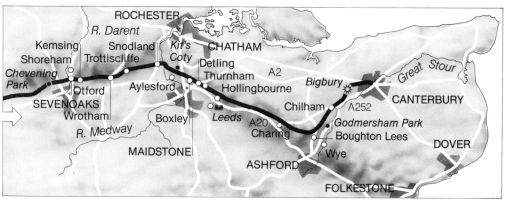

ampton, he rode eastwards to make his penitence at Canterbury, three and a half years after Becket had been murdered. The King took five days on the journey, living only on bread and water. After arriving at Canterbury he put on sackcloth and ashes and went barefoot. His feet were cut by the stony streets, leaving a trail of blood. Once inside the cathedral he prayed for a long time, first in the north transept where Becket had died and then in the crypt before the coffin. His clothes were then drawn down from his shoulders and he was flogged, five strokes from the prelates there, and three each from the monks of whom there were at least eighty. He then spent the entire night at prayer in the crypt, ending with a mass as day broke. Every episode in the Becket story has a theatrical quality to it, and this more than any other. To understand the significance of Henry II kneeling at the tomb of a man now martyred who was once his friend, being subjected to a beating at the hands of the bishops of England and the monks of Christ Church Canterbury, one must remember that he was the most powerful man in Europe, and held that position by unquestioned divine right. This, moreover, was as punishment for a crime he may for a second have deeply wished, but in no way ordered, and actually tried to prevent, but which happened nonetheless by a kind of inexorable momentum of its own.

It is necessary to keep the historical idea firmly before one on the Pilgrims' Way if the whole walk is not to disintegrate into something slightly ludicrous, particularly in Surrey, where you thread your way from golf-course to back-garden to golf-course again. It is all too easy to feel foolish standing in Guildford High Street in great boots and carting a rucksack. You cannot expect the exposure of other long walks on the North Downs today. To do so leads only to frustration and a hatred of suburban life. You must resolve either to love the putting-greens themselves or carefully exclude them from your mind, filling it instead, as a medieval traveller would have done, with the strange story of Thomas à Becket.

Winchester to Farnham 28 miles

Though the starting point of a walk is usually unimportant, Winchester cannot be so easily neglected. Pilgrims had also come here in the Middle Ages, to visit the tomb of St Swithun. This modest ninth-century bishop, the tutor of Alfred, was first buried at his own request on the damp north side of the cathedral, but in 971 he was translated to behind the high altar. The disturbance produced a rain storm lasting forty days, which Englishmen have talked about ever since. Both before and after Becket's martyrdom Swithun was the object of national and even international pilgrimage, and it is very likely that some pilgrims at least came

down the Pilgrims' Way in the wrong direction to visit him. His shrine was destroyed at the Reformation, but a replacement has been built, in the east end of the cathedral, and here surely is the place to begin on the Pilgrims' Way. As you go back down to the west door you will pass the transepts which, almost uniquely in this country, preserve the Romanesque style of just after the Norman Conquest. The Canterbury Cathedral in which Becket was killed would have looked like this. But it is the nave that holds your attention. It is by coincidence an exact contemporary of the Canterbury nave, both being built at the end of the fourteenth century. Its enormous, rather narrow length slides off down to the west end, one of Auden's

> Luxury liners laden with souls
> Holding to the East their hulls of stone.

In the north aisle a dark slab marks the grave of Jane Austen, who died in College Street in July 1817.

From Winchester to Alresford, about nine miles, the Way is along the Itchen, a smooth, sleek river, divided into several channels by

A corner of Winchester Cathedral: the Norman tower is all but concealed by the later Perpendicular additions.

slivers of islands that are covered in dry rushes or sometimes smoothed out into bits of lawn. The most likely route for pilgrims leaving Winchester would have been on the river's right bank, which is higher and better drained than the other, but this is now occupied, as far as King's Worthy, by the Winchester-Basingstoke road, and after that by the road to Alresford. Both are busy and it is far preferable, if less correct, to keep to the footpaths and lanes on the left bank. These may have been used by pilgrims in the summer anyway.

Head for Easton church tower, a kind of French cloche, that stands plainly above the river meadows. When you get there, you will find a very good saw-tooth Norman door and inside an odd horseshoe chancel arch, which is the result of the walls bulging at the top, not part of the Normans' original design.

After Easton you follow a lane passing a pretty trellissed lodge that marks the beginning of the Avington estate. Emerging from a wood into a shallow valley you come into sight of Avington House itself. The whole valley was once laid out as its park, with carefully grouped trees and a lake in front of the seventeenth-century house. Most of it has now been turned back to agriculture, and the rest has an air of decay. The still neat house standing in this landscape of neglect once housed Charles II and Nell Gwynn for the week-end, but has now been turned into flats inside.

Two miles of a barish landscape bring you to Ovington, where there is a pub down by the river among trees. The Way now crosses the busy A31 to come to a ford over the Itchen, whose source is at Hinton Marsh three miles to the south. The immaculately clear chalk stream water is ideal for cress, which is grown in the valley here in reeking mattresses contained in concrete beds.

New Alresford, which is just to the north, was new in about 1200, when Bishop Godfrey de Lucy of Winchester built a market town to accompany his scheme for making the Itchen

Easton church and the Itchen: an almost French view.

navigable from here to the sea at South-ampton. The depth of water in rivers on chalk is notoriously variable, and to counteract this the Bishop built a great embankment across the Alre, damming behind it a two-hundred-acre lake, with gates and sluices going down to the Itchen. The profit the Bishop was after lay in the wool that came off the Downs to the north. He succeeded in having Winchester nominated a staple, one of the few markets in the country from which the export of raw wool to the Flemish and Italian clothiers could be conducted. His Itchen navigation scheme prospered for a century and a half until in 1353 the staple was moved to Calais, and the Itchen waterworks were neglected. All but sixty acres of the lake have slipped away, and the rest is now a coot-infested marsh. The road north to Basingstoke still runs above the wet ground on the thirteenth-century dam.

From Alresford to Farnham is nineteen miles. This is over a watershed between the Itchen, which flows south to the Channel, and the Wey, a tributary of the Thames. For almost the whole distance the supposed line of the Pilgrims' Way is occupied by the modern London–Southampton road. This is a lesson in

itself. It is very easy, but wrong, to think of old roads as narrow grassy tracks deeply hidden between dark hedges. Economic and technical change may have left a few previously vital routes in this balmy state – it has happened to the Pilgrims' Way in Kent – but far more often a once important road will be important now, and will show the massive and genuine improvements made in the science of road-building in the last two hundred years.

All the same, the A31 is horrible walking. There is, though, another way to Farnham which Neolithic herdsmen or pilgrims might themselves have used. This way is, besides, through lanes and greenways that fit one's expectations closer, as well as revealing more of Hampshire than could be found on the hard shoulder of a dual carriageway.

In some ways the official Pilgrims' Way, particularly as it nears Farnham, is not like a prehistoric route at all. Just beyond Alton the edge of the chalk kinks to the north, to be replaced by a surface of impermeable clay, which old roads always avoid. In addition, this valley route passes *through* settlements, forming the main streets of Alton, Bentley and Farnham, as the Pilgrims' Way almost never does anywhere else. Hilaire Belloc tried to explain away these anomalies by claiming that primitive man would have preferred the heavy trudge in the valley to a route high up on the chalk because here the hills were so deeply indented that any higher path would have meant exhausting ups and downs. This is not true. Between Alton and Farnham the high route climbs no more than 250 feet in the ten miles, with total descents of only sixty feet per mile in between. For today's walker at least this is far better than attempting the footpaths in the valley. There, within a matter of yards, your boots contract a kind of earthy elephantiasis, doubling their size in minutes and tripling their weight with clods. It is no fun.

To reach the high road from Alton itself means a steep climb up the front of the escarpment. Any traveller would want to avoid this, and on the map there is a clear line of connected lanes and footpaths that do so, striking north-east directly from Alresford, via Bentworth and Shalden, passing very close to the highest point in Hampshire, at 738 feet, just north of Holywell Down, to reach the Harrow Way at Well, which it then follows into Farnham. This is the way to go.

From Alresford you start out over the Bishop's Dam to Old Alresford and then up the long straight track leading north-east. Characteristically, it leads to nowhere of any significance; it is a good chalky road, sometimes in trees, but more often open and up on Hampshire. The landscape is neither comfort-ing like the Cotswolds or Dorset, nor abrasive or stimulating. It is surprisingly empty, but without a suggestion of vehemence or bleak-ness – just slightly coloured in coordinating browns and greens and blues which have in them more darkness than colour.

After seven miles you will come to Bent-worth, an open village arranged around a square of lanes, and after another two and a half to Shalden, part of the way down a long curving coombe, open on one side and with a hanging wood rising steeply on the other. Bentworth was the birthplace of George Wither, a seventeenth-century poet who spent his early life in and out of prison for what was considered his scandalous poetry on vice and himself. He later turned Puritan, holding Farnham Castle for Parliament in the Civil War, and then sentimental, wanting to return to his birthplace to die, but collapsing instead in London.

From Shalden it is five and a half miles to Well, all of which, after a first small descent to the Alton–Reading road, are along the top of the chalk ridge that drops gradually away to the north, but is flat on top and has no great views over the Wey valley. After Well you pass down towards Farnham along the Harrow Way by the site of a Roman villa and the Norman motte-and-bailey called Barley Pound. Powderham Castle looks an exciting prospect in gothic lettering on the map, but it too is only an earthwork. You cross into Surrey and within two miles arrive in the centre of Farnham.

Farnham to Merstham 30 miles

Farnham is inescapably Cobbett's town. It still looks much the way it did when he was born here in his father's pub, the Jolly Farmer, in about 1762. Most of the houses in the Borough, and off it in Castle Street, show fine and firm Georgian fronts, the image of urbane prosperity. These handsome streets were the visible dividends of a famous corn market, the biggest in England except for London. According to a man Defoe met, 44,000 bushels of wheat, drawn by eleven hundred teams of horse, had once been brought to market here on a single day.

By the early nineteenth century such abundance must have seemed the product of a golden age. By then the Speenhamland system and the private enclosure of over four million acres of common land had combined to polarise rural wealth, so that as Cobbett hurled in his *Political Register*, 'We are daily advancing to the state in which there are but two classes of men, *masters* and *abject dependants*'. This transformation of independent yeoman farm-ers into enslaved hands and the substitution

The Maltings in Farnham: Home Counties prosperity.

of a divided for a carefully graded rural society was Cobbett's constant theme and constant anger. His championing of the cause against it makes him one of the heroes of the nineteenth century, a conservative radical whose fight was to return England to the kind of country into which he had been born.

Rural Rides, where his love of southern England is seen to grow out of this moral concern and a deep practical knowledge of soils, crops and the management of the land, were all done on horseback. He was no walker, thinking 'to tramp it ... too slow, leaving the labour out of the question, and that is not a trifle'. He died in 1835 and is buried in Farnham churchyard.

The Hog's Back humps up to the east of Farnham, rising to 500 feet above sea level and about 200 feet above the expanse of Surrey fields and heaths that stretches to the north. This hog of a hill, almost equally steep on both flanks, was produced by the combination of a fault to the south and vertical bedding planes

in the chalk. Along its back runs the A31, but the Pilgrims' Way steps down a little, about a third of a mile to the south, to get more sun and the better drainage of a slope.

To reach this lower road, which runs through the villages of Seale and Puttenham, it is best to go south from Farnham and cross the River Wey by Moor Park before climbing the Hog's nose. Moor Park is now a college, but in the seventeenth century was the home of Sir William Temple, who for a while employed the young Jonathan Swift as his secretary. Here Swift wrote *The Battle of the Books* and met Esther Johnson, known to the world as Stella. Few places can have been more profoundly civilised than Moor Park in these years. Temple himself had had a brilliant diplomatic career but at the height of his success he suddenly quit public affairs to devote to his garden all the talents with which he had served the nation. William III came here to implore him to become Secretary of State, but nothing could take him from his garden on the banks of the Wey. Its design was conventional enough, with straight up and down gravel paths and the kind of pleached trees he would have found everywhere when on his embassies to Holland.

The Pilgrims' Way descends in sand from St Martha's Hill near Guildford, with the remains of the Wealden forest to the south.

But in the book on gardens he published in 1685 Temple describes – and he is the first Englishman to do so – the beauty of a less rigid kind of garden, in which the earth is more gently and more subtly moulded – the landscape garden, in fact, of the next century.

As you make your way up and along the Hog's Back the sand will show through in the fields around you, but the country is very pretty and looks fertile. Cobbett loved the landscape here: 'The road is good; the soil is good; the houses are neat; the people are neat; the hills, the woods, the meadows all are beautiful. Nothing wild and bold, to be sure: but exceedingly pretty.'

This comfortable landscape appears intermittently during the tree-lined four miles to Puttenham, which is a pretty brick-and-clunch village, crowned by the church that stands at the end of the street. Several of the houses have brick in-fill between the timber uprights in the walls; this is called nogging. Others, more rarely, have little ironstone chips pushed like raisins into the mortar, a process called galletting, which gives a charming twinkle to the face of a cottage.

From Puttenham it is three and a half miles to the recrossing of the Wey south of Guildford. En route, a short detour to the south is worth making to Compton, whose Norman church has a curious double chancel; but this oddity is overshadowed by the terracotta Mortuary Chapel of G.F.Watts, the Victorian painter and sculptor. It was designed by his wife in 1896 in an extraordinary mixture of gilt angels, art nouveau curls and tendrils and impenetrable Celtic symbolism.

Two miles of sandy track lead from here to another chapel, this one dedicated to St Catherine, a grey ruin. Below is the River Wey, now safely channelled, but previously spreading untidily over the whole valley. John Bunyan may have lived at Shalford, half a mile to the south. It is said that here was the original Slough of Despond, and that the Pilgrims' Way itself was the imaginative source of the whole of *Pilgrim's Progress*.

There is now a footbridge immediately across the river which allows you to bypass Guildford. This would be a mistake, because

Guildford's cobbled High Street is one of the best things in Surrey. In it are buildings – like the 1683 Guildhall, with its clock that hangs yards out into the street, and nearly opposite the Tunsgate (1818), a giant Tuscan portico that used to front a now demolished corn exchange – that are far more adventurous than anything in Farnham (which seems demure by comparison). This ambitiousness could so easily have been pretentious, but instead it is a visual thrill, mainly because these slightly grandiose buildings are all pushed up one against the other and all on a very steep slope that drops sharply to the Wey.

You must go back down to the river to reach the Way again, turning east at a road of smart modern houses, and then climbing up into Chantries Wood which is heavy with the smell of pines. The path climbs for nearly two miles to the tiny church of St Martha's on the summit. From there you descend in pure sand and emerge from the trees to a broad swooping valley, on the far northern edge of which you see for the first time the long wall of the North Downs. Of all the English chalk hills these downs have the messiest line, broken everywhere by woods and bushes, but the valley is lovely, there being 'very few prettier rides in England' Cobbett thought, although when he came here in October 1825 all was not well, since he had 'heard of no less than five people, in this vale, who have gone crazy on account of religion'.

The source of this new lunacy was at Albury, two miles from St Martha's, where you will find an extravagant church of very yellow sandstone, dotted all over with large gallets. The church was not built until 1840, but for fifteen years before that Albury had been the centre of the Catholic Apostolic Church, which took from its founder Henry Irving an extraordinary amalgam of austere Presbyterianism and the wildest kind of romantic mysticism and arcane ritual. In Albury Park, just to the south, the twelve new apostles spent most of the nineteenth century in careful and excited preparation for the second coming, but by 1901, when the last surviving apostle died, Christ had not yet reappeared and the Catholic Apostolic Church quietly faded away. The church building at Albury is now permanently locked.

The way leads clearly on to the village of Shere, prettily arranged around the Tillingbourne, but eastwards the line of the Pilgrims' Way – if there ever was such a single thing – has been lost, and so the choice is open. One possible way is through Abinger Hammer, named after the iron works or bloomeries that were once here and whose furnace ponds still are. From there you can climb on to a ridge that rises between the

Tillingbourne and the Downs, mostly owned by the National Trust, and covered in places with islands of old beechwood. About three miles ahead the spire of Sir George Gilbert Scott's church on Ranmore Common prods above the trees. You make for this, crossing the valley below the Downs and then climbing steeply and greasily up them.

Half-way up, the Pilgrims' Way survives as a terrace, darkly crowded and overhung with yews. Legend – fostered by Belloc – claims these trees mark the line of the Old Road, but in fact yews grow everywhere and anywhere on chalk. The legend is helped by the look of them. In the crypt-like darkness beneath a stand of yews their trunks of twisted and blackened sinew – exaggerated if a scar of chalk happens to be showing through – look ages old. But the yew is wizened before its time and is rarely as ancient as it looks. What seems to be a single immense trunk is actually a spiralling rope of many separate stems all the same age and all growing up from ground level.

You emerge from their dark tunnel on to Ranmore Common, at the head of which is Scott's church, built in 1859 for the Cubitts. They lived a mile away at Polesden Lacey, a Regency Greek villa which was later converted into a classic of Edwardian taste. It now belongs to the National Trust. The outside of the church is covered in round flint cobbles and the interior filled with cold marbly details. It feels unused.

The Way comes down in two miles to the sharp gap made in the Downs by the River Mole. The Roman Stane Street from Chichester to London squeezed through here, as the trunk road and railway do now. The River Mole was, until the eighteenth century, famous for burrowing underground here to appear again several miles later at Leatherhead. Knowing this, it is disappointing to find that its lovely name was given it by an Elizabethan geographer, not some poetical Saxon. Before the sixteenth century, rather less prettily, it was known as the Dork, hence Dorking.

But although it was so famous for this sinking and underground flow, the truth is – and Defoe the rational topographer was firm about it – that it never disappears at all. There is a slight leakage into its bed as it runs over the chalk, but William Camden's story that someone pushed a duck in at one end to retrieve it at the other with its feathers rubbed off could not possibly be true. The myth of the Mole nevertheless persisted: Spenser, Milton, Celia Fiennes and Pope all repeated it. It is a classic case of not finding untrue what you enjoy finding true.

On the far side of the Mole, which you can cross by stepping stones, Box Hill, England's best picnic spot, rises steeply above you, covered in beech and the box trees by which it is named. It is owned by the National Trust. Of all the thousands of picnics that must have happened here the most famous is the disastrous expedition in *Emma*. Emma's party arrives and leaves by coaches up the back way – as many do now – but if you have crossed the Mole by the stepping stones there is a very steep climb to the open grass at the top where picnics are best and the views over to Leith Hill and the Weald are widest. As usual, though, to follow the Pilgrims' Way there is no need to go as far as the top; you can contour round the hill lower down, following a path on the edge of the wood for about three miles, passing three vast chalk quarries. In the bottom of one of them – and this you stumble across quite unannounced – is an incongruous collection of small steam engines and tenders.

Immediately beyond this pit the escarpment of the Downs steepens and one must follow either the crest or the foot of the slope for the next three miles. Box, juniper and yew line the

whole way. At Colley Hill if you have been going along the lower path you must climb to avoid Reigate and then cross the London Road on a footbridge above a deep cutting. Going down a small lane you soon enter Gatton Park. Gatton until 1832 was one of the rottenest boroughs in England, returning two members to parliament from a village of 23 houses. The best thing here – and to find it you must go round the back of some dull modern school buildings – is the minute town hall, built by the owners of the place in 1765 as a cynical political joke. The 'elections' were held in this little Doric temple in the park. It shelters a large urn on which the Latin inscription, when translated, reads:

> The urn remains when the lots have been drawn.
> Let the well-being of the people be the supreme law.
> The Place of Assembly of Gatton 1746.
> Let evil deception be absent.

Cobbett, predictably, did not get the joke and thought Gatton 'a very rascally spot of earth'.

It is about a mile to Merstham from the gingerbread cottage at the park gates. The

Stepping stones over the River Mole under Box Hill.

Private railway tracks under the Downs near Bletchworth Quarries.

footpath across the fields arrives at Merstham's show-piece: Quality Street, a traffic-free backwater lined on each side by comfortable Home Counties houses, most of which are from about 1700, but with some discreet insertions from early this century. Everything is tile-hung or tactfully half-timbered. This street of separate, rather grand houses is now less remarkable than it must once have been – acres of Surrey and North Kent are now covered in streets whose whole aim is to be like this one.

Merstham to the Medway 27 miles

This part starts badly. Within three quarters of a mile you have to cross two motorways, two railway lines and a dual carriageway. Between them all the Way is along reproduction Quality Streets. After the last motorway is crossed, though, the Way is not bad at all. On the map the buff smear of Croydon creeps dangerously close to the edge of the Downs, but stops short and leaves the path clear through beech-woods which are not grey-trunked as they are in the Chilterns, but damply green. The ridge of the Downs rises slowly until at Botley Hill, just north of Titsey, they reach their highest point, at 882 feet. Only a large communications aerial marks this as a summit, but the view over to the south is wonderful. The greensand is here a long wooded ridge, parallel to the Downs but not as high. Beyond it are the Forest Ridges in the middle of the Weald, and on the far horizon, slightly east of south, the clean level brow of the South Downs.

Titsey is the first of the parks which have obliterated the line of the Pilgrims' Way. The same geographical feature – the edge of the Downs – that for physical reasons brought prehistoric travellers here provided exactly the variety, neither rude nor craggy, which

appealed to the landscape tastes of the eighteenth century. Between here and Canterbury five parks – Titsey, Chevening, Eastwell, Godmersham and Chilham – divert or interrupt the way.

There is no way through Titsey Park and you must follow the high and wide main road along the Downs crest from Botley Hill, passing the isolated Tatsfield church after about a mile and then diving into a woody lane where the main road goes down the edge. After three-quarters of a mile you cross into Kent and whoop with delight. This is the last county and the best. Here the sound of electric hedge clippers is exchanged for shears. In Kent the Pilgrims' Way is a much more definite thing – no archaeological resurrection, but a continuous thread of lanes, both on the Downs and below them, which has been broken only by those few parks. There is a historical reason for this. After about 1200 London took over from Winchester as the capital of England. The most direct route from London to Canterbury would have been down the Roman road through Rochester (now the A2), but the Pilgrims' Way (which would have been joined at Otford) was a popular alternative. The Archbishops of Canterbury had a string of palaces along it, at Charing, Wrotham and Otford itself, where they could stay when travelling between Lambeth and Canterbury.

This traffic kept the Way open in Kent, where in other places it disintegrated in neglect. But development was arrested there. As land-drainage and engineering improved the easier gradients of the parallel valley roads – now the A20 and, further along, the A25 – kept most of the traffic off the Pilgrims' Way, which has been left in an ideal state for the walker – a definite track that is easily followed but almost free of traffic.

East from the border with Surrey the Downs are again not smooth along the front but wavy. There are two ancient trackways which avoid the ins and outs, one by following the crest, the other the scarp foot. The lower one after four direct miles through arable fields comes up against Chevening Park gates, and has to make a long detour to the south, round three sides of a mile-wide square, in the middle of which sits Chevening Park. It was originally a seventeenth-century house but was greatly altered and enlarged by Lord Stanhope in 1717. The history of the English country house is very much the retreat of the occupants from their servants' and the public's gaze. By 1792 the third Lord Stanhope found intolerable what all his predecessors had accepted, and had the ancient right of way across the front of his house abolished by Act of Parliament.

The detour which Lord Stanhope's need for privacy made necessary can be avoided by

*The carefully arranged landscape around
Avington House near Alresford has been
allowed to drift into romantic decay.*

taking the high track along the Downs. For most of the way trees block out any view to the south, but when you arrive above Chevening itself you find a sudden sharp hole has been cut through the woods pointing straight down at the grand house about a mile away. So narrow is this cut – called the Keyhole – that only the original central block can be seen. All the way down on either side the great beeches have for centuries been precisely shaved to a height of about forty foot, as neat as a garden hedge but five times as tall. The whole Chevening estate is as immaculate as this.

About a mile beyond Chevening the Downs pull back to reveal the valley of the Darent, which cuts through them on its way north to the Thames. Two miles down the valley on the bank of the river is Shoreham, which in the 1820s was the centre and inspiration of a group of painters (of which Samuel Palmer was a member) known as the Shoreham Ancients. Blake was their hero and occasional guest, and following him they resisted the realist drift of their contemporaries and aimed for a beautiful Platonic ideal. The lovely full downs in Palmer's pictures are quite unlike the real thing, but once you know that this is Palmer's valley it becomes impossible to dissociate the look of the Downs themselves – actually quite flat – from his great bosomy representations of them. It produces an odd kind of double vision.

The Pilgrims' Way crosses the Darent at Otford, which was the scene in 774 of one of

Oast houses near Otford. In essence no more than giant chimneys, capped by draught improvers called cowls, these symbols of Kent are increasingly being converted into houses. Chemical additives in beer have replaced the hops that were once dried in them.

Offa's battles with the men of Kent. No one knows who won. The best thing in the village now is what is left of the Archbishop's palace. It lies at the end of a broad street going south from the village pond. The palace was once substantial, 440 feet long and 220 feet wide (as big as Knole), all of Tudor brick with stone quoins. It was built at enormous expense in the early sixteenth century by Archbishop Wareham, but after being confiscated by Henry VIII was soon neglected, had the lead stripped off its roof and began to fall apart. It is an almost unnoticed ruin, with plants growing out of it and a tatty fence in front. The tower at the west end is empty, but most of the range that survives is now filled with cottages, in front of which, quite unselfconsciously, lean-tos have been built and washing is now hung. This looks just like a nineteenth-century print of a ruin, twice as romantic because it is treated as everyday.

It is just over five miles from Otford to Wrotham. The Pilgrims' Way is at first rather busy and lined with bungalows, but both traffic and houses gradually diminish, until past Kemsing you will probably be on your own between the hedges of the lane and below the small woods on the hills. From the north will come the high whine of Brands Hatch motor racing track. A mile and a half from Kemsing the way passes in front of St Clere, a contemporary of the original Chevening and a very small version of the familiar pattern of great house and park below the Down. Soon afterwards the metalled lane turns south and the Pilgrims' Way continues as a grassy track towards Wrotham, edging past an orchard and dominated by the white scar made across the Downs by the new M20. Wrotham, just to the south of the Way, has the roofless remains of another 'palace', which can never have been bigger than an average-sized manor house.

From Wrotham the Way begins to turn slightly north, following the edge of the Downs as they start to open up for the wide valley of the Medway. In two miles you pass above the pretty village of Trottiscliffe (pronounced Trosly). Its church is another half-mile to the east, left stranded there with only one good house and a couple of cottages by it when in the fourteenth century the Black Death drove most of the villagers away down the road. There is some perfect nineteenth-century knapped flint in the church walls, and

inside an enormous pulpit that was once in Westminster Abbey.

About a mile east of Trottiscliffe church down a gravelly track are the Coldrum Stones, a Neolithic long barrow in great collapse. They are owned by the National Trust. This is the first of a small group of such tombs which are clustered around the Medway crossing. They have structural similarities to tombs in Scandinavia and north Germany, and were probably built by people from there who had penetrated up the Medway.

From the Coldrum Stones you can look out across the six-mile-wide Medway gap. This flat and once marshy expanse would have been a major problem to prehistoric travellers and even to medieval pilgrims. Where did they cross? As ever, there is probably no one single answer. Some pilgrims may have gone as far north as Rochester and from there taken the Roman road to Canterbury. There were probably ferries at Halling and at Snodland,

The burial chamber of the Coldrum Stones Long Barrow. Kit's Coty, its twin on the far side of the Medway, is on the hills in the distance.

LEFT *In Kent, the Way often runs below the Downs, on the very edge of the chalk, a few yards from the Wealden clay, as it does here near Wrotham.*

BOTTOM LEFT *Blackthorn in flower on the Way near St Clere in Kent.*

RIGHT *On the Pilgrims' Way in Kent.*

BELOW *The Way between Detling and Boxley.*

but there are none there now, and the only modern way of crossing the river is by the bridge at Aylesford. A good compromise is to walk to Snodland and to get the train for two stops down to Aylesford. The way down to the river is through the tiny hamlet of Paddlesworth, consisting only of the plain brick Comfort Manor and the shed-like Norman church of St Benedict's, roughly built of herring-bone flint, but repaired all over with brick and clunch and ragstone patches.

Snodland itself is Kent's Middlesbrough, all hard red brick leading up to the smoky cement works and paper mill on the river. Embedded in Snodland are two neglected churches and a harshly restored Wealden house. The river itself is a strip of water the colour of cold tea between tidal mud banks. On the far side a reedy marsh stretches towards the Downs. Trains run regularly to Aylesford.

The Medway to Canterbury
31 miles

Cross the medieval bridge at Aylesford to the narrow streets of the village built tightly on the bank of the river. The Downs are two miles away across the flat valley, with their edge now heading south-east towards Folkestone. If you head straight for the hills from the river you

Kit's Coty, a Neolithic tomb, now caged.

arrive below Kit's Coty, the most famous of the Medway group of Neolithic monuments. (Nearby are two more, the Countless Stones and the White Horse Stone.) You have to climb up the down a few hundred yards to reach this giant tripod, which most likely is all that is left of a long barrow whose earth mound has been eroded away. From here the industrial works on the Medway stand up largely. Beyond them the nearest point of Down on the other side is the site of the

Coldrum Stones. It is conceivable that these great communal tombs served as markers for the shortest good route from hill to hill across the Medway valley.

The Way now crosses the A229, the Roman road from Rochester through the Weald to Hastings, and then continues below the hills through a succession of villages – Boxley, Detling, Thurnham and Hollingbourne – which were all dependent on the Pilgrims' Way, but significantly lie just south of it. The Way keeps to the very edge of the dry chalk, while the villages are grouped along the line of springs which rise at the junction of the chalk and the clay. As before, the Pilgrims' Way is paralleled by an equally ancient trackway that follows the top of the Downs, while yet another line of rights of way south of the main route connects the villages themselves. Any of them might have been used by medieval pilgrims.

At Boxley, about three miles from Kit's Coty, pilgrims would definitely have left the Way to go to the Cistercian abbey a mile to the south. Only an enormous barn – once the guest house – now remains of Boxley Abbey, but until the Reformation it was a big, rich place, built from the donations of those who had come to see its most famous possession – the Boxley Rood of Grace. This was a life-size model of Christ on the cross, which, when various wires and levers were operated by hidden monks, would nod and roll its eyes, wag its head and wave its hands. Most importantly it could pull faces of extreme displeasure if the pilgrim's offering was too mean, and of divine relief and grace when he finally produced enough. It was dismembered and burnt at the Reformation.

The Way winds on, rising and falling slightly in easy sweeps. This part is one of the gentlest on the walk. About four miles from Boxley you reach Broad Street, a hamlet in which almost every building has a hipped roof, with sloping rather than vertical gables. Aesthetically there is no better way of covering a house than this; the building is somehow pegged down into the landscape by it.

A mile and a half further at Hollingbourne it is worth going a little off the Way to Leeds. The village is one of the prettiest in Kent, but Leeds Castle is even better. It is made of the Kentish ragstone that changes from grey to yellow according to the light, and is built on an island in an artificial lake fed by the waters of

TOP RIGHT *Leeds Castle, near Maidstone: made to look more romantic in the nineteenth century, now a conference centre.*

RIGHT *The fourteenth-century ragstone bridge over the Medway at Aylesford.*

Len. The harmonious look of the castle from the north is as much the product of the nineteenth century as of the thirteenth.

The way is nearly all unmetalled for the eight miles from Hollingbourne to Charing. Except for a modern tile factory at Marley Court and a new hospital two miles further it is quite uninterrupted. The A20 has taken all the traffic and building, leaving the old road unimportant and bare. It is one of those rare stretches along which, not needing to map-read, you can drift through an unthinking afternoon, or perhaps better a few hours of the night.

Charing has several places in which to stay. The main street of brick and weatherboarded houses runs between the Canterbury and the Folkestone roads which join just to the west. This was a natural place for a market, which used to be held in the wide street leading east to the tall grey fifteenth-century church tower. On the north side of this open space are the remains of another of the archbishops' palaces, whose fragmentary flint buildings are now used as a farm. There is still a very roughly arranged courtyard in which hens peck and tractors are parked. The eastern side of it is made up of what was once the Great Hall, a very large building of about 1300, which is now used as a barn. Wisps of hay and straw stick out through its delicately cusped windows.

The Pilgrims' Way itself avoids Charing and moves on west past the large chalkpit at Burnthouse Farm, following the fringe of the wood. In early spring this is an arrangement of subtle differences in colour. Against the darkness of the yews and the leafless bushes the slight greyness of last year's Traveller's Joy is very near the just-yellow of the new catkins. None of it is far from the monochrome.

About four miles from Charing the Way passes the ruined Eastwell church, a coolly romantic thing by a water-lily lake. The house of whose park this lake was the chief ornament has been demolished.

Just beyond, the Way reaches a turning point at the Valley of the Great Stour. Canterbury is north-east down the river. Pilgrims would either have kept above the damp valley ground or maybe have taken to the river itself at Wye. (This, incidentally, is still a very good way to get to Canterbury. You can float effortlessly down in a small boat on the clear stream right to the West Gate of the city itself.) Neither of these would have been

The vibrations from artillery positioned too near Eastwell church in World War Two so weakened its foundations that most of it collapsed during a storm in 1951. Only the tower still stands.

taken by prehistoric men. They would have continued on the edge of the Downs to the sea at Folkestone, a route which can still be picked out in lanes, and which one branch of the Countryside Commission's North Downs Way follows.

If you are to continue on foot to Canterbury you turn up through Boughton Lees and head for the squat tower of Boughton Aluph church, prominent on the skyline ahead. This massive flint church with a light and roomy inside was built all at one time in the fourteenth century. Why should such a cavernous church be here in a village of just a couple of houses?

In a mile the Way climbs sharply up into King's Wood, once said to be full of thieves and a terror for travellers. At first it is yew and old beech, but these soon give way to coppiced chestnuts, a commercial crop and an ugly kind of woodland. Down to the right, though, are the green open slopes of Godmersham Park. The Palladian house to which this land is attached is down by the river and invisible from the path. Jane Austen's brother lived here, and she often came to stay, enjoying herself far more than in the modest house at Chawton in Hampshire. 'Kent is the only place for happiness,' she wrote. 'Everyone is rich there.' Godmersham has been claimed as the model for Mansfield Park and for Pemberley, Darcy's house in *Pride and Prejudice*, but any description in the novels is so vague that one cannot be sure.

Past Godmersham Park you drop to a lane which in a mile comes to Chilham, with the last few hundred yards along a puce and plum coloured wall, the boundary of the Chilham Castle estate. If you have begun the morning in Charing, Chilham will be lunch. The little village square, where there is a pub, is a perfect piece of town planning. The church closes off one end and the gateway to the castle the other, while at the corners of the square are lanes dropping away like the pleats at the corners of a table-cloth. The 'castle' is in fact a great Jacobean brick pile built around five sides of a hexagon and standing next to the much older stone keep which by the early seventeenth century had become obsolete. As if to point this out Sir Dudley Digges, the builder of the new, civilised and unfortified house, had a stone tablet set above his front door saying 'The Lord is my house of defence and my castle', with his name, his wife's name and the date, 1616.

Mercery Lane in Canterbury: the last few yards of the Pilgrims' Way bring you to the Christ Church gate into the Cathedral precincts. Refreshments and souvenirs have been sold in this street since the twelfth century.

The last afternoon is from Chilham to Canterbury, about six miles. The way is not clear to start with, and you have to take a lane which is almost certainly not on an old line to the village of Old Wives Lees (a good name, which is rather an odd corruption of Oldwood's Lees, meaning old clearings from the wood). From there, though, there is a continuous line of footpaths leading via Nickle Farm and Chartham Hatch straight towards Canterbury. It is all through orchards and past a hop garden. You pass Bigbury, a large Iron Age fort on a ridge between the Stour and one of its small tributaries. The banks are hidden in a wood. This may have been the site of pre-Roman Canterbury, or at least a refuge for its inhabitants. A little further on you get the first sight of Bell Harry, the great tower of Canterbury Cathedral, and with it the first inkling of that wonderful finishing feeling. Harbledown, now a suburb of Canterbury, soon closes the path in on both sides. Only the top of Golden Hill, owned by the National Trust, is clear of buildings, but the famous

Boughton Aluph, near Wye, and a field of rape.

view of the cathedral from here, which was meant to have been preserved, has now been obscured. You cross the A2 and make for the Westgate of the city. The nearer you get the older the buildings become until you are suddenly confronted with the two grey ragstone drums of the fourteenth-century Westgate.

You hurry on and move up the High Street through crowds of shoppers indifferent to the fact that you have walked half-way across England, over a tiny branch of the Stour overhung with buildings, and then left into Mercery Lane, the image of a cramped medieval street whose upper stories jetty out towards each other. At the end of it is the brilliantly heraldic Christ Church gate into the cathedral precincts. There is a wonderfully welcoming sensation of arrival, of being more and more enclosed the deeper you penetrate – by the city wall, the close wall, and then the cathedral wall itself, all these in onion layers.

To enter the perpendicular nave of Canterbury Cathedral must be one of the great architectural experiences in the country, but even this is not the final arrival. If you have walked the Pilgrims' Way the place to go is

A Norman passage in the Cathedral.

surely the North Transept, where Becket was martyred. This is quite bare and architecturally unimportant, but is the heart of the place. Here on 29 December 1170 the four knights found the archbishop and murdered him by slicing off the top of his head as he knelt on the floor. As a final barbarity one of the knights, Hugh Horsea, put his sword in Becket's open cranium and flicked out his brains on to the flagstones.

There is of course far more to the cathedral than this solemn place, so much in fact that one should stay in Canterbury for several days to see the wealth of artistry that Becket's martyrdom both inspired and paid for, and to hope perhaps for a miraculous cure to all the aches and blisters which the journey will no doubt have produced.

MAPS: OS 1:50,000 Numbers 179, 185, 186, 187, 188, 189

GUIDES:
Sean Jennett, *The Pilgrims' Way*, Cassell 1971
C. J. Wright, *A guide to the Pilgrims' Way and North Downs Way*, Constable 1971

BACKGROUND:
Hilaire Belloc, *The Old Road*, Constable 1904
D. J. Hall, *English Medieval Pilgrimages*, Routledge 1966
Jonathan Sumption, *Pilgrimage*, Faber 1975
Richard Winston, *Thomas Becket*, Constable 1967

INFORMATION:
North Downs Way Information Sheet, from the Ramblers' Association

The South Downs Way

Eastbourne to Buriton in Hampshire 80 miles

The South Downs Way is a chalk walk. During the week that it takes to go the eighty miles from Beachy Head to Buriton in Hampshire the chalk is always with you. It is the most homely and unrock-like of rocks, as though it were the best that Sussex could do when rock was demanded of it. Only at Beachy Head do the Downs reveal their depth of whiteness, but this image once seen remains with you, so that the mind, as if with a cheese-wire, is continually cutting sections through the whole height of the Downs, making Beachy Heads and Seven Sisters all the way to the Hampshire border.

The geology of the South Downs is simple. From about 100 million to about 70 million years ago a shallow sea covered most of Britain. The lands that bordered this sea were probably parched, almost deserts, so that there were no rivers, which would have brought heavy sediments down with them, flowing into it. Minute marine plants precipitated the pure calcium carbonate which was in solution in the sea and the fine white dust that was produced settled on the seabed to build up at the rate of one foot every thirty thousand years. It was not a snowstorm. The marine conditions around the Bahamas now are in the process of creating downland. Also in this sea were sponges, whose silicate skeletons, dissolved, sifted and concentrated in nodules, came to form the lines of flint which seam the chalk.

Forty million years later Italy collided with Europe, and a small outer ripple of this cataclysm which built the Alps bumped Kent and Sussex into a dome of chalk. The top of the dome was probably cracked in the upsurge, and water then carried away both the chalk and the underlying clays and sands. On the Downs you must imagine yourself on the lower slopes of a great chalk pimple whose other edge is forty miles away in Surrey and North Kent. The slight rise of the Weald is all that remains of what was between the North and the South Downs. The rivers – the removal agents – still flow through the chalk hills in gaps disproportionate to their sluggishness. The sources of these rivers were once higher than the present chalk escarpment. As the Weald itself was reduced the courses of the rivers out to the sea had themselves to be lowered. The

The Seven Sisters: only here do the Downs reveal their full depth of whiteness.

gaps they have made in the Downs were not cut through the hills, but worn down from above.

It may seem strange that the crumbly chalk should have resisted the immense eroding forces which have removed so much from around them, but it is precisely because rain can percolate through the chalk that the Downs have not been worn away. The impermeable layers of clay and sand which are exposed in the Weald are, in varying degrees, carried away by the water which cannot soak through them.

The physical and chemical nature of chalk has always influenced what people have done on the Downs. Life has been dictated for millennia by the absolute lack of surface water, and the strong acidity of the soil, which comes from its being constantly drained or 'leached'.

There were hunters in Sussex 400,000 years ago, who wandered over from the continent. (The English Channel did not come into existence until extremely recently in geological time, about 10,000 years ago.) These Palaeolithic nomads left no mark on the land, which cannot have changed from its natural state until the first farmers arrived from Europe in about 5000 BC. Recent experiments have shown that small patches of down, fenced off and left untouched for several years, consist-

Cocking Chalk Pit: about 100 million years ago a fine white dust accumulated at the rate of one foot every 30,000 years.

ently revert to woodland. This must mean that the bareness of the eastern Downs is not their original state, but the result of prehistoric clearance. The chalkland wood was probably never as thick as that in the Weald, and could easily have been cleared with stone axes. From the first this relative bareness and the good drainage will have attracted men to the Downs who used them as a ridgeway, and it is a real pleasure to know that the way you follow here is not an artificial construction, but one of the natural highways of England. Until the coming of the turnpikes in the eighteenth century it remained the recommended route for travellers going the breadth of Sussex, avoiding the mire of the Weald to the north.

Stone Age man left little evidence on the Downs. There are a few long barrows, their communal tombs, and some 'causewayed camps', which were probably stock enclosures. The most interesting remains are at Cissbury, where over a wide area the ground is pockmarked with the pits and small spoil heaps of a Neolithic flint-mine. This was more than mere surface-scratching. One of the shafts, when excavated in the nineteenth century, was found to be forty-two feet deep and tapped six seams of flint.

The Downs are covered with lynchets, or Field Systems as the Ordnance Survey calls them, some of which may be as much as three or four thousand years old. These banks are produced when steep slopes are ploughed. The earth tends to slip down the hill and if the same

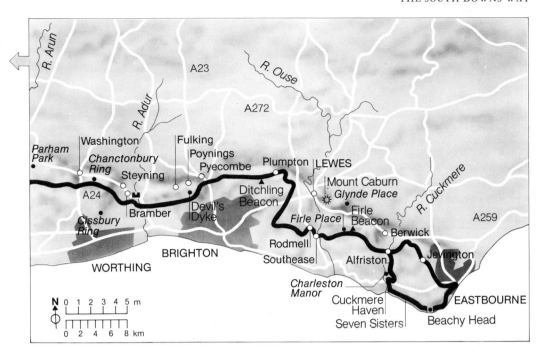

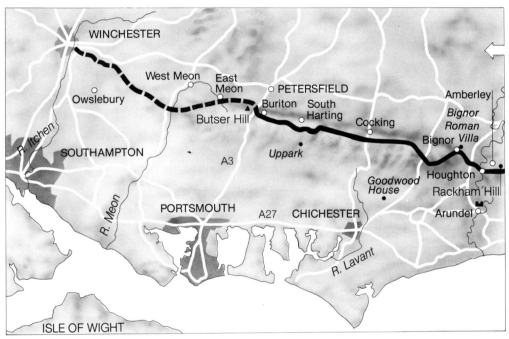

land is worked for a long time a bank builds up at the bottom of the hillside field and at the top a corresponding 'negative' bank is eroded. That there are so many on the Downs may mean that prehistoric men were hill-dwellers. It may be, however, that equivalent evidence in the richer soils below has been wiped out by later, more intensive farming there. Photographs from the air have in fact discovered ancient field-systems on the coastal plain of Sussex and in the flat river valleys which cut the Downs. The previous orthodoxy that the heavier lowland soils were too tough for prehistoric farming methods may have to be changed. The remains on the Downs may have

been produced in periods when population pressure made the cultivation of marginal lands necessary.

The Bronze Age greatly altered the look of the Downs. Between Eastbourne and Buriton the Way is lined with more than four hundred tumuli, the round barrows in which the Bronze Age people buried their dead, singly, at first in a foetal crouch with a pot beside them, containing food for the after-life; and later, after they began to cremate bodies, with the ashes actually in the pot. Their mounds now are nothing but grassy warts in the middle of fields, often with a depression in their centre, where robbers or archaeologists have dug.

131

Some of them may have been thirty foot high originally, and before the grass grew over the newly-dug chalk must have been brilliant white. They were probably the centre of a dramatic ritual of burial, in which the ditch surrounding the mound played an important part. It had a vertical inner face, and a ramp down into it from the outside. This barrier could not be crossed with ease and grace, and the body, brought down into the ditch by commoners, was probably handed up to the elect within the circle, who then laid it on a rug or a pillow of fur in a pit in the centre.

The life of the Bronze Age left other remains. These are the cross-dykes or 'covered ways' which link the heads of dry valleys. It is not known what they were for, but they may have been either estate boundaries, defence-works or, more unlikely, protected routes across open land from one valley to the next.

The Iron Age emerged from the Bronze Age, continuing its mixed farming. As before, people probably lived both in small villages and single farms. The major contribution to the landscape of the new, more violent age were the hillforts of which there are nineteen on the South Downs, most of them very small, no more than stockaded farms. The chief of them all, however, is Cissbury Ring, north of Worthing, which is a massive fortress, covering sixty acres. Most of them were probably built by mutually hostile tribes in 300 BC, but they were almost certainly strengthened in common defence against the Belgic invasions of the last century BC.

The forts share with all other habitations on the Downs the problem of water. Elaborate and innovatory seventeenth-century technology allowed Uppark to be built on top of the Downs and still have running water. Its owner Lord Tankerville displayed his wealth and ingenuity with a water garden in which fountains carelessly sprayed the precious liquid that had been brought up 350 foot from a spring a mile away, before it was rerouted through the kitchens.

A simpler alternative existed in the dew-pond, which may have been invented in the Iron Age. This, in effect, is an artificial puddle, the bottom of which is sealed with clay or concrete so that the water does not seep away. Most dewponds are probably no older than the eighteenth century, and collect their water from the rain and mists which regularly cover the Downs. Such ponds are to be found on all English chalk hills. Many of those in Sussex were made by men from the Yorkshire Wolds who in the nineteenth century were the acknowledged masters of the art. Richard Jefferies drank from them but warned that 'The water has a dead flavour; it is not stagnant in the sense of impurity, but dead, even when

quite clear. In a few moments after tasting it, the mouth dries, with a harsh unpleasant feeling, as if some impalpable dusty particles had got into the substance of the tongue. This is caused probably by suspended chalk, of which it tastes'. Most of the water that falls on the Downs sinks through the chalk to the impermeable layers below, where it forms a reservoir. This can be tapped directly by wells, such as the one at Gumber Farm on Stane Street, which is four hundred feet deep. Otherwise it emerges at the scarp-foot in the form of springs, next to which many of the villages and great houses below the Downs are built.

From the coming of the Romans until 1914 one process dominated the history of the Sussex landscape. With the increasingly efficient plough more and more of the heavier but more remunerative soils of the Weald could be cleared of their forest cover and turned over to arable. On the Downs sheep took over where men had ploughed before, reaching a peak in the eighteenth century of 400,000 ewes between Eastbourne and Hampshire. A South Down breed was developed which had short wool, but whose meat, lightly flavoured with the wild thyme it cropped, was the most delicious of all muttons.

During the Napoleonic Wars food shortages and high prices briefly made tillage of the Downs profitable, but with the fall in prices later in the century most of it returned to pasturage. In the First World War the same forces brought the land under the plough again. Improved fertilisers and higher yields meant that this time there was no reversion. Today you hardly meet a sheep on these Downs, which are covered in cornfields that can seem at times as wide as the American Prairies.

The Pier at Eastbourne, built between 1872 and 1888 to grace the 'Empress of Watering Places'.

Eastbourne to Alfriston

From Eastbourne to Alfriston there are two possible ways: either inland via Jevington or along the Seven Sisters and then up the Cuckmere valley.

---

1 **By Jevington** 8 miles

Eastbourne was the last of the big Sussex resorts to be developed and is more coherent than most. It was almost entirely owned by the Duke of Devonshire who in the ten years after 1877 created what became known as 'The Empress of Watering Places'. Eastbourne is still grand and feels like the place where Empire-rulers would water. Its hotels along the Promenade, all white and pearl grey, themselves looked dressed for the bowling green; rucksacks are greeted with frowns from old ladies.

You are soon out of this and on to a furzy down, on which it is surprisingly easy to get lost. Keep north and away from the sea. There is a golf-course here which uses Bronze Age barrows as bunkers, but after a mile this ends too, and you are on a good white chalk road heading north. Down to the right are the

Pevensey levels, a bay in Roman times which turned into a salt-marsh when the natural drift of shingle eastwards cut off the mouth. In the Middle Ages, helped by the construction of dykes, the marsh gradually dried out to become agricultural land.

But the Downs themselves fold you in. In August the entire slope of the hills is covered in ripe wheat or barley, apparently continuous to the sea. It all looks so fertile that it is surprising to find that the corn is often only eighteen inches or a foot high. To produce even this much the soil has to be heavily limed. On the crest line which the Way follows, crops are not now grown because the exposure to sea winds here is more than in the combes and deans, the downland words for valleys. Nor is it the famous downland turf, but thin spiky grass, called 'gratton grass', to which downland reverts if it is returned to fallow after being cultivated. Here it is the legacy of the brief cultivation during the Napoleonic wars.

On Willingdon Hill you come to a crossing of greenways marked by stones which look as though they come from Baghdad or Istanbul. They are in fact the remains of Barclays Bank

The Long Man at Wilmington, decently emasculated.

in Eastbourne. Over this crossroads the Way goes down into a small dry valley in which, among trees, is the flint and brick village of Jevington. Just north-east of it on Combe Hill is a Neolithic causewayed camp, made in about 3000 BC. Bronze Age barrows are everywhere, while just east of the village is a pattern of lynchets which are possibly the result of Iron Age farming. In the Saxon church tower are some Roman bricks. With all this Jevington is no museum and no showplace, but a typical village equals of which are found the length of the Downs.

It is four miles from Jevington to Alfriston, above which, on Windover Hill, you get the first view to the north over to the Weald. Beneath you, but invisible from the path, is the Long Man of Wilmington, also known as the Lone Man or the Lanky Man, a figure 231 feet long once cut in the turf, but now marked out in white bricks. His hands are outstretched and in each of them he holds a long stave. He has been identified as Baldur the Beautiful, Beowulf, Woden, Thor, Varuna, Boötes, Apollo, Mercury, Mohammed and St Paul, but no one really knows. He may have once looked more like the Cerne Abbas giant, and been decently emasculated in the nineteenth century.

Beside the spire of Wilmington church below can be seen the roof of the vast medieval barn belonging to Wilmington Priory. Its size shows how productive this country must have been in the Middle Ages, and it is known that the Battle Abbey estates at Alciston, just below the Downs a mile and a half away, yielded at least sixteen bushels of wheat an acre, which was twice the medieval average.

From above the Long Man's head the Way goes down a white chalk road edged with ragwort and scabious around the sharp valley of Ewe Dean to Alfriston on the banks of the Cuckmere. Just to the south is the thirteenth-century Lullington church, the smallest in the country, capable of holding a congregation of twenty. It was not built this small, but is part of the chancel of a once larger church which fell victim to the stagnation and economic retreat of the later Middle Ages.

2 By the Seven Sisters 11 miles

At Beachy Head the sea has cut the South Downs clean open, interrupting the hills in mid-course. Before the English Channel broke through the chalk ridge, it continued as far as Boulogne where its eastern end can still be found. The subtle moulding of the contours along the Seven Sisters continues without hesitation to the cliff edge, where it drops – at Beachy Head – 532 feet. These cliffs are clean because they are moving steadily inland. The sea eats away at the bottom, taking away the support from the cliff higher up, which then falls off, leaving a vertical face. The Iron Age earthwork at Belle Tout, just beyond the old lighthouse, was originally a mile or two inland on a hilltop. The National Trust, which owns the whole area, are looking after what is basically a vast self-destruction machine.

Richard Jefferies loved the breeze on Beachy Head. 'The glory of these glorious Downs is the breeze,' he wrote. 'It is the air without admixture. If it comes from the south, the waves refine it; if inland the wheat and flowers and grass distil it. The great headland and the whole rib of the promontory is windswept and washed with air; the billows of the atmosphere roll over it.'

As you slide along from one Sister to the next – there are in fact eight – you will see lines of flint at regular intervals in the cliffs. They were not laid down like this, but are the result of a natural sifting by which the silica comes to settle in the narrowest of pin-stripes along slightly harder beds in the chalk. Prehistoric man may have got the idea of mining for flints from the sight of these seams well below the surface.

At the end of the Sisters you come to Cuckmere Haven, the only river mouth in Sussex on which no port has been built. The Cuckmere valley as it nears the sea is as soggy and as lined by drainage channels as those of the other Sussex rivers, but above the flood-line is the anomaly, on these almost entirely bare eastern downs, of a large wood, called Friston Forest. You push into it and find hidden inside Westdean village, and, just on its northern edge, Charleston Manor, which has a double tithe barn whose wavy field of a roof was made to protect the produce of thousands of acres. Roofs in Sussex, although rarely the stupendous size of Charleston's barn, often undulate like this, particularly in the river valleys, where transport was easy, and a heavy, beautiful, yellow stone called Horsham slab could be brought from the Weald for the roofs. It was cut as thick as bread at the eaves, with the slices thinning to the ridge. The weight of the roof was often too much for the framework beneath, and although many houses once covered in this lovely stuff have since been thatched or tiled, the sags of the roofs remain. From Charleston it is two miles along the embanked meandering Cuckmere as far as

Plonk Barn, where you join the other path from Eastbourne and cross the river into Alfriston.

The Cuckmere to the Ouse 7 miles

Alfriston is a pretty place with a wide green between the river and its main street. Next to the green stands the Saxon church, faced with flint which has been 'knapped'. This was a technique which was developed in the Middle Ages both in Sussex and in the chalklands of Norfolk. Each nodule of flint is precisely chipped so that when set in a wall it presents as neat a face as a brick. But it looks better than brick, because it is so shiny, so obviously hard and, Hilaire Belloc thought, because it is so obviously an expensive process. Compared with this painstaking precision most flint walls look like nothing more than banks of rotten teeth.

Next to the church is the Clergy House, the first building to be owned by the National Trust, bought for £10 in 1896 when under threat of demolition. It was built in the middle of the fourteenth century and is a nearly typical 'Wealden' house, with a central hall rising to the roof, and a section on either side of two storeys, of which the upper projects slightly. In two ways, though, Alfriston Clergy House is different. As it was made to house priests – who were theoretically celibate before the Reformation – it does not have the usual inner door between the Hall, where the priests lived, and the housekeeper's quarters at the north end. The house also has an extraordinary floor. It is made of rammed chalk, bound and sealed with sour milk. From its appearance this bizarre process is not evident. It is as though the turf has simply been scraped away and the house laid directly on the chalk of which the Downs are made.

From Alfriston the South Downs Way climbs straight up a white track between, in August, giant swiss rolls of straw, the product of a baling process well suited to the enormous fields. Instead of this track, it is worth going along the lane and field-path to Berwick, whose church can be seen in the trees a mile and a half to the north. You pass the brick-and-flint New Barn of which the tiled roofs come down on one side to chest-level in extensions called catwalks. This early nineteenth-century barn was built to house both the crops from the new tillage on the Downs and the ox-teams which worked it, which in turn provided manure close to the place where it was most needed. Behind the barn and contemporary with it are the remains of chalk pits quarried to provide tons of lime for the acidic downland soil.

The interior of Berwick church is covered in murals done mainly by Duncan Grant and Vanessa Bell during the Second World War. Although they were both atheist to the bone, this did not stop Bishop Bell of Chichester from commissioning them, nor the artists accepting the idea with alacrity. Years of wrangling with conservative parishioners delayed the work, but once it was finished Sir Charles Reilly, the instigator of the project, wrote to the Bishop: 'I have seen it. I have been to Berwick. I went yesterday with Duncan Grant. It's wonderful. It's like stepping out of a foggy England into Italy. I felt such a happy heavenly feeling as I sat there.' On every panel, behind the bright biblical scene in the foreground, the artists have included the darker green shapes of the Downs.

Cuckmere meanders.

The Berwick murals were painted on canvases which were then attached to the walls of the church. The painting itself was done in a barn at Duncan Grant's home, another Charleston, three miles to the north-west under the Downs. It was the centre of what became known as Bloomsbury-by-the-Sea, when several members of the Bloomsbury group, among them Virginia and Leonard Woolf and Maynard Keynes, bought houses in this part of Sussex, all just below the Downs, to enjoy, as Quentin Bell has described it, 'the aesthetic comfort of Sussex gardens full of flowers in which plaster-casts from the antique slowly disintegrated from year to year; high studios that were also living rooms in which were painted decorations of a kind that would now be considered dreadfully fussy and old-fashioned; rooms made for ease rather than show, on the walls of which hung the spoils of more adventurous years.' The site of this lotus-eating lies below you as you walk from Berwick to the Ouse. Here too are the first of the great houses and parks that fringe the Downs on their northern side. Firle Place is right under the main edge, while Glynde Place is a mile to the north under Mount Caburn, an island of down, on top of which is a small Iron Age camp, probably a single enclosed farm. The parks conceal the change from bare hill to wooded and watered plain with plantations of sycamore and beech.

Firle Place has, since the fifteenth century, been the home of the Gage family, most of whom have been politicians or soldiers, but of which one member permanently benefited humanity by developing a particularly delicious green plum, which ever since has been known as the greengage.

The edge of the Downs moves into combes and out again in round noses. You pass two dewponds and the wide valley of the Ouse, criss-crossed by drainage channels, comes into sight, with Lewes – squeezed between the cheeks of the hills – at one end, and Newhaven's derricks at the other. The Ouse is an ugly river, embanked with concrete slabs on which it leaves muck at low tide. Against the piers of the bridge by which our path crosses it the body of Virginia Woolf was washed up in 1941 after she had thrown herself into the river about a mile upstream.

Rivers usually contain the oldest elements known in English place-names. Strangely, of the five rivers that cross the South Downs – the Cuckmere, the Ouse, the Adur, the Arun and the Lavant – only the last has a Celtic word embedded in it. The others are all as recent as the sixteenth or seventeenth century. The name 'Ouse' may simply have been applied to the river which flowed by Lewes.

From the Ouse to the Adur 22 miles

Over the river the path comes to Southease, which must rival a hamlet in Kent called Smugley for the most comfortable place-name in England. The church and few houses round a small green are very quiet, but it was once a much busier place. Norman Southease was a major centre of the herring fishery, paying the appalling rent of 38,500 herrings to the Lord of Lewes, compared, for instance, to the 4,000 due from the fishermen of Bristelmestune, the village which was to become Brighton.

Half a mile along a busy road brings you to Rodmell. At the bottom of the village, next to the church, is the low-browed weather-boarded cottage called Monks House (NT) in which Leonard and Virginia Woolf lived. The novelist's ashes are buried in the garden. From Rodmell the path turns up Mill Lane and climbs to the height of the Downs. The small

fort on the Caburn can be seen contouring its hill on the other side of the valley and above Lewes pokes the grey Norman castle from which William de Warren, a son-in-law of William the Conqueror, administered the Rape of Lewes, one of the six areas into which the Normans divided the county, four of which were in the hands of members of the Conqueror's immediate family. The Normans were particularly aware of the need for keeping Sussex secure, since they themselves had landed at Pevensey and conquered the whole country from there. The river valleys were the points of weakness, and castles were built to control each of the river gaps through the Downs.

In 1822 William Cobbett came to Lewes, where he found 'the girls remarkably pretty, with round faces, features small, little hands and wrists, plump arms and bright eyes. The Sussex men, too, are remarkable for their good looks'. All this was in contrast to the lascivious decadence of the fashionable crowd at Brighton, where Cobbett felt so uncomfor-

Southease Church: one of only two round towers in Sussex.

table and out of place that he left after a single night.

Lewes stays in view as the path makes its way north-west above the small goat-ridden village of Iford until it reaches a lovely horseshoe bottom called Cold Coombes, on whose western edge is a small sycamore and beech wood shaped by the prevailing westerlies. From the side it looks like an aeroplane's wing in section. Hilaire Belloc loved the Downs because the same wind that shapes these woods seems to have shaped the hills too, so that 'The roll of the Downs stands like a monstrous green wave, blown forward before the south-west wind.' The sight of Cold Coombes, with this dark wood on its edge, just as the barley is being cut, is one of the loveliest on the Downs.

The Way crosses the Lewes–Brighton road by a pub and climbs for a mile and a half back from the edge, up Balmer Down, to meet the scarp again on Plumpton Plain. This is the official route, since the corner it cuts off is infringed by Lewes, but by going this way it misses out the only place where the Downs and national history have ever met. A mile to the east of the path is the site of the battle in 1264

when Simon de Montfort, his son Henry and the Earl of Gloucester met the forces of Henry III coming up from Lewes to meet them. The rebels won, capturing the King and his brother. The royal forces were driven in total confusion across the Ouse, and several knights were drowned. The victory made de Montfort virtual dictator of England, but it was a tyranny with an eye to democracy, and famously the parliament of the following year included for the first time, in addition to the prelates and barons, representatives from the boroughs and shires.

It is two miles from Plumpton Plain to Ditchling Beacon. The distant view is of the apparently solid wood of the Weald rising behind the more open country of the Vale of Sussex between. The fields immediately below form a regular rectangular grid, laid in the sixteenth and seventeenth centuries on what had previously been common land. A lane runs down the hill to Plumpton, overhung with trees and from centuries of use sunk below the level of the surrounding land. There is a pub and shop in the tiny village at the bottom, and it is good to follow the lane down, since to keep only to the crest of the Downs is to miss

their character – or an important part of it – which is their connection with the villages below. To go down to the spring-line and climb back up again has been the usual movement of men in Sussex since the Stone Age.

At Ditchling Beacon the Downs only arch their neck, rising slightly to 813 feet, the third highest point of the hills and the highest on the South Downs Way. From here you sink gradually in two miles to Pyecombe, crossing into West Sussex and passing two windmills, known as Jack and Jill, which are almost the only survivals of the hundreds that spattered the Downs in the nineteenth century. Pyecombe, which means 'the valley infested by gnats', was where the crooks were made with which shepherds from all over the Downs controlled their flocks; the gate into the churchyard has a crook for its latch. The London–Brighton road crosses the Downs here, not, as might have been expected, through one of the river valleys, because they were always too wet.

You climb West Hill, only to come down

Brick barns at Plumpton below the Downs.

again to another slight hollow called Saddles-
combe, occupied by a collection of buildings
half way between an overgrown farm and a
small hamlet. There is a pond and beside the
road a big ash tree.

The landscape becomes more dramatic. For
the first time you see, nine miles away, the
distinctive raised nipple of Chanctonbury
Ring, which is almost exactly the central point
in the Downs between their leaving the sea
and their disappearance at Butser Hill in
Hampshire. In the foreground is the Devil's
Dyke, a great trench cut into the hill from the
north, half a mile long and three hundred foot
deep, turning a right angle half-way through
its course and so almost isolating a block of
downland, which men in the Iron Age
reinforced into a substantial fort. The Devil
intended to cut right through the Downs in
one night to let the sea flood into the Weald
and drown the churches there. He was
disturbed by an old woman holding a candle,
which he mistook for the dawn, and so left his
work unfinished.

But all this is not what holds your eye. For
almost every day in summer above the Devil's
Dyke float two or three hang-gliders. On the
ground these machines are as ungainly as
geese, but when in the air they glide in and out
of each other's paths in impossibly slow turns
that mesmerise the crowds sitting on the
hillside here.

From the Devil's Dyke to the Adur is five
miles, almost all along white chalk tracks and
between cornfields. You cross a series of old
roads coming up from the villages to the north
and passing down the dip-slope to the sea. The
long accumulation of building on the seaside is
mostly invisible from the South Downs Way.
On this stretch more than any other it is
possible to feel the famous isolation of the
Downs. You may hate it, like Dr Johnson,
who thought it was enough to make a man
want to hang himself, if only he could find a
tree. The Weald as always is with you on the
right, but to the left there is nothing but the
strangely grey cornfields and beyond them an
equally grey sea. It is a very hard landscape.
The chimneys of the power-station at
Portslade-by-Sea and the pylons carrying the
high-voltage lines from it are the only verticals
in a landscape of horizontal austerity. Above
Fulking the way passes beneath two of these
lines. They fit this scene and contribute to it.
The Downs are large enough to take them and
they are no defacement; the wires as they sag
between the pylons mirror the shapes of the
land itself.

*One of the windmills above Clayton, with Wolstonbury
Hill beyond it.*

At Truleigh the Way reaches a slight summit and the two miles from here to the Adur are downhill all the way. The view opens out, with the wide spread of Steyning on the river's far bank, and three miles to the south the almost square profile on the skyline of Lancing College Chapel, which is 190 foot long and 150 foot high. Although this neo-perpendicular building was begun in 1854, work is still being done on the west front.

As you coast down the hill to the river, you pass on the right a wide staircase of cultivation terraces going down the hill, which may have been cut in the Iron Age. These are above the village of Upper Beeding, which as Belloc pointed out 'lies in a hollow, damp all the year round', while Lower Beeding is miles away and higher up. The names probably mean that Lower is a daughter village of Upper. The path crosses the Shoreham road and comes to the Adur, a typically muddy Sussex river, to which the Downs have given way with grace. A new footbridge takes the path across.

From the Adur to the Arun 13 miles

North of the path as it crosses the Adur is the extraordinary ruin of Bramber Castle, built in the eleventh century to guard the Adur gap by William de Braose, who also held the key frontier castles of Skenfrith, Grosmont and

The Devil's Dyke, and the little hamlet of Saddlecombe beyond it: the Knights Templar ran a hostelry here until the fourteenth century, when they were suppressed for disgusting practices.

Monmouth in the Welsh Marches. One wall of the keep, seventy foot high, not very thick and fifteen foot long is all that remains of Bramber. It sticks into the air like an only tooth and is owned by the National Trust.

Steyning (pronounced Stenning) is half a mile away, and is worth the detour for the pretty curve of its main street and its amazing Norman church. The economic decline of the late Middle Ages affected Sussex badly and little church-building was done after the middle of the fourteenth century. Earlier work, obliterated in many other parts of the country, was in this way preserved here. So the nave of Steyning church, built in about 1150, remains in its original Norman state. It is in Caen stone, which takes fine detail better than anything Sussex can produce, was familiar to the Norman monks, and was probably cheaper than an equivalent English stone because sea-transport was easier than bringing heavy stone-laden wagons along the appalling twelfth-century English roads. The whole building, in both style and material, is a package imported from Europe, and it has a panache that shows it. Four round arches make arcades on either side of the nave which ends in a single chancel arch forty-foot high. All are supported by clean round columns with cushion capitals, each slightly different in its decoration. The whole is grand without being stolid, the result of a strict control of mass.

Both Bramber and Steyning are north of the Way, which from the river goes through Botolphs, a once thriving village which shrank in the fifteenth century to the church and four houses. From here to the Arun is the best part of the South Downs. The Way follows as always the northern edge, but the hills now begin to grow in width to the south, and as they are covered in footpaths it is worth wandering to the south of the designated route. Only then will you get the impression of the Downs themselves driving a broad way westwards through Sussex.

Annington Hill and then Steyning Round Hill on to which the Way climbs are empty except for two barns, but just to the south on Park Brow large lynchets mark the site of a settlement which seems to have been continuously inhabited and farmed from the Late Bronze Age until Roman times. This uninterrupted use of the same land over as much as fifteen centuries means that prehistoric farmers must have evolved some kind of land regeneration, either by crop rotation or by marling.

It is a mile from the lynchets over empty down – marked as 'No Man's Land' on the map – to Cissbury Ring, the largest man-made structure in Sussex. This vast earthwork was built in about 250 BC and its dimensions are staggering: the fort is two thousand six hundred feet long and one thousand three hundred feet wide, enclosing about sixty acres. Sixty thousand tons of chalk were quarried and piled to make the rampart, which was revetted on the outside to present a vertical wooden wall to the attackers. Eight to twelve thousand logs, each fifteen foot long, would have been needed. It takes twenty-five minutes to walk Cissbury's complete circuit, during which you will come across, in the south-west corner, the remains of the famous flint-mine which may have been worked as early as 3390 BC. The whole area is owned by the National Trust.

From Cissbury Ring, which may have been the centre of an Iron Age kingdom bounded by the Adur and the Arun, a track leads northwards over the Middle Brow directly to what was once a much smaller dependent fort, but is now the centre of the Downs and their

The singular remain of Bramber Castle, an only tooth in the Adur Valley.

most famous landmark. This is Chanctonbury Ring. Half-way along a walk is always a good point, but to have it so clearly and beautifully marked makes it better. Besides, the Ring is a magical place. From a distance the clump is like a solid, thick-trunked mushroom, and until you are quite close it appears impenetrable. Then, in a moment, it opens and the two-hundred-year-old trees separate from each other to allow you entrance. The ring was planted in 1760 by a Charles Goring, who lived at Wiston House just below. The sycamores and beeches grew well from the beginning, except in the centre. In 1908 the foundations of a third- and fourth-century Roman temple were discovered to be the cause of the ground's infertility. The resulting space in the middle of the Ring is still there and on a bright day has the luminous air of a temple.

Just west of the Ring is a dewpond, recently rebuilt by the Society of Sussex Downsmen, and containing the most wholesome looking water of any on the Downs. The route then descends between scruffs of ragwort to cross the London–Worthing road. It is better to take the official detour which bends two-thirds of a mile northwards to cross the road by a footbridge on the edge of Washington village. Just by the bridge is the church which contains a beautiful little seventeenth-century alabaster memorial to John Byne, his wife and their entire progeny. The Latin inscription says 'suscepit ex ea quinque filios filiasque duas', meaning literally 'he took out from under her five sons

Chanctonbury Ring, the centre of the Downs: an eighteenth-century plantation on the site of an Iron Age fort and a Roman temple.

and two daughters'. All nine of them kneel in the panel above, each in a cartwheel of a ruff.

You climb back on to the Downs, where the Way passes through a small wood, one of the first signs of the blanket woodland which covers the hills at their western end. The previously constant expanse of the view over to the High Weald, which for miles and days you have taken for granted, becomes intermittent as the trees begin to close in on the path. At the same time the familiar view begins to change as the high ground made by the band of the hard Lower Greensand peaks in the wooded Blackdown (918 feet) invading the Low Weald from the west.

Most of the way stays free of wood, however, until the far side of the Arun. From above Washington to Amberley in the Arun valley is about six miles of clear, straight, often grassy down, which you can breeze along without effort in a couple of hours. On Sullington Hill is the only building, a Dutch barn, the inside of which is covered with fascinating graffiti describing people's various experiences there.

You pass on the nose of this hill a strange arrangement of dykes for which no one has yet accounted; certainly the solution of 'ranch boundaries' cannot fit, while there could be no possible defensive use for ditches arranged in a T set askew on the hill. It may be a combination of two schemes, possibly of different dates.

Neither these problems, nor the fact that a famous area of Celtic fields on Chantry Hill is invisible under sprouts, will bother you much. The South Downs take you along with a wonderful rhythmic momentum, as their northern edge blows in and out of combes, flirting with the plain. To the north the red brick-clays of the Weald are exposed in a pit near Storrington, while southwards you see the sea and the eastern end of the Isle of Wight.

On Rackham Hill you must stop your rapid progress west and sit down. Below you is Parham House, looking tiny in its park full of powder-puff trees. Parham is a typical product of the boom in country house building that followed the transference of wealth to the gentry after the Dissolution of the Monasteries. Because of its nearness to Westminster, the source of court patronage, Sussex is particularly rich in these houses. Parham was built in 1577 by a parvenu London merchant on land previously owned by Westminster Abbey. The park was made at the same time and was very little altered in the eighteenth

The Byne memorial in Washington Church.

Glass, lead, freestone and unknapped flint in Washington Church.

century, so that it looks untidier and less of a perfected landscape than most.

From above Parham two miles downhill bring you to the Arun, the last of the rivers that cut the Downs. Arundel Castle, four miles away to the south, looks like a castle should, in silhouette on a woody bluff above the meandering river. The path is between wire fences which catch loose straws as they are blown across the hill. Very soon this turns the path into a long yellow straw mattress which crunches under your feet. Do not follow the official path straight to the Arun bridge at Houghton, but turn down instead to Amberley, a thatched Sussex village, whose inhabitants and houses both look retired, with a castle at the river end built by the Bishops of Chichester and now full of fuchsias and white roses. Officially, it is only open a day or two a year.

From the Arun to Butser Hill
21 miles

The clays overlying the chalk west of the Arun mean that thick woods cover much of the Downs. From Houghton village you soon climb into this woodland and within three miles arrive above Bignor, where a collection of thatched buildings house the remains of a

Earth works on Sullington Hill.

sumptuous Roman villa. From calculations based on the size of the farm buildings found here it is estimated that Bignor was the centre of a 2,000-acre estate, whose main product may have been the wool for which Britain was famous throughout the Empire. (There was a state weaving mill at Winchester.) The mosaics at Bignor are amazing, and their state of preservation so immaculate that it almost puts Cissbury Ring in the shade. Some of the mosaics have an astonishing immediacy. The figure of Winter, in particular – all that is left of a pavement showing the four seasons – has an air of absolute desolation. Those in other rooms are gayer. A bright Ganymede covered the floor of the dining-room where, as the guide book says, 'people reclined on the couches flinging their jests across the room between mouthfuls of food'.

Bignor villa lay just to the west of Stane Street, the Roman road which in three perfectly straight alignments covered the fifty-six miles between Chichester and London Bridge, crossing in the process two ranges of chalk hills and the almost impenetrable forest of the Weald. The South Downs Way crosses Stane Street at a heathy place, called Gumber

Corner, now owned by the National Trust. For Hilaire Belloc this place was the centre of the world. It was the inspiration of one of his most famous poems:

Lift up your hearts in Gumber, laugh the Weald
And you my mother the valley of Arun sing.
Here am I homeward from my wandering,
Here am I homeward and my heart is healed.

If you have time on your hands – you only need a day spare – walk down the Roman road to Chichester or to Goodwood from here; both are about eight miles away.

The scarp of the Downs turns north at Gumber, only resuming its westward course in two miles at Barlavington. The South Downs Way cuts this corner, joining the scarp again at Woolavington Down. It is just over four miles from here to Cocking, for almost every yard of which the path is tightly shut in by trees. The ground is slithery mud for most of the year. The trees are not old beeches, but scrubby cobs and hazels. You need to be in the right mood to think of these woods as Belloc's 'strongholds of silence and desertion ... exhibiting the once unconquerable nature of the country'. Beside the path the bushes are covered in the wild clematis-like flower called traveller's joy that turns in late summer into the hairy mass of old man's beard. Nearer the ground grows the purple nettle-leaved bellflower, darker than its relation the harebell which is everywhere on the open down. You will find here too the prettiest flower of chalkland, the scabious, whose slightly purple heads have in them the pallor of chalk. This beautiful plant has such a horrible name because it was, apparently, 'long thought efficacious in scaly eruptions'.

In this wood you are walking along the northern edge of Charlton Forest, which was the area covered in the seventeenth century by the most famous foxhunt in England, the Charlton Hunt. The Duke of Monmouth thought the chase such fun here that he intended when he became king to hold his court at Charlton.

You pass Tegleaze Farm, totally isolated in the wood, and three miles later emerge on to the open top of Manorfarm Down, where Sussex is again as open as a map below you. The Way descends over a mile beside a large chalk pit to the A286 near Cocking. The ten miles from here to the end of the path at Buriton are on a narrow strip of open down between woods on either side. At Monkton House, three miles from Cocking, you turn south into the wood, past a line of Bronze Age round barrows, known as the Devil's Jumps, to come out again by Buriton Farm, which is as cut off as Tegleaze. These solitary farms have long been a feature of the landscape of the Downs, the legacy either of medieval depopulation or the earlier unsociability of the original settlers.

A mile from Buriton Farm you curl round an Iron Age fort on Beacon Hill and then cross over Harting Down to come, by a small wooded lane, to where the South Downs Way should end. This is Uppark, the seventeenth-century red-brick house that sits on the Downs as though it has grown out of them, as their natural culmination. Alone of all the great houses associated with the Downs Uppark is up on them. Its position is dependent on the hydraulic technology invented in the middle of the seventeenth century. This is Uppark's artificial lifeline, but you would not guess that it needed it. Strangely there is no awkwardness between the red brick, Dutch shape and classical vocabulary of the house and the rolling green of the down which comes without interruption or decoration right up to the south front. Uppark fits its place not by being rustic or provincial, but by its clean confidence and clarity.

The most exciting moments of Uppark's history were during the time of Sir Harry Fetherstonhaugh who inherited the house in 1774 when he was just twenty. He was vastly rich and out for a good time, which he found in the fast set that gathered round the Prince of Wales. In 1780 Emma Hart, a 'showgirl' in the Temple of Aesculapius, a nightclub in London, and of a transfixing beauty, was brought to live at Uppark. There she danced on the dining-room table to a mesmerised circle of England's most fashionable men, one of whom, Sir William Hamilton, was later to marry her, only to lose her to Nelson. Sir Harry's entertaining continued unchecked and Uppark became 'the Rendezvous of all that is gay and fashionable in the country. The Duc de Chartres, the Duke of Queensbury, Lord Grosvenor, etc...' as the *Craftsmen* reported in 1785. All this came to a sudden end in 1810 when Sir Harry quarrelled with the Prince Regent and may have lost heavily at gambling. This was not the end of it all, however. In 1825, when over seventy, Sir Harry suddenly married his head dairy-maid, whom he had seen at work in the little dairy just west of the house. He lived another twenty-one years with her and died in 1846 at the age of ninety-two. His widow and her sister stayed on, the one dying in 1874 and the other, always dressed in black velvet because she thought that it suited the house, living until 1895. During this time H. G. Wells lived downstairs as a boy – his mother was housekeeper there.

From Uppark to Buriton the Way is on a track enclosed between hedges, crossing the

Uppark, the only great house on top of the Downs. The Duke of Wellington refused to live here because his horses would have been ruined by always having to climb up and down hill.

county boundary into Hampshire, where the style of fingerposts changes, but apart from that all is the same as before. Finally the path drops down the steep scarp, covered in a hanging beechwood, to the village pond at Buriton and the end of the South Downs Way. Edward Gibbon lived in this village in his youth. It is a pleasant place, but you may feel it is too insignificant an ending to a long walk. If you have one day left, go on to Winchester. There are no Countryside Commission acorns or arrows, but you can thread your own way by public footpaths across the Hampshire chalk to the Itchen. On Butser Hill, just west of Buriton, the long chalk finger of the South Downs is absorbed into the undifferentiated mass of the Hampshire chalkland. At once you lose the impression of being on top of the hills; in Hampshire you walk in amongst them. If this is a loss, Hampshire's rivers put those in Sussex to shame. While the Cuckmere, Ouse, Adur and Arun were all slow and brown, the Meon and the Itchen are heavy, dark chalk streams full of trout and green weed. (It may be significant that the rivers of Sussex have names invented only four or five hundred years ago while 'Itchen' and 'Meon' are words from the language spoken in Britain before the arrival of the Romans.)

It is 23 miles from Buriton to Twyford Down, the last hill above Winchester. From it you drop to the banks of the Itchen, and on a series of thin islands, between the playing fields of Winchester College, you can make your way beneath willow trees to the middle of the city. This is a proper end to a walk.

MAPS: OS 1:50,000 Numbers 185, 197, 198, 199

GUIDE:
Sean Jennett, *South Downs Way*, HMSO 1977

BACKGROUND:
Quentin Bell, *Bloomsbury*, Weidenfeld and Nicolson 1968
Hilaire Belloc, *The County of Sussex*, Cassell 1936
Hilaire Belloc, *Sonnets and Verse*, 1954
Peter Brandon, *The Sussex Landscape*, Hodder and Stoughton 1974
David Harrison, *Along the South Downs*, Cassell 1958

INFORMATION:
The Society of Sussex Downsmen,
93 Church Road,
Hove, Sussex BN3 2BA

The Cotswold Way

Bath to Chipping Campden 95 miles

Like most of the hills in southern England, the Cotswolds are lopsided, with a steep sharp face on one side, and a long steady descent on the other. The Cotswold Way goes along the steep western edge, and as a result hardly sees typical Cotswold country at all, which is all on the dip-slope of the hills. That long Cotswold backside was the landscape that Sydney Smith in the early nineteenth century found 'one of the most unfortunate, desolate countries under heaven, divided by stone walls and abandoned to the screaming kites and larcenous crows: after travelling really twenty and to appearance ninety miles over this region of stone and sorrow, life begins to be a burden and you wish to perish. At the very moment when you are taking this melancholy view of human affairs, and hating the postilion and blaming the horses, there bursts upon your view, with all its towers, forests and streams, the deep and shaded Vale of Severn'.

On the Cotswold Way Smith's Badlands to the east are not visible and the soothing Vale of Berkeley (with its extension northwards, the Vale of Gloucester and Evesham) is the steady accompaniment to the five or six days it takes to go from Bath to Chipping Campden. The edge itself is not usually as sharp a division as where Smith reached it at Birdlip, but is cut back by small streams into warm, woody valleys, which have sometimes left isolated fragments of hill standing out in the plain.

This fretted edge, incredibly, is slowly on the move. It is perfectly conceivable that the sea should be eating into the Pembrokeshire Coast or Beachy Head, which look so frail and friable, but it is almost impossible to imagine that the elements here in Gloucestershire are gradually pushing back the Cotswold escarpment. It looks so buffered by trees and grass and settlement and seems too rounded to be under attack. But the facts are undeniable. Four miles south of Bristol is Dundry Hill, six miles from the present position of the edge. Dundry is a bit of Cotswold that has been left behind, capped by a beautiful kind of Cotswold limestone, which was quarried to build St Mary Redcliffe in Bristol. The Severn plain has several such outliers – like Bredon Hill near Evesham – all of which show that the Cotswolds once covered the entire area the plain now occupies.

Near Chipping Campden.

The process is this: the Cotswold stone is only a top layer resting on several thicknesses of the softer Lias clays, which are relatively easily removed by weather and streams. Erosion undermines a section of the cap which, unsupported, breaks off. Over millions of years the edge slowly recedes. The attack is led by the streams, which, falling fast down the scarp slope, cut their valleys back into it. But who would have thought that the little stream in Ozleworth Bottom or in Tyley Bottom, just next door, would have been so knife-edged?

Cotswold Stone

Cotswold Stone is firmly lodged in our imaginations; as J. B. Priestley identified, it makes walls 'faintly warm and luminous, as if they knew the trick of keeping the lost sunlight of centuries glimmering about them'. This is what is special about Cotswold Stone: the combination of a material and the history of the place where it is found. Geologically, Cotswold Stone is indistinguishable from the band of limestone of which it forms a part, stretching in a narrow S-bend from Lyme Bay in Dorset through Gloucestershire, Northamptonshire and Lincolnshire to finish up in a clot on the North Yorkshire Moors. They were all laid down about 160 million years ago, as the floor of a shallow sea.

Even within the Cotswolds, where the limestone reaches its greatest width, there are several kinds of stone. At the bottom end of the scale is the ragstone, which contains hundreds of fossil shells, and can usually be broken in the hand. It is only good for field walls and the roughest of buildings. Next come the freestones, whose grain is much finer; they can be cut into smooth ashlar blocks, or sculpted into finials and other decorations when new from the quarry, but they then develop a hard protective crust. The best quarries for freestones are some way down the dip-slope, where the finest kind of limestone, called the Great Oolite, outcrops. A few quarries (there are no longer any working in the Cotswolds) produced stone which could be split into roofing 'slates'. They were left out in a frost, when the moisture in the stones turned to ice, expanded and split the blocks along their cleavage lines.

The colour of the stone gradually darkens as you go north. Painswick is nearly white, Stanway and the villages round it are an almost bright yellow, while much of Chipping Campden is brown. The variation is due to a rust-coloured substance in the rock called limonite.

It is a marvellous chance that this same material should have as many different grades. Field walls, barns, cottages and manor-houses can declare themselves for what they are, using

The Cotswold Way approaches Stanley Mill near Stroud, built in the early nineteenth century when the Cotswold cloth industry was at its height, but now, like most of the others, defunct.

the appropriate material. The result is an automatic visual unity, but one with a progression in it, from rag to ashlar.

Wool

The Cotswolds have their fair share of Iron Age camps, and far more than their fair share of Neolithic long barrows, but the prehistoric past does not thrust itself on you here as it does on the Ridgeway, for example. The shadows of Neolithic men were inescapable there, but on the Cotswolds it is the woolmen's ghosts that rise in every village and town to meet you. You hardly see a sheep now, but in William Camden's day at the end of the sixteenth century, the Cotswolds and sheep were inseparable: 'Cotswould takes its name', he wrote, 'from the hills and sheep-cotes (for mountains and hills the Englishmen in old times termed Woulds). Upon these hills are fed large flocks of sheep, with the whitest wool, having long necks and square bodies ...'. The wool of these strange animals, with that from Shropshire and Hereford, was thought the best in England, and English wool incontestably the best in Europe. In the early Middle Ages the finest Flemish and Italian cloths were exclusively made from it. Only the white and curly merino wool from Spain could hope to challenge the English product, which nevertheless held its position by being softer and by felting more easily. Medieval England was a wool state: in 1421, when the export of raw wool was already falling off, it still provided seventy-five per cent of all customs dues. A century before, a poet from Artois had spoken of 'carrying wool to England' as we would say coals to Newcastle now.

One up from the sheep on the commercial ladder which rose from these unenclosed,

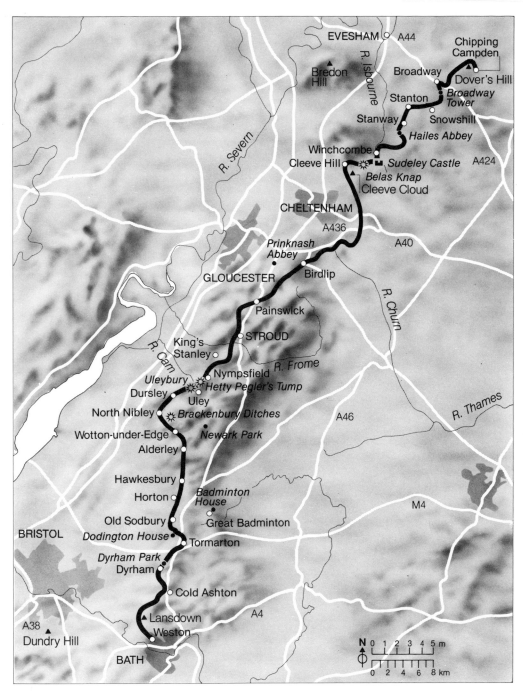

unwalled hillsides to the cloth factories of
Flanders and North Italy was the shepherd. A
thirteenth-century book on estate management advises flock-owners to employ 'discreet
shepherds, watchful and kindly, so that the
sheep be not tormented by their wrath, but
crop their pasture in peace and joyfulness, for it
is a token of the shepherd's kindness if the
sheep be not scattered abroad, but browse
around him in company. Let him provide
himself with a good barkable dog and lie
nightly with his sheep'.

At this level nothing can have changed from
the twelfth century to the seventeenth. Above
it, though, all was change and harsh com-

petition. The wool trade in the Middle Ages
has been described by Eileen Power as 'a
pocket of capitalism in a pre-capitalist world',
and many of the wool-tycoons were Cotswold
men. For these *grands bourgeois* the boom period
was in the thirteenth and early fourteenth
centuries, when free trade, low taxation and a
voracious foreign market – whose representatives came here to buy – made whole-
sale contracts of raw wool a goldmine. The
whole clip would be sold *en bloc* to foreign
buyers in 346 lb sacks. In 1310, 35,500 of these
sacks were exported. By the early fifteenth
century the recession had arrived.

Although the market in raw wool never

entirely collapsed, Englishmen began to manufacture cloth themselves. From the beginning of the fifteenth century cloth was the important thing. In 1447, for example, when the economy as a whole was at a low ebb and only 7,654 sacks of wool were exported, as many as 13,425 sacks of cloth went out. The middleman (or wool 'brogger') and the clothier, a general entrepreneur, now became the men with the economic clout. The raw wool market had been controlled by a few great figures who amassed vast fortunes, and if lucky entered the nobility. The wealth from the cloth trade was more widely spread, creating a middle class which never rose beyond that. It was these people who built their good houses in Wotton, Painswick, Winchcombe and Chipping Campden, and the so-called 'wool' churches in those towns. If anything they are really 'cloth' churches.

Gloucestershire became famous for superfine broadcloth. It was mostly sold 'white', to be finished abroad or in Coventry, but some was dyed, and later Stroudwater Reds and Uley Blues became famous all over Europe, especially for military uniforms. They were dyed in the piece, not in the wool, and after being steeped in the dye were laid out in long ribbons on the valley sides above the mills and dye-houses that had come to cluster round the fast-flowing scarp streams.

The only special buildings that medieval cloth manufacture needed were a dye-house and a fulling mill, in which the cloth was washed with soapy fuller's earth and beaten with heavy water-driven hammers until the wool felted and the woof and warp disappeared. All the many other processes could be carried out at home.

With the mechanisation in the eighteenth century of carding, twillying, scribbling, spinning, weaving, gigging, shearing and pressing, large mills were built, especially on the Frome and its tributaries near Stroud. By 1824 there were over 150 mills here. Depressions in the 1830s and 1870s, as well as competition from the north of England and abroad, almost entirely wrecked the Cotswold textile industry. Today there are only six mills which still make woollen cloth, and their proprietors can hardly make the claim, as their predecessors did in 1802, that 'It is pretty

Bath: the ideal of an urbane city still in touch with the fields that surround it. The Palladian bridge in the foreground decorates the landscape around Prior Park, the mansion built for one of Bath's creators, Ralph Allen, by another, John Wood the Elder. Together they made fashionable the yellow Bath stone, and changed Bath from an untidy and uncomfortable town into the most beautiful city in England.

generally understood that we have had the Market of the World in our Hands . . .'.

The Royal Crescent in Bath – an oval piazza sliced in half and exposed to a spread of lawn.

Bath to Old Sodbury 18 miles

The Cotswold Way starts in Bath, which is not a Cotswold town by any stretch, but this does not really matter. It is a place to come to on its own account. Stepping out of the train from Paddington at Bath Spa one has the sensation of having arrived not in the provinces, but at another rather more elegant and more poised capital. It has a busyness in its streets which goes well with the rather austere architecture.

Bath has probably never felt better. Its social heyday was in the first few decades of the eighteenth century, when royal visitors to the waters drew the fashionable crowd after them. At that time, though, Bath was rather a mess, difficult to get to, ugly and uncomfortable. Of its architectural showpieces only Queen Square was finished in time (1728) to house the aristocracy it was meant for. By the 1750s Bath had begun to fade as the in-place, and started to fill up with un-chic middle classes. It was just at this moment, in 1754, that the Circus was begun, while the Royal Crescent was not built until 1767, and Lansdown Crescent until 1793. All this architectural elegance and genius was to decorate a city which yearly was becoming what R.A.L.Smith has described as 'the last refuge for half-pay officers and retired civil servants'. Bath seems much smarter now.

The city would not exist at all if it were not for the waters, which bubble up from the ground at 120°F. Bath had been, with Buxton in the Peak District, one of the main therapeutic centres of the western Roman empire. There were five Roman Baths here, and two swimming pools, combined with a temple to Sul-Minerva. Their remains are some of the most impressive Roman relics in Britain. The lead-lined Great Bath would have been the centre of social life in Roman times, its spatial magnificence and cleanness doing something to make up for the cramped filth of the rest of the Roman city. It would also have been the acknowledged pitch for sexual adventures.

The Saxons, when they arrived, ignored the sumptuous ruins. Not until the seventeenth century did the idea of the spa as a healing place take on again. By the time Celia Fiennes came here in 1687 things were a good deal more decorous than the Romans must have had them: 'The Ladyes go into the bath', she wrote, 'with Garments made of fine yellow canvas, which is stiff and made large with great sleeves like a parsons gown; the water fills it up so that its borne off that your shape is not seen, it does not cling close as other linning. . . .' Unlike the Romans, who indulged almost entirely in immersion, visitors in the seventeenth and eighteenth century drank the waters as well. Celia Fiennes said simply that 'its very hot and tastes like the water that boyles eggs, has such a smell'.

The Way begins just next to the Roman Baths, in front of the Abbey, a late fifteenth-century Gothic building with a fine fan-vaulted ceiling. The exact choice of way out of the city is yours. You need to head vaguely north-east, and you can easily take in the best parts of Bath's eighteenth-century design by making for the Circus, a tight ring of thirty-three houses, pierced by roads in three places and with a tall clump of plane trees in the middle. This was once entirely paved over and was said by its designer, John Wood the Elder, to be intended for sports on the Roman model, like a toy Colosseum. Today this cool and shady place looks as if it was always intended to house old ladies. The architecture is almost undecorated, very plain, but softened by the trees.

The deep and tree-filled valleys near Cold Ashton are produced by water acting on a rock which is quite soft but impermeable. Streams cut down into the hills but the valley sides are rounded.

Leading to the west is Brock Street, towards an open space which drops off to the south. Reaching the end of the street one suddenly finds, stretching away and hidden until now, the long half-ellipse of of the Royal Crescent. This was designed by John Wood the Younger, a decade after his father's Circus. It too is made up of individual houses, but here they are treated as a palace, with giant Ionic columns along the whole line of the Crescent. The grass in front of it is now a park, but until quite recently used to be fields. This is the place where one can best see what makes Bath unique. Very tight and ordered but imaginative architecture on adapted classical models is arranged on the steep sides of a tree-filled English valley. The two elements – the uncompromisingly urban and the still rela-tively rural – are brought sharply up against each other. This, together with the unexpected and subtle articulation of Circus, street and Crescent, makes this part of Bath the best bit of town-planning in England.

The Way goes westward from this middle of Bath, through Weston and then immediately up on to Kelston Round Hill. You pass the end of the Bath Lansdown racecourse and then

loop back to the east, making for the village of Cold Ashton. For the first mile or two the view out over the Avon towards Dundry Hill and Bristol, with the Mendips in the south-west, gives you the impression of being on the edge of things, but after leaving the trig point on Hanging Hill, four miles from Weston, you lose this wide outlook and begin to get in between the deeply cut hills. The movement now is from one small valley to the next, with high, narrow, flattish spaces between them. Nothing could be more different from the unbroken back of a chalk ridge, where rainwater sinks immediately underground and has no chance to cut these steep and lovely valleys.

Few people count these southern hills as Cotswolds, but they are. Here already you come across one of the things that make this such a good walk, and which is a product of the Cotswolds themselves. Many of the farmhouses have smooth ashlar fronts, grey with a bloom of yellow on them. This is the result of having a good material to work with and enough money to use it. There is no great gap between the style of these farms and the rather grander houses that the Way so often comes to. The local tradition of building comes confidently up to the point where the ideas and practices of international architecture can take over. Hamswell House, for example, sitting squarely on the valleyside two miles from Hanging Hill, is basically a Dutch design, but there is no qualitative difference between it and the farmhouses in the valley below. In just the same way the far grander Dyrham, a few miles from here, does not seem to be a foreign insertion either.

A mile from Hamswell the way comes to Cold Ashton, a village high on one of the ridges between the valleys and with a beautiful seventeenth-century manor looking down into one of them. Unfortunately it hides itself behind high walls from the stares of those on the public road. You turn north here, crossing a sloping field of elbow-high barley to a hamlet called Pennsylvania, where there is a pub.

It is two miles to Dyrham Park, along the slight edge to which the hills have returned. Only trees are visible as you approach the house and village. The way in from this side is not the best, as you arrive end-on, at the stable block. It is better to come from the east, down the edge of the Cotswolds, where you find the house tucked in under the hillside, which is now all grass, but in the seventeenth century was covered in flower gardens, with a cascade falling down from a statue of Neptune at the top. The house itself is really two houses back to back. The one facing the hill is the later, built from 1698 to 1704, rather heavily, with swags and pediments above the windows. The other side is prettier and lighter, built about six years before, and facing a smooth lawn spreading out to the road. The National Trust now owns Dyrham, and you can have tea in the greenhouse, built in 1701, one of the first in England.

After eating your ginger cake you go round to the lane that runs along the end of the garden, and find that there is no high wall to conceal the house, like at Cold Ashton, but a grille of iron railings to display it. This is the difference between the beginning of the seventeenth century and the end, and is the result of French influence.

North of Dyrham you pass a spectacular set of lynchets, as unblurred as if they were cut yesterday. Here in AD 577 the Saxons won a decisive battle against the Celts, killing three of their kings, Conmail, Condidan and Farinmail, and taking Gloucester, Cirencester and Bath as a result. The Britons were pushed back into Wales and Somerset.

The way climbs the gradual slope of the edge and moves through a series of stone-walled fields filled in summer with a variety of crops – hay, barley, wheat – each one of which gives the land a different nap, like cloths. You cross the M4 and soon dive into Dodington Park, which was designed by Capability Brown in 1764. According to Pope, Nature had already done most of the work for him, providing 'woody hills, stumbling upon one another confusedly, and ... a valley betwixt them with some mounts and waterfalls'. The house in the middle, unseen from the Cotswold Way, was designed by James Wyatt as a massive Neroesque palace in 1795. It is now surrounded by a caravan park, a motor museum and other things. None of these impinge on the still great beauty of the Park as it is seen from the Way. Oaks, sycamores, beeches and the occasional copper beech, all now in their prime, are grouped on and below the grassy edge of the Cotswolds.

Old Sodbury is just a mile north of Dodington Park. You could end your day from Bath here if you wanted, but if you still have the energy and the curiosity go east for three miles, on footpaths that lead away from the edge, to Badminton, one of the great ducal estates of the country. The village you come to outside the gates of the big house is almost wholly made up, as might be expected, of estate cottages, but this is only the beginning. For hundreds of acres around here the country has been turned into a kind of toy kingdom. Little castles and gingerbread cottages, miniature temples and triumphal arches, as well as a barn like a lead-soldier fort, dot the rather flat but heavily and beautifully wooded landscape. It was quite incidental that some of these buildings provided housing for the estate

workers. Their main purpose was visual entertainment for the Duke when riding in his estate. The grandest of all these buildings, designed by William Kent, is Worcester Lodge, which stands in a direct line with the centre of the main Palladian house (on which Kent also worked) at the end of a three-mile ride through woods. This is a wonderful walk to take, with the hay rattling against your shins; as you drop occasionally into slight hollows in the land, both house and lodge disappear, to reappear again a minute or two later, one nearer, one further away. The Lodge is a tall, heavily rusticated arch, with above it a domed and pedimented pavilion. On either side are two miniature pyramids, which somehow serve as an estate cottage for a family to live in. The large single room above the arch is a clear, lucid space in which shooting parties have lunch from time to time.

Old Sodbury to Uleybury 20 miles

If you made the detour to Badminton and Worcester Lodge you can continue on down to rejoin the Cotswold Way at Lower Kilcott. Otherwise you must cover those six miles

The front of Dyrham Park facing the edge of the Cotswolds. Built at the beginning of the eighteenth century, it is an example of architecture imported from France running into an English hillside.

along the Way itself. This follows the edge up from Old Sodbury past an Iron Age fort which the Romans reinforced and where Edward IV camped with his army on 1 May 1471. He was campaigning against Henry VI's Queen Margaret of Anjou, who was marching with her army along the Severn to Gloucester. She found the city shut against her and was forced to move on up river to the next bridge at Tewkesbury. Here on 4 May the armies met and fought. Edward IV won and Prince Edward, the son of Henry VI, either died fighting or, as William Shakespeare the Tudor propagandist dramatised it, was taken prisoner by the Yorkists and foully murdered.

A mile and a half from Little Sodbury is Horton, where the National Trust own Horton Court, an unusual mixture of a Norman Hall, perhaps originally a priest's house, and a Tudor house belonging to the Bishop of Bath and Wells. From here the Way climbs the sharpening edge above Hawkes-

bury and then drops into the tree-clad Kilcott valley, where it meets the lane coming over from Worcester Lodge. A tiny stream has cut this valley and used to provide the power for an eighteenth-century corn mill about half a mile downstream towards Alderley. You take a field lane just beyond the mill and here pass from Avon into Gloucestershire. Alderley, just a mile further, is a village almost entirely made of large houses behind the now familiar concealing walls. Nothing beyond the glimpse of a rose is revealed to the uninvited.

Alderley stands on the lip of Ozleworth Bottom, which extends east in alternating bands of wood and hay meadow. Hidden away at the top of a side valley up here is Newark Park, a sixteenth-century house which was gently gothicised by James Wyatt (who also designed Dodington). The position is wonderful, in woods high above the Ozleworth valley with views all over. The National Trust owns the house, but only a path through the estate is open to the public.

From both Newark and Alderley it is just over a mile to Wotton-under-Edge. The name is significant. This is the first real Cotswold town the Way has reached, and here the edge

Worcester Lodge in Badminton Park: William Kent's triumph of incidental architecture is now an estate cottage.

has at last really become one. Many of the houses are rather unexpectedly colour-washed, and not all of them are made of stone. 'Wotton' means wood-town, and several of the buildings have a timber framework, although none reveal it. This may sound strange for a town surrounded by England's best building stone, but until the middle of the sixteenth century most secular buildings in the Cotswolds were built of wood. Only then was it first realised that England was using up her timber reserves. Restrictions on felling were imposed, which, with the general shortage, raised the price of wood and for the first time stone became the more economical material. One of the best things about Wotton is the view of the woody edge one gets from between the shops in the High Street. Here is the first of the 'wool' churches, paid for by Wotton's cloth manufacture, which was finally extinguished by the slump in the 1830s. Only a couple of mills down the road in Kingswood could be said to continue the tradition, and they, rather ignominiously for this one-time centre of superfine broadcloth (the stuff of hunting jackets and billiard tables), now only make elasticated textiles.

Climb up Wotton's Edge from the western end of the town, and then, in thick wood, contour round the top of the ridge, past the banks of a fort called Brackenbury Ditches, for about a mile. Trees hide everything to the west, which is good theatre because unknown to you the first thrilling view of the walk is about to burst. You emerge from the wood on to a grassy space. Over in the west is the Severn. By a good chance from this hill, called Nibley Knoll, you are looking up one of the river's widest loops – the Noose by Frampton-on-Severn – and, glazed by an evening light, the river fattens into a bright inland sea. Further down – and the sharpness of it is so unexpected – the two square blocks of the Nuclear Power Stations at Berkeley and Oldbury-upon-Severn jut out darkly into the lit river, while still further downstream, over eleven miles away, is the unmistakable shape of the motorway suspension bridge at Aust, marking the beginning of Offa's Dyke. The sudden change from the domestic scale of Wotton and Ozleworth Bottom to this universal prospect inevitably brings out one of those 'bursts of admiration' at a view which Jane Austen thought so ludicrous. You will experience one again on realising that on the far western horizon are Welsh mountains, the Black Mountains and Brecon Beacons. It is very odd to find the Cotswolds – so heartland English you would have thought – so near Wales.

On the end of Nibley Knoll is a 111-foot-high tower, erected, mistakenly, in 1866 'in grateful remembrance of William Tyndale, translator of the English Bible', who was thought to have been born in North Nibley, below. There *was* a Tyndale who lived there at the right time, but he was no relation of the translator, who came from somewhere in the Welsh Marches.

It is extremely steep down to North Nibley, which is famous as the site of the last private battle in England, when the Berkeleys and the Lisles, with two thousand retainers, fought here in 1469 over a disputed inheritance. The edge is more broken here than anywhere since Bath. You have to go down a rather busy road and then climb again on footpaths past the charming landscape of Stancombe Park, which curves down a coombe with a lake and some cottages arranged by it. It is easy to see why there are so many quite grand houses on this border of hill and plain: if that transition is included in a park it gives it, literally, an added dimension, and lifts it an aesthetic and even a social notch.

At the top is a golf-course, on Stinchcombe Hill, an attenuated peninsula which is in the process of being cut off from the main body of the edge, as Cam Long Down and Downham Hill, just to the east, already have been. The path goes round all three sides of Stinchcombe Hill, repeating the view from Nibley Knoll (which is worth doing), and then drops down the far side to Dursley.

Dursley was one of the main cloth centres when the manufacture became industrialised, as well as having a famous butter market, which was attended by dealers from Cheltenham and Stroud; this was killed by the arrival in 1856 of a branch railway. It still has, down by the river Cam, the large R.A.Lister engineering works which give the town a slight industrial air, from which Wotton, just over the hill, seems centuries away. Dursley's Queen Anne Market Hall, on columns, and the several good eighteenth-century clothiers' houses now seem a little lost.

From Dursley to Uleybury is two miles, at first up a lane and then over the two steep and turfy outliers, Cam Peak and Cam Long Down. To end the day well, climb up on to Uleybury, an Iron Age fort above Uley, a cloth village, which was known worldwide for its blues. In summer the Iron Age banks of the fort, ringing a whole promontory, hold inside them, like a shallow saucer of milk, a field of waving barley.

Uleybury to Birdlip 21 miles

Half a mile north of Uleybury, on the very edge of the Cotswolds and in another field of barley, is Hetty Pegler's Tump, a near-perfectly preserved long barrow. The door to it is locked, and the key is in a cottage on the Uley–Stroud road. Hester Pegler owned the field – and the Tump – in the late seventeenth century, when antiquaries first came to notice and to name such things. The barrow was built in about 3000 BC, probably by people who had come from South Brittany, where there are several tombs very similar to this one. The pattern, of a central passage with one or more burial chambers opening off it in pairs, is also repeated all over southern England. It was plainly a cultural image that had great hold on this race of Neolithic men, and almost certainly is a symbolic representation of the womb of the earth-goddess. In primitive cultures architecture and sculpture merge.

You go on along the edge, moving in and out of woods, which is typical of a great deal of the Way now; the scale of what you can see shrinks and expands from moment to moment. You reach another long barrow, north of Nimpsfield, with just one pair of chambers, but this is very ruined, with the stones and chambers exposed, not shut in as they were meant to be by a smooth tummock of the earth.

Now the edge turns east, where the Frome has cut it back, and you turn with it for a while, emerging from Stanley Wood below the edge and then going downhill towards the river itself, through Middleyard and past King's Stanley. You reach the river-banks by the tall brick buildings of Stanley Mill, the first fireproof building in England, built in 1813. Everything – doors, columns and trusses – was made in iron, with the floors in brick and stone. The history of this mill is typical of what happened all over these valleys. In 1629 there were fulling mills and corn mills here. By 1660 a gigg mill (in which the nap of the cloth was raised by moving specially grown teasels across it) had been added, as well as a warping room, shear shop and dyehouse. In 1813 came the great rebuilding with iron. It was now to be only a cloth mill, but with dyehouses, wool lofts, wool stoves, cloth rooms and counting houses as part of the complex. In 1833 there were five water wheels here, on a fall of sixteen foot and together producing 200 hp, as well as a 40 hp steam engine. The mill specialised in worsted, a lighter material than broadcloth, unfulled and with the weave still visible in the finished cloth. Stanley Mill was one of the twenty in Gloucestershire still going in 1900; it eventually closed in 1954.

Past the mill you cross the Stroudwater Canal, built in 1779 to bring raw wool up and take finished cloth away. Later, as power looms took over, coal quays were built on the canal banks. The change from water to steam-driven looms was one of the things that destroyed the Gloucestershire textile industry. It was plainly cheaper to operate steam looms in Yorkshire and Lancashire, where coal was near to hand.

Road and railway both come through here. The Way crosses them, and, avoiding the brick proliferation of Stroud to the east, continues through a field of cows on up to Standish Wood on the crest, owned by the National Trust. Coming out from the wood you follow the capes and bays of the edge in and out. Above Standish park is the first of several

The yews and box tombs in Painswick churchyard.

Painswick, where the Cotswold stone is whitest.

excellent topographs on the Way, identifying to the south Stanley Wood, the heavy separate bulk of Cam Long Down and beyond it Stinchcombe Hill.

Haresfield Beacon is three-quarters of a mile from the topograph, and is owned by the National Trust. (Would a fire lit here have been seen on the Brecons?) It is four miles to Painswick, along easy tracks and lanes for the most part, but encountering a few difficulties just short of Painswick itself. Never mind about these, because the sight ahead is too good for fussing to destroy it. Painswick is a pale and beautiful town on a slight hillside, with the spire of its church the only vertical, and with dark valleys all round it. Rather than following the official Way and having to deal with its difficulties, take the lane that drops to the main road and cross it to find a charming area of what used to be Painswick's business end, a gathering of mills, now converted, along the Painswick stream. This area suffered in the 1830s slump more than any other. Until 1820 there were twenty-one mills working on this stream and its tributary, Wash Brook. By 1849 there was one. This was King's Mill, just by the main road, three stone storeys high and

with long weavers' windows on the top two floors. You can follow the stream along, past the remains of Mason's Mill, and the tiny Cap Mill, as far as Brookhouse Mill, which stands opposite its dye-house, and from there climb steeply up into Painswick itself. It is hard to imagine that these good stone buildings in a damp green valley are the relics of a depressed industrial landscape.

The town above, though, is rich. One of the houses, the Beacon, may have been designed by John Wood (the Younger) of Bath and it is a measure of Painswick's style that it does not appear extraordinary here. Painswick is a splendid place, originally a medieval town, but now full of clothiers' houses built or refaced in the seventeenth and eighteenth centuries. Its several streets, all as good as each other, make a pocket of urbanity in Gloucestershire. Only occasionally can one detect what is at the heart of it all, as in New Street, which is fronted by some of Painswick's best houses, but behind which, rather set back, is a nineteenth-century warehouse. Painswick was proud of its trade.

163

On the many beautiful table tombs in the yew-filled churchyard are fixed smart copper plates, on which occupant after occupant is described, in curly eighteenth-century script, simply as 'Clothier'.

You leave by Gloucester Street and go along a golf-course on a ridge between two roads, coming to Painswick Hill, where there is an Iron Age camp. From here you see Gloucester for the first time, in its wide and varied plain. If the light is right you will see its cathedral tower. If not, the only thing that appears to stand up at all is a blue gasometer.

From Painswick Beacon to Birdlip is five and a half miles. It is almost entirely in woods, or along the edge of them, on paths overhung with oaks that the deeper soil can sustain here, as chalk downland soil cannot. Below the edge a mile from the Beacon you pass above the new Prinknash Abbey (pronounced 'Prinnish'), a building like an office block, in a horrible orange stone, which is proof that local material alone does not guarantee the good looks of a building. It houses a chapter of Benedictine monks, who came from Caldy Island on the Pembrokeshire Coast.

The path is all through the woods, with a gap in them a mile from Prinknash where two tree-lined meadows are kept unsprayed and flowery by the Gloucestershire Naturalists' Trust. In another half-mile, where the edge is precipitous, you arrive at Cooper's Hill, where there is a tall, cock-crowned and worm-eaten maypole, which every Whit Monday is dressed in ribbons and flowers. At the same time a race is held down the hill after what should be a Double Gloucester cheese, but is actually a wooden drum made to represent it. A real cheese could burst with its bouncings on the way down. The hill is much steeper than the Manger at Uffington, where the same thing used to happen, so steep in fact that you would think no one could catch the cheese before it got to the bottom.

The footpath's way down the slope zig-zags a little to the left, and then follows along the foot of the edge. To Birdlip is three miles around the head of the beautiful Witcombe valley. Here are the remains of a Roman villa, which, if the evidence from nearby Roman Cirencester is anything to go by, is likely to

Wadfield near Winchcombe: sureness and plain, unaffected grace.

have been maintained and ocupied well into the fifth century. It is now housed under some small neat buildings.

Birdlip is at the top of the edge, here very tall, on the Ermin Way, which was the Roman road from Cirencester to Gloucester. Birdlip has rather a grand inn, the Royal George.

Birdlip to Belas Knap 18 miles

From Birdlip to Belas Knap, as good a long barrow in its way as Hetty Pegler's Tump, is nine miles as the crow flies, but the Cotswold Way doubles that, to avoid road walking, to visit Cleeve Hill and, mainly, to avoid Cheltenham. The whole day, in fact, feels like a cautious circling of Cheltenham, as though some horrible urban contagion were there. The head office of the Countryside Commission is in Cheltenham.

Immediately east of Birdlip is a spare, tall beechwood, covering a small promontory of hill. Through this the Way comes out on to the open Barrow Wake, where there is a topograph with which to look out over Gloucester, this one with some geological explanations on it. It was here that Sydney Smith found relief from the stony Cotswold desert.

The way crosses the road from Gloucester to Stow-on-the-Wold and climbs on to Crickley Hill (owned by the National Trust), with yet another Iron Age camp on it. You head on along the edge for a mile, but from there the Way is a little unsatisfactory. It chops and changes direction for a frustrating two miles. Eventually you come to the Devil's Chimney, a stack of rock on the edge above Cheltenham, and then you go east along the furzy Charlton King's Common to come in two miles to Seven Springs. This is the Source of the Thames; though it is not usually stated with such certainty, there is no doubt that the dribble you see here travels further on its way to Canvey Island than any other. From here to the mouth is 210 miles. From Thames Head, fifteen miles to the south near Cirencester, it is only 201. (The Windrush and the Cherwell take respectively 199 and 198 miles to reach the sea.) Unfortunately for the record, the water that emerges at Seven Springs becomes the River Churn for twenty miles before it joins the so-called Thames at Cricklade.

From the Source of the Thames there is a mile-long slog up the A436, going slowly uphill, at the end of which you turn sharply north and drop very steeply to the valley of the Chelt, now filled with the Dowdeswell Reservoir, and edged with rhododendrons. There is a pub just downstream of the dam.

Up through a wood on the far side the Way goes on unbrokenly through wide arable fields. From here to Cleeve Hill for the first time on the Cotswold Way you get into the way of striding along. The more broken and detailed kind of walking which the Way has involved until here certainly has its pleasures, but this long sweeping afternoon to Cleeve Common is a fine break to have. At the far end of it the way goes below the yellow cliffs of the hill called Cleeve Cloud, a beautiful name from the Anglo-Saxon for Cliff Hill, *Clif Clud*. The village of Cleeve Hill has a hotel, The Rising Sun, and a youth hostel.

Now the Way climbs back almost the way it has come, this time going on Cleeve Common, above the Cliff, on to another golf-course, where there is yet another beautifully made topograph of the view west, which ever since Nibley Knoll has been yours. The best outline to be seen is the long broken spine of the Malverns, nearly twenty miles away. There are two small Iron Age forts here, but they are nothing to the 160-acre monster on Nottingham Hill that appears on the Ordnance Survey a mile to the north. You head away from it, over the rough grass of the common towards the aerials that are prominent there. Just south-east of them is the highest point of the Cotswolds, 1,083 feet above sea-level. The way turns east through walled pastures to what is left of Wontley Farm, with no farmhouse but some old barns and, for once, masses of sheep. The stony road running through the old yard is the same yellowy grey as the buildings themselves.

From Wontley it is about a mile to the Neolithic long barrow called Belas Knap, in the corner of a wheat field and discreetly placed by a wood, not standing out largely on the edge. Like Hetty Pegler's Tump, it has two horns at one end, lined with dry-stone walling. (This walling, though admittedly restored, is beautiful here. Very narrow, almost tile-thin stones were used in a way that makes the wall look like tweed.) Between the two horns at Hetty Pegler's was the entrance to the gallery and transepts of the tomb. Here too, apparently, is a great door made of megaliths between the horns of the barrow, but this door is false. Only solid stone was found behind it. The three separate burial chambers are relatively crudely burrowed in to either side of the mound.

Archaeologists have decided that this is a development, and rather a decadent one, from the earlier Hetty Pegler's Tump. If you compare Belas Knap with the West Kennett barrow – a parallel development – it is quite clear that in Wiltshire skill and energy and commitment to the culture were still very much alive when the barrow was built, while Belas Knap, avoiding the constructional problems of building several connected internal chambers, but wanting nonetheless to

Wadfield Farm: impossible to escape the image of the Cotswolds as a golden landscape.

make a good show, seems to be taking short cuts.

A pair of gargoyles on Winchcombe church: the precipitation into stone of evil and ugliness may have induced a sense of security and even of heightened sanctity in the medieval mind.

Belas Knap to Chipping Campden
19 miles

The last day is the best. The Way goes along the wood behind Belas Knap (what names there are in England! This wood is called Humblebee) then drops steeply to some cottages at the head of a valley that runs down to Winchcombe. Just visible in the trees on the far side are the golden walls of Sudeley Castle, and to their left Winchcombe church tower standing clearly above the roofs of its town. There is a sense that everything is here in this valley, which is made complete when you come to Wadfield, the farm a little way down towards Winchcombe. Without show and almost without ornament this clean, calm house was built here at the very end of the seventeenth century, with wide eaves and a hipped roof. Here is the understated perfection of the Cotswolds, as beautiful a building as anything between Bath and Chipping Campden for its position, sureness and plain, unaffected grace.

You will breeze down the valley after this, through the clover and buttercup hay, to the lodge gates of Sudeley Castle. This is a great showplace now, and for a time was the home of Katherine Parr, after the death of Henry VIII. She herself died here in 1548. There is a very good Victorian sculpture of her in white marble in the church attached to the castle.

Follow the lane that goes north away from the castle gates to Winchcombe, crossing the Isbourne, and arriving in the town up Vineyard Street. The main part of Winchcombe curves away to the right, but you must turn left to the church. This, following the pattern, was built in the mid-fifteenth century, at least partly with cloth money, but there was not quite enough of it and both the Benedictine Abbey that was here and Ralph Boteler, Lord of Sudeley, contributed. The church is almost entirely of the one date, and should be classic Perpendicular Gothic, but is heavier and stonier inside than one would expect.

What matters about Winchcombe church is on the outside. At gutter level, but not acting as water-spouts, are forty of the best gargoyles in the country, some of which are joke figures and some hideous devils. The gargoyle is inconceivably alien to our minds. Why put these horrors and gross cartoons on a church?

It is two miles from Winchcombe church to Hailes Abbey. Go down the main street of the town, over the Isbourne again, and then down Puck Pit Lane, which soon turns into field paths over the low hills between Winchcombe and the Abbey, surrounded by orchards. Hailes was once a stupendous place, founded in 1251 by Richard Earl of Cornwall, brother of Henry III and King of the Romans, as the result of a vow made nine years before when he was nearly drowned off the Scillies. The Abbey was well endowed, but things went badly at the start and the monks were soon in debt. A permanent source of funds arrived in 1270 when the Abbey was given a phial of the Holy Blood of Christ, which became one of the most famous relics in the country. Even as late as 1533 flocks of pilgrims were coming to see it. Five years later Henry VIII's Commissioners took the phial to London, where it was found to be 'honey clarified and coloured with saffron'. The Abbey was closed on Christmas Eve 1539.

Only a part of the cloister now stands to any height, but the museum explains what was once here, as well as displaying some beautiful bosses from the vault of the Chapter House. It is owned by the National Trust.

Now follows a lovely stretch of about five miles below the hills, along the spring line and through three small villages whose yellow stone and carefully unspoilt look make them all of a piece. The first is Wood Stanway, three miles from Hailes via the Cotswold Way, but little more than a mile across the fields. It is the least careful of these villages, with some bits of dung and straw still left about between its seventeenth and eighteenth-century cottages. Stanway, half a mile further, is hardly a village at all, but an excellent aristocratic collection of church, house, gatehouse and enormous fourteenth-century tithe barn, whose roof is a miraculous stretch of stone tile. The public road is forced to make a sharp double bend to get round this group, an indication of what the local priorities are. Where the road first kinks the way into the house moves smoothly on, under a three-storeyed Jacobean gateway, a house in itself, with scallop-shell finials on top of its gables. The main house, which is more restrained, is rather over-shadowed by its flamboyant gateway.

A foot-path goes through Stanway's park to Stanton, the perfect village with an almost

Now blotched like the skin of a trout, the stone tiles of this Cotswold roof in Stanway were laid in about 1400 on the tithe barn owned by Tewkesbury Abbey.

*Sudeley Castle, originally built in about 1440 by Ralph
Boteler with booty picked up in France during the
Hundred Years' War.*

Hills that were once covered in sheep are now given over to cereals and forestry.

A Cotswold wall: topstones placed vertically are more difficult to remove.

inhuman neatness. Come here on a weekday morning in May and you will see nothing move. What makes it even more unreal is the complete absence of signs. This is a conservationist's triumph, and the consequent removal of the village from the twentieth

ABOVE *A too-perfect house in a too-perfect village: part of the hoovered street in Stanton.*

century was perhaps intended. There is an expensive pub at the top of the hill, from which you can look out over orchards and a rare newly-made Cotswold stone roof.

From Stanton to Broadway is about four miles. The Way climbs the edge steeply on to Shenbarrow Hill, and then turns north along it, keeping to a ridge between what is now the Vale of Evesham on the left, and a sharp Cotswold valley on the other side. If you have time, go down there to your right, to the village of Snowshill, where you will find Snowshill Manor, a late fifteenth-century house, which in about 1700 was given the same kind of pure face as Wadfield near Winchcombe. It is owned by the National Trust and contains a quirky collection of armour, lace, weaving tools, penny-farthings and so on.

As you go from Snowshill to Broadway, you cross into Hereford-and-Worcester. The towers of both the old church at Bury End and the newer one in Broadway itself stick up above the trees. Over to the right the folly tower on Broadway Hill stands still taller. As

BELOW *The edge of the Cotswolds and the Vale of Evesham.*

the end of a walk approaches the compulsion to finish gets stronger and the interest in things on the way more peremptory, but do at least look inside the church at Bury End to see the Norman nave.

In Broadway are signs galore; hard-edged commercialism here exploits our taste for the quaint. Now is the moment to indulge the end-of-walk hurry and walk on out into the fields and up to the tower on Broadway Hill, built in 1800 by the Earl of Coventry so that when he was at home near Worcester he could identify his Cotswold estates from the drawing room. The outlook from the foot of the tower is as good as any since Nibley.

But this will only get half a glance. It is four miles to Chipping Campden, on turf and then through a wood, emerging near the Fish Inn, on to the Broadway–Chipping Norton road, opposite which is the best of all the topographs, a model of the landscape in slate. The Way from here, back into Gloucestershire, is along a mile of wide straight green track, between old beeches. It comes to Dover's Hill, owned by the National Trust, and the site from 1605 until 1851 of the annual Cotswold Olympicks. The games included skittles, leaping, the quintain, wrestling, cudgel-playing, coursing and shin-kicking. They were stopped when the common was enclosed, but have been revived recently.

It is a mile from Dover's Hill to Chipping Campden, whose wonderful brown ogee curve of a High Street you enter at its western end. Like Painswick, Chipping Campden is full of seventeenth, eighteenth and nineteenth-century houses, but has kept more of its medieval air, perhaps because it is arranged like an overgrown village. There is a medieval informality in having the Market and Town Halls standing in the middle of the street. Go down the High Street, past the medieval Wool Stapler's Hall and the house of William Grevel, the greatest wool merchant in England at the end of the fifteenth century, and nearly opposite turn off into the street that comes up to the church. The disposition of buildings around the foot of the tower creates yet

A slight rise in the land lifts Chipping Campden church above the roofs of the town. The perpendicular tower, remodelled in the late fifteenth century, still embodies the idea, lost in many villages, of the spiritual rising above the secular.

ABOVE *Sir Baptist Hicks' almshouses in Chipping Campden, the culmination of the Cotswold vernacular, cost as much as £1,300 when they were built in 1612.*

LEFT *Broadway Tower, built by an Earl of Coventry in the late eighteenth century, was visible from his home near Worcester. William Morris, Rossetti and Burne-Jones rented it for holidays.*

another of those scenes which sum up the Cotswolds. (Perhaps that characterises this walk. Again and again you see exactly what you expect to see; these hills are without incongruities.) On the left is a row of almshouses, built in 1612 by Sir Baptist Hicks in the familiar Cotswold style of sharp flat gables. Opposite are the lodges and gateway to Sir Baptist's own house, destroyed in the Civil War. They are almost exactly contemporary with the almshouses, but are the product of the international and aristocratic traditions, with wonderful onion-shaped roofs to the square lodges, all carved from the limestone. To the left of the gatehouse is the church itself, a harmonious remodelling of an earlier building done from 1450 to 1500, with pencil-thin

bands of stone running up the pinnacled tower at the west end. For the wealth that made all this as so much else in the Cotswolds, you must look to the sheep, of which you have hardly met one since Bath.

───────

MAPS: OS 1:50,000 Numbers 150, 151, 162, 163, 172, 173

GUIDES:
Mark Richards, *The Cotswold Way*, Thornhill Press, 2nd Edition 1979
Richard Sale, *The Cotswold Way*, Constable 1980

BACKGROUND:
G.R.Crosher, *Along the Cotswold Ways*, Cassell 1976
Charles and Alice Mary Hadfield, *The Cotswolds: a New Study*, David and Charles 1967
Eileen Power, *The Wool Trade in English Medieval History*, OUP 1942
Jennifer Tann, *Gloucestershire Woollen Mills*, David and Charles 1967

INFORMATION:
The Ramblers' Association, *Cotswold Way Handbook*, annual

A Coast to Coast Walk

Robin Hood's Bay to St Bee's 190 miles

This east-west walk crosses the whole breadth of England, from the coast of Yorkshire to the coast of Cumbria. It was pioneered by Alfred Wainwright, Britain's most famous walker, whose guides to the Lake District are classics of the genre. This is England's best walk because it runs against the country's grain. Unlike the routes along the limestone and chalk ridges, on the Pennines or the coast, it defies the structure of the land. Throughout, and most intensely when crossing the watershed, you sense the division of Britain into two halves, like water-wings. Our habit of thinking of Britain as running north and south is deeply ingrained. We speak of 'up north' or 'down south' far more often than 'out west', and almost never, as Americans do, of 'back east'. The Coast to Coast Walk seems to realign the country, as if the island had been tipped on its side, like Crete or Java. On no other walk described in this book will you be so stimulated by the views ahead of barrier hills, and on no other will you feel less enclosed by the landscape at hand. Instead, the whole thing is seen as if from in space, as a journey across a mental map.

The reason is the clarity of the landshapes involved. Beginning on the North Yorkshire Moors, you descend after fifty miles to the absolute flatness of the Vale of Mowbray. Just over twenty miles of that brings you to the edge of the Pennines at Richmond. From there the crossing of the great watershed (thirty-five miles) takes two days, which are followed by a second flattish interlude of low limestone hills leading straight to Shap on the edge of the Lake District. The Cumbrian mountains reach almost to the sea, leaving only a narrow strip of lowland before you arrive at St Bee's on the west coast. This basic shape, the rhythmic alternation of high and low ground, is so dramatic that it seems almost incidental you should pass through three National Parks – the North Yorkshire Moors, the Yorkshire Dales and the Lake District. You are not confined to a beaten track. Mr Wainwright is careful to call his guidebook 'A Coast to Coast Walk'. He encourages his followers to find variations for themselves, and to branch off his route to the many diversions which the National Parks offer.

Nethermost Cove Beck and Helvellyn seen from Grisedale.

It is Viking country. The path bisects the territory that they overran from east, west and south. For three-quarters of a century they merely raided the coastal plains, sacking the Northumbrian monastery of Lindisfarne in 793, and Jarrow a year later. But the invasion of Yorkshire from their East Anglian base in 866 was a much more serious and lasting affair. The Danish Vikings conquered and occupied the country, settling there as farmers. In the course of time they embraced the Christian religion and established a kingdom centred on York. The Norwegian Vikings were simultaneously establishing an empire in the west. They hooked a great arm round the north of Britain, first occupying the Orkneys and Shetlands, then spreading south-west to the Hebrides, the Isle of Man and the coast of Ireland, where they looted the monasteries and carried off the population as slaves. From Ireland they colonised the west coast of Cumbria, and penetrated over the Pennines to the West Riding. They hoped to avoid the long sea-route round northern Britain by creating a land-corridor to the Yorkshire coast, from where the journey to Stavanger in their fast longships would take only thirty-six hours. By this route, roughly the line of the Coast to Coast Walk, they could more easily transport home the booty they had amassed in Ireland. But the scheme failed. The physical nature of the country was against them: the Pennines were a genuine barrier, but more important the differences between the Danish and Norwegian kingdoms of York and Dublin were too great for any amalgamation to work. The Norsemen had dynamism and mobility, but none of the necessary political cohesion, while the Danes had already acquired a life-style more in tune with the English than their fellow-Scandinavians. The turning point came in 937 at the battle of Brunanburh, somewhere in Yorkshire, when an enormous Norwegian army was crushingly defeated by Athelstan, king of the English.

The Viking period of British history lasted some 250 years, and it is surprising that it should have left so little mark on the country. One must seek evidence of the Danelaw in northern museums, in their ornaments, chalices and stone crosses, or more theoretically in the character of the people, their independence, wordly wisdom and capacity for hard work, for the settlers remained to become the Englishmen whose lands were ravaged by the invading Normans. The most obvious Scandinavian legacy is in the place-names which you will constantly encounter on the Coast to Coast Walk, in both the Danish

Swaledale sheep, the most beautiful in Britain: not much wool, but good mutton.

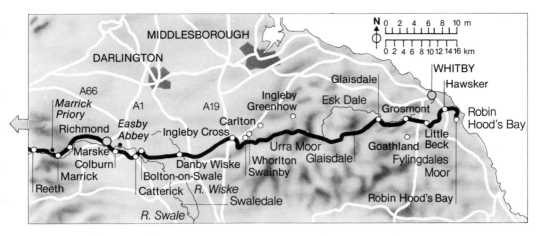

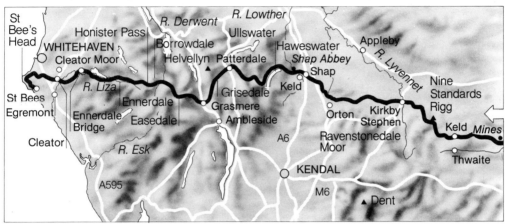

and Norwegian halves. Fell, beck, force, dale, kirk – all of which dot the maps of the north – are Scandinavian names for what Anglo-Saxons called hill, stream, waterfall, valley and church. It is on this linguistic level that the Coast to Coast Walk has a unity. You will pass one Keld at the top of Swaledale and another near Shap. These are where Vikings found springs. Thwaite near the Yorkshire Keld and the countless -thwaites in Cumbria are all places where they cleared a meadow from the indigenous woodland.

Place-name science is extraordinarily precise. It is possible to draw a line, for example, through the barrier of Great Gable and Kirk Fell, west of which the Danes did not penetrate, but east of which places ending in -thorpe and -by (the Danish for farm and village) cover the map. The Kirkbys are the most significant of all, immediately identifiable as Danish and as Christian, and quite different from the places of the independent Norwegian pagans. Kirkby Stephen, it is thought, records a personal act of piety by a defeated Dane. But the two were cheek by jowl. Just north-west of Kirkby Stephen, near Appleby, is a tiny village called Hoff, with next to it a wood called Hoff Lunn. In Old Norse this means 'the grove of the heathen temple where sacrifice is offered'. Wordsworth has the last word:

Mark! how all things swerve
From their known course, or vanish like a
    dream;
Another language speaks from coast to coast;
Only perchance some melancholy stream
And some indignant hills old names preserve
When laws, and creeds, and people all are lost.

The question remains of which way the Walk should be done – west to east or east to west? Wainwright prefers the first because the weather usually comes from the west and is good to have at one's back. But there are reasons why it is better to have the Lake District at the end of the walk. Cumbria is visually the most exciting part of northern England, and is a better climax than the North York Moors. But more important, the Lake District is very steep. Unless you are perfectly fit before starting on a long walk, you will find your stamina, morale, enthusiasm, drive and love of England all sinking to an unthought-of low three or four days after the beginning. This is the time to have flowery meadows and purling brooks, not Helvellyn. From that nadir, though, your body will start to pick up, and after nine or ten days the world will lie at your feet, and any number of mountains will be easy prey. It is kinder to yourself to start on the east coast.

179

All this is practical enough. On a more elevated plane there is the example of the American poet, philosopher and walker Henry David Thoreau who, before going on a walk, used to stand outside his house and let the natural magnetism of the earth turn him in any direction it chose: 'My needle is slow to settle,' he wrote, 'it varies a few degrees . . . but always settles between west and south-southwest. The future lies that way to me, and the earth seems more unexhausted and richer on that side . . . Eastward I go only by force; but westward I go free . . .' Surely this is persuasive enough to make you start the Coast to Coast Walk at Robin Hood's Bay.

Robin Hood's Bay to Ingleby Cross
50 miles

At the bottom, Robin Hood's Bay is all narrow streets and passageways, with cafés, in a cleft that climbs from the wide foreshore of the bay. The bay itself is famous – to geologists – for its reefs of sandstone that stand up as ridges where the softer clays have been picked out from between them. This is the edge of a gentle dome which has its centre about a mile out to sea; the top of it has been sliced off by wave erosion.

Sea villages as prettily placed as Robin Hood's Bay have all gathered their suburbs, and it is through these brick buildings that the path starts out, heading north. Roses and fuchsias hang out from the gardens into the path, which continues through cliff-top barley fields. The view to the south is of the guano-dripped roofs of the village on a naked North Sea coast. Three miles along the coast path brings you to Maw Wyke Hole, where a signpost points west to Hawsker. Here you turn inland, through caravans and then along a lane to Hawsker village.

Beyond it you continue westwards, climbing a little, and seeing to the north the outlines of Whitby, with the silhouette of hotels on one side of the harbour, and on the other the ruin of the Abbey. You can see through its windows three miles away. The way now turns south and on to the first heather moor of the walk. This can be exhausting if you do not pick your way from one burnt and denuded patch

May Beck spatters over Falling Foss in the North York Moors. Fos is the Danish for waterfall.

to the next. This moor, surrounded on all sides as it is by the neat border of cultivation, emerges from Yorkshire like a bald man's pate from his hair. It has been reckoned that the moment of most extensive cultivation in North Yorkshire came as early as AD 1300, since when the history of agriculture on the moors has been one of retraction and depilation, of the substitution of heather and ling for waving barley and oats.

Four miles from Hawsker you cross the B1416 and in another mile come to the first of the dales in the moors that characterise this first part of the crossing of England. As far as Ingleby Cross the dale alternative will always be at hand, not only if fog or cold make the moor inhospitable, but if at any time the darkness and featurelessness of the high ground gets too much. Given the different characteristics of the Danes and Norwegians, it is not surprising to learn that the Danes were Dale men, and that the Norwegians – once they had spread over from the west – were content with the upper valleys and the moor itself on which to pasture their sheep.

You pass New and Old May Beck, two farms beyond which, on a good path through a beechwood, you come to Midge Hall, a plain building surrounded on three sides by the stream which spatters over a waterfall called Falling Foss. In half a mile the way passes a massive rock, which has been hollowed out, leaving a circular bench inside. 'The Hermitage 1790' is carved in large letters beside the Gothic door.

Little Beck is just under a mile away, a neat collection of stone cottages, a chapel and old mill, with petals from the roses littering the lane. There is no shop or pub. This tiny hamlet is first recorded in 1100, but is certainly older, possibly a Norse settlement. Beyond it the way climbs to and crosses Sleights Moor, on top of which is a tumulus called Flat Howe, with a stone kerb around it. Not far away are two groups of standing stones called the Bride Stones, one in very reedy ground. All these monuments (although to call them that is mere flattery) are probably from the early Bronze Age.

South from here are the three vast white globes of the Ballistic Missile Early Warning Station on Fylingdales Moor, which is run jointly by Britain and the United States. People have moaned about vanishing countryside and mentioned requiems in connection with these monumental objects. But it is a recipe for rigidity and death to approve only of the visually conservative, and of what fits in rather than what reshapes. There is no need to be terrified of the monumental.

Grosmont is about three miles from Little Beck, steeply down from the moor in Eskdale,

No. 80135 at Grosmont, the northern terminus of the North York Moors Railway. The tunnel on the left takes trains south on to the line through Newtondale to Pickering.

the valley that splits the North York Moors in half. Grosmont is a railways place. One of the two stations here is on the Whitby to Middlesborough line, run by British Rail. It is unstaffed and greatly overshadowed by the other one next door, managed by a crowd of steam enthusiasts. This is the northern terminus of the North Yorkshire Moors Railway, which twists southwards through Goathland and Newtondale to Pickering. The line was engineered in 1836 by George Stephenson, as a horse-drawn railway. In 1845 it was converted to steam and finally closed by British Rail in 1965. A preservation society has now reopened it, using the still vastly impressive engines. At times engulfed in steam and ear-blastingly loud, these were the first of the new machines to enter the life of the rural population of the moors in the mid-nineteenth century. What is now the object of preservation societies produced the same kind of reaction in the 1840s as the Fylingdales Balls have recently.

From Grosmont (pronounced without the s) to Glaisdale is three and a half miles along the woody valley of the Esk. A good wide track leads along by the river to Egton Bridge, the tone of which is set by its Manor, firmly exclusive behind walls and dark, thick foliage. There is an elaborate Roman Catholic church just up the road to Egton itself, which is famous for a gooseberry fair.

To get to Glaisdale you cross the Esk on a graceless box of an iron bridge and walk on the road past two massive red-boled sequoias for about a mile, when you turn off on to an old pack horse track through Arncliffe Wood. The middle section in the wood is paved with stone slabs that have been worn into deep U-troughs through use. The way emerges at the seventeenth-century Beggar's Bridge (over a branch of the Esk), whose purity of form puts the clay-footed iron object at Egton Bridge to shame. The village of Glaisdale is just beyond. In the nineteenth century there were three blast furnaces in this disjointed village, which is spread over the entrance of the Glaisdale valley into Eskdale, not evenly, but in oddly urban spurts. The stone in the terraces is harshly and mechanically cut. It makes sense in Glaisdale to refer to something being 'at the end of the block', which is hardly thinkable in other country villages.

The twenty miles from Robin Hood's Bay to Glaisdale have seen the easy alternation of low moor and dale. Beyond it the way makes its first major excursion on to the high ground, with which it stays officially for the next thirty miles. Until the western end of the Cleveland Hills on the verge of the Vale of York the path comes to precisely three buildings – a couple of farms in Huthwaite Green and the Lion Inn on High Blakey Moor. That is an average of one building every ten miles. This may be the kind of isolation you are looking for, but unless you have with you your food, stoves, pots, tents and other countless necessaries, a descent and a detour to the more hospitable parts of the North Riding is unavoidable. This, after all, is not the Appalachian Trail. Walking in England, in fact, is quite different from walking in the States. There the idea is to become the solitary figure in a natural landscape, which involves a shedding of the cultural past and an adoption of nature. In America to go for a trek is an attempt to emerge from culture; in Britain it is an inevitable immersion in it.

The dark – at times monotonously dark – moors west of Glaisdale illustrate this as well as anywhere else. The track that climbs on to Glaisdale Rigg, which is grassy at first and then coated in heather, would seem to be nothing more than a pleasant walker's route above the yellow fields of Glaisdale to the south, until you find a stone saying 'Whitby Road 1791' standing on the verge. The traffic from the Vale of Pickering to Whitby now crosses by Sleights Moor near Grosmont, but this track was once the main artery. The moor has many other standing stones on it, uninscribed, and these probably mark estate boundaries. The track joins a tarmac road and then turns off it again, keeping westwards above Great Fryup Dale Head, to come to another tarmac road which leads you consistently westwards. This is now Danby High Moor, covered in Bronze Age barrows. The moors are fairly often sunk in a heavy mist that blows in from the sea-coast, a damp and depressing thing called a roak (a Scandinavian word). Walking in this can give you a soaking.

You will have arrived near Rosedale Head, perhaps unaware of the great prospects that

Fat Betty, a welcome incident in the dark monotony of the North York Moors. The rudimentary cross is probably a guidepost of sorts erected in the Middle Ages.

should be opening for you north and south-wards, to the sharp peak of Roseberry Topping on the one hand and down Rosedale on the other. If you have seen nothing for a few miles but grey-tongued and grey-wooled sheep and the occasionally whirring grouse, and are in crying need for something to enliven the steady plod westwards – the beautiful conception of crossing England coast-to-coast is all too susceptible to erosion during a day's drenching in blanket roak – out of the mist comes Fat Betty. This unfortunately is not the warmly mothering figure her name suggests, but a squarish block of whitewashed stone sitting on the moor. It is one of about thirty 'crosses', only a few of which are cross-shaped, which stand next to old routes across the North York Moors. In quarter of a mile from Betty are two more, the Ralph Crosses, which actually are cruciform. They are probably medieval, possibly set up by the monasteries to guide their servants from the mother abbey to the outposts or granges from where the great flocks were managed. These stone guideposts have names like Percy, John, Ana, Redman, Ralph and Betty.

A single monolith down the road from Rosedale Head, marking a district boundary, is called Margery Bradley, and a mile beyond it is the Lion Inn, nine miles from Glaisdale village. Like the Tan Hill Inn on the Pennines, what was once a soak for desperate miners now caters for the more refined pleasures of motorists and walkers. Here is a place to pause. Beyond, if Wainwright's route is followed exactly, are twenty miles of refreshment-less hard going.

It is quite likely, though, that by now you will want to see a dale. Just south of the Lion Inn is Farndale, which, parallel with Rosedale and Bransdale, pushes a long way into the moorland block. The streams of all of them are gradually cutting back their daleheads, so that one day the narrow valleys will divide the moors into a series of regular strips. To come down into Farndale is a blessed relief. Beautiful trees, buildings, a pub at Church Houses, fields full of cereal crops, excellent stone walls – all this is marvellous after the moor above.

From Church Houses a lane leads up the deeply settled landscape of Upper Farndale to the Dale Head, where the track coming directly from the Lion Inn, along the disused mineral railway, can be joined. This railway was closed in 1929, but still provides a firm, level surface that contours carefully for about two miles before dropping 1,300 feet in a mile, to the agricultural land below the moors. The Coast to Coast Walk does not go down with it, but joining the Cleveland Way follows that route along the Cleveland escarpment, with Middlesbrough and Yorkshire's broad acres spread out to the north.

This stretch is a confluence of walkers, since the Cleveland Way, the Coast to Coast Walk and the Lyke Wake Walk – a forty-mile cross-moor marathon which is done by thousands each year in under twenty-four hours – all crowd on to the one well-used path. But if you have already walked either or both of these, why not go down the railway incline and follow the lanes and footpaths that run below and parallel to the hills? Rather than the usual great views you will see things like the strangely shed-like church in Ingleby Green-how, remodelled in 1741, with capitals on the columns inside showing a bear and a pig and cartoon faces, all of which have all proved a puzzle to architectural historians. (The name Ingleby, which recurs at Ingleby Arncliffe and

Arncliffe Hall, on the edge of the Vale of Mowbray. Inside is a plaster ceiling which depicts Plenty hovering over Roseberry Topping, with next to it a cow and a cottage.

Cross means, in Danish, 'English village', which looks like firm evidence of the cohabitation of the two races next door to each other. The arrangement of villages west of here, with the almost regular alternation of -ton and -by – Great Broughton, Kirkby, Great Busby, Carlton, Faceby, Whorlton, Swainby, Ingleby Arncliffe – is an almost schematic interlarding of Angle and Dane. One obvious question suggests itself: If so many villages have Anglian names, why did the Danes name just two of them 'the English place'? Were these the odd exceptions, where Danes took over pre-existing settlements, rather than squeezing themselves in between?)

All the villages are now indistinguishable in tone, and all are visibly under the influence of Middlesbrough. They act as dormitories for the management of Teesside industry. The result is often an exaggerated and affected villagey style. Carlton-in-Cleveland is the best of them, drawn back on either side of the Alum Beck, whose little valley is filled with tall beeches and chestnuts. The strangest is Whorlton, wrecked by plague in the Middle Ages, and now little more than a rotten castle and a ruinous church.

Ingleby Cross to Richmond
23 miles

The Cleveland Hills end, or rather their escarpment turns south. At the corner stands Arncliffe Hall, a solid mid-eighteenth-century mansion in ashlar. The Coast to Coast Walk leaves the high ground and heads straight across the Vale of Mowbray. Wainwright apologises for this interruption to bare highland walking, and advises us to hurry over the flat ground as quickly as possible. But it is a good thing, in a way, to walk for a day and a half through country which is not a show area of England, but one of its granaries. This is middle England, almost all barley, a little wheat, some timber, some sheep and very few cows. The economies of scale have meant that even here you come across ruined farms, but there is nothing like the sense of desertion and of abandoned struggle that you find on the Pennines. Here the illusion is of man in control of his environment – trunk roads, railways and national grid lines all drive directly to their destinations, in contrast to the windings of communications on the moor and the hopeless meandering of streams here in this contourless flatness. All the fields are hedged with thorn, or post-and-rail fences. The farms are of brick, and the rock of the earth is buried in good soil.

At Ingleby Cross is the Blue Bell Inn; leave it and cross the violently busy A19 to plunge off into agriculture on the far side. A good track zig-zags through five right-angles between the grid of enclosure fields and farms (one, Brecken Hill, in ruins) and then heads steadily westwards. This is and always has been excellent horse country. Defoe was wildly enthusiastic about 'the gallopers of this county', which for combined speed and strength he reckoned would beat any in the world. Moor House Farm, which you come to five miles from Ingleby Cross, keeps race-horses in its paddocks. Catterick, Thirsk, Ripon, York and Redcar are all within easy distance.

At Oaktree Hill, a slight roll in the flatness of the Vale of York, the Pennines appear to the west. This should be a great moment, but it is not. Although they make a wide brown streak down the middle of England on maps, in purely physical as opposed to geographical terms the Pennines are really very insignificant. The highest, Cross Fell, is just under five-ninths of a mile high, while England here is 130 miles wide – the proportion of height to width is 1 to 234. That is just the impression you get standing on Oaktree Hill. This is virtually a horizontal country; what counts is the breadth of barley, not the blue shadowy rise in the distance.

Danby Wiske, an all brick and pantile village round a green, comes in two miles, and has a good pub in it, as well as a church with an interesting Norman door, and a scene above it of three robed men said to be weighing a soul. From the village to Richmond is thirteen miles on the flat. Perhaps the endless fertility of it – the Vale of Mowbray is like one enormous fleece laid out – will begin to pall, but an incident at last occurs when you come to Ellerton Hill, five miles from Danby Wiske. There you turn off the road and along the banks of Scorton Beck for about a mile to Bolton-on-Swale. The church here, St Mary's, is itself only interesting for an entirely chance but good pattern of gables at its north-eastern corner. Inside, though, is a tablet to the extraordinary memory of Henry Jenkins, who was born in 1500 and died in 1670, aged 169. In the churchyard is a clumsily lettered obelisk put up in 1743 in appreciation of this achievement.

On an embankment above the flood meadows a lane leads to the Tancred gravel pits by the Swale. The pits are crossed by conveyor belts converging on shudderers that sort the gravel into different grades. The Swale, if it has been raining in the hills, will be full and a lovely dark brown, the colour of hot chocolate. This is the first encounter with the Pennines, since it is Pennine peat that makes the river brown. The way will be along this, the best of English rivers, for the next thirty miles. The word 'swale' in northern dialect now means cool or chill, but the river's name is

probably related to *swallow*, the bird, both of them coming from a Germanic root word, meaning something like move, whirl and rush.

From the gravel pits it is about a mile to Catterick Bridge on the river bank, with a stretch of ancient wall at one point, thought to be a Roman embankment of the river. There was a Roman town here, called Cataractonium, after the rapids in the Swale. Cross the bridge and continue on the far bank past the racecourse and a clump of wild raspberries and under the thundering A1. Somewhere here is the line of Dere Street, the Roman road to the north, which in rather different circumstances the Pennine Way crosses at Chew Green in the Cheviots. It is two miles to Colburn, well above the river, and in and out of woods. These slight hills are the toes of the Pennine foothills. The Hildyard Arms at Colburn is a welcoming place, but perhaps it is better to push on to Richmond, which is only another two miles away, much of it on filthily muddy paths in the wood.

You pass the ruined Hagg Farm, and after half a mile emerge at a sewage works. On the other side of the river is Easby Abbey. This was founded in 1155 for the Premonstratensian Canons, an order very much like the Cistercians in thinking manual labour not liturgy was the way to God, and in their preference for remote places. Shap Abbey was theirs too. To judge by the look of Easby today their sense of place was unfaultable, even though the effects have been heightened by eighteenth-century landscaping and the building of a good Georgian brick house at the focal point on the hill above. This genius for choosing the right place, which is evident time and again at abbey ruins, may be a chance effect. The monastery needed a stream or river to fill its fish pond and maybe to drive its mill. It needed some good flat land, but since the best would probably not be given it by the founder, it was likely enough that some high and initially unproductive land would be included in the grant. (It was exactly this unsuitability to the plough of so much of their land that turned the Cistercians in particular into the great sheep-farmers and wool-producers that they became.) These are all practical and economic factors, but they add up to the marvellously picturesque recipe of an abbey standing on a grassy meadow in a deep valley by a stream, with high land nearby. One can immediately think of Llanthony, Tintern, Rievaulx, Valle Crucis, Marrick, Shap, Kirkham, Strata Florida – and Easby – all of which more or less fit this pattern.

After so much sameness in the Vale of Mowbray, incidents now crowd in. Only a quarter of a mile from Easby, Richmond appears on the far side of the Swale. This excellent town can lay a fair claim to being

Britain's best. It is small and cannot hope to compete with Bath or York, but in its class is without equal. The first look you get at it, from a line of villas, shows Richmond as it is. The castle keep is on a cliff above the brown and broken Swale at the west end, and spreading out down from it are the mixed stone and brick buildings of the town, steeply decked on the hillside. This mixture of the hill and the valley materials expresses exactly Richmond's role, as an exchange market between the two economies that meet here at the edge of the Pennines. The great castle, imposing as it is, has been a strategic irrelevance ever since it was built in the 1070s. Swaledale, which it controls, has not proved a crucial Pennine crossing – people have gone by Wensleydale or the Stainmore gap – and the main north-south arteries have stayed east of it in the plain. But as a market Richmond has boomed. The cobbled sloping market place is the centre of town. In the middle of it is the church of Holy Trinity,

Easby Abbey near Richmond: the same factors which, for practical reasons, dictated the siting of an abbey appealed to an eighteenth-century taste for the picturesque.

which Pevsner thinks 'the queerest ecclesiastical building one can imagine'. The church is joined to its tower by an office building, and is itself on the first floor. Until 1971 there were shops under the north aisle. All this is an old arrangement, and in Richmond obviously God and Mammon have always walked hand in hand. The other sights of Richmond are the ruined priory and a Georgian theatre, but more than these it is the general tone which is so good. Richmond has a wholesome beauty, with a strong economic function still providing the dynamo for its social life; it avoids the stagnation which can so easily kill a good-looking town if it is treated too preciously. The day Richmond decides that buses can no longer park in its beautiful market place will be the end of what is best about it.

Richmond to Kirkby Stephen
35 miles

The way to leave England's best town is by its best street, Newbiggin. Leave the market place by Finkle Street which at its far end opens out on to Newbiggin. There are good houses behind the limes which run the length of this

Yorkshire boulevard. One of the prettiest and almost the first you come to is No 11, in quite a rough grey stone, but with delicate white and blue decoration framing the windows and doors.

From the end of Newbiggin it is uphill, the first proper slope of the Pennines, on a tarmac road with villas on one side. In front is Swaledale, curving wonderfully away as it pushes into the hills. It is all green and woody. You leave the tarmac behind and lose sight of the Vale of Mowbray and the Cleveland Hills beyond it. One of the undeniable pleasures of long walks is seeing behind you a vast distance over which you know you have walked, step by step. The lane goes into Whitcliffe Wood, and then along below a small limestone scar, in the middle of which is a monument where in 1606 Robert Willance fell over the cliff when out riding. The horse was killed but he survived.

Three miles from Richmond you come to the hamlet (if it could be called that) of Applegarth. The name is straight from the Old Norse for apple orchard, and the place consists of three farms, about a quarter of a mile apart, with a barn or two between them. They are called West, Low and East Applegarth, and although they are part of one place it is a very tentative and typically Viking sociability. There are rabbits all over it. Of course the actual buildings are all much more recent than the age of the settlement. West Applegarth has good stone mullions in its windows and old, slightly bowed panes between them. It is here that you enter the Yorkshire Dales National Park.

The Swale makes a wide sweep to the south. You drop to the valley floor and, crossing Clapgate Gill, make for Marske across the fields, squeezing through a series of squeeze stiles. This is half hedge and half stone-wall country. The junctions between hedge and stone are never vertical, with the stone stopping abruptly and the hedge taking immediately over. Instead, the stone slides gradually to the ground with a branch of the hedge bush stretching out over it.

Marske sits with ease in the little valley of its beck, with the Hall on the far side carefully screened from the public stare. Beyond it is a steep and long climb up the lane, but the reward at the top is worth all the effort. The country shifts gear. On the wide expanse of moorland grass to be seen from the top of the hill are no trees, but an endless sculptural bareness of walled pasture. Two miles follow of the best walking in the world. The grass in the fields is typical of sheep country. Unlike

Richmond: a market town on the frontier between the hills and the Vale of York. The first of the Pennines rises behind it.

cows, sheep are very selective eaters, and where a cow will crop indiscriminately sheep will leave the more brittle of the grasses untouched, so that a meadow mown by them has two layers to it – the well-cropped floor and a thinnish scattering of higher grasses. This is the ideal combination: a smooth sward underfoot and the regular brushing against your legs of taller stalks. You pass three farms – Hollins, Ellers and Nun Cote Nook – before coming to Marrick, a mess of a tiny village, which has the air of brown nineteenth-century photographs of children playing in rural Yorkshire streets. At the bottom end are a church and a chapel (now converted into a house), both of which would be indistinguishable from the barns in the fields, were it not for the windows – round-headed in the chapel, pointed gothic in the church.

After crossing a nose of high land which the Swale swings round, the way now drops to the river again, on a partially flagged but muddy path through a wood, to emerge at Marrick Priory. Some sensible modern buildings, an adventure centre for the Diocese of Ripon, and the Abbey Farm now cluster at the foot of the 1811 church tower, which was built from the

Marrick Priory in Swaledale preserves exactly the atmosphere of smaller abbeys in the Middle Ages – not every one a Fountains.

materials of a twelfth-century priory. Marrick again demonstrates the infallible monastic sense of place, while the modest and homely nature of the farm and dormitories is a good reminder that not every abbey was a Fountains. The tone now must be similar to what it was in 1150.

It is two miles from the Priory along Swaledale to Reeth. The moor edge to the north still shows the scars of lead-mining, but nothing could look less maltreated than the valley floor, a nurtured, almost pampered landscape. Reeth is strung around a large sloping green, tipped so that sitting outside one of its four hotels you can look the length of the green dale and ignore the bitterer implications of the once wrecking and now wrecked industry which has made a stony desert of the top edge of the valley.

From Reeth to Kirkby Stephen is twenty-four miles. It is possible, in a long and tiring, but hugely exhilarating day, to walk from one to the other. It is, in effect, the crossing of the

Pennines from side to side. To do it in a single day gives a kind of central hub to the Coast to Coast Walk, a middle day in which the back of England is broken.

You leave Reeth by the Kirkby Stephen road, past a good new housing estate, with stone slab roofs, but then turn off uphill to come out above the intake wall of cultivation, on a path through bracken and heather. The line between field and moor is precisely defined by the stone wall, but islands of field, surrounded by their own walls, float out higher than the main moor/cultivation boundary. Seen in isolation they can look like the first fields to be cleared in an otherwise intractable land.

Agriculture soon ceases to matter. The path turns up Mill Gill and in about four miles from Reeth comes to the ruins of Old Gang Smelt Mill, of which only the chimney and a few walls are standing. From here to Keld the path is never out of sight of some relic of the lead-mining that has been carried on here since before the Romans, but which only in the eighteenth and nineteenth centuries reached Klondike proportions. Collapse was almost total at the end of the nineteenth century, as the failure of seams coincided with cheap foreign imports. The consequent human wreckage was worse than the physical destruction of the landscape that the boom years had brought.

Two miles from the mill ruins the way crosses an entirely grassless, heatherless, lifeless area of gravel, which was thrown aside as spoil by the lead-miners, but is now itself being dug, sorted and carried off for driveways. After this you come to a sharp valley, about 500 feet deep, called Gunnerside Gill. There is no avoiding the horribly steep down and up of this. On the far side of it can be seen a good example of a 'hush'. This is where, to remove soil and expose mineral-bearing rock, a dam was built across a stream and a small lake allowed to build up. The water was then released in one gush, sweeping away before it everything on the surface to reveal what is called (now, at any rate) the pay-dirt. As can be imagined, this leaves an almost irreparable scar. In the bottom of the gill is another smelt mill, with an arcade of unexpected delicacy in this hard and exploited landscape. There is nothing that makes the land look more used or

The Swale near Keld.

*Crackpot Hall and beyond it Upper
Swaledale, a gentle slice into the Pennines.*

more slutty than this kind of surface mining that leaves so much rubbish around after it is done with the earth.

Regretting perhaps that you did not follow the banks of the Swale you climb the far side of the gill and make an easy way on a track over the moor to Keld, about three miles away. The heavy hump of Great Shunner Fell, which you may know from the Pennine Way, forms the horizon to the west. The path drops down from the moor again into Swinnergill, where there are hushes, yet another smelt mill, and the entrance to a mine level. Just around the corner is the ruin of Crackpot Hall, once a big farmhouse but now abandoned because of mining subsidence. Its rooms are open to the sky and the stone roof-slates stacked against the walls. No house could have a better position, looking down over Upper Swaledale, with the regular dotting of laithes in walled fields. Crackpot Hall, with its obvious but now destroyed solidity, has an almost novelistic significance. A permanent and regenerative way of life here has been literally undermined and destroyed by a temporary and exploitative one.

It is just over a mile to Keld, where you cross both the Swale and the Pennine Way. The village is small and sweet, too famous for its own good, and rather antiseptic. There is a youth hostel, but no shop, café or post office. It is usually filled with cars and is a place to leave, especially because the Swale above it is so good, the peaty water falling regularly over rock steps in its bed.

At Smithy Holme, just over a mile from Keld, you leave the Swale for the last time and head north up into Whitsundale. The landscape changes into typical Pennine gritstone moor after passing Raven Seat, a lonely farm with a spread of moor all round it. It is a four-mile Pennine trek from here to Nine Standards Rigg, at 2,170 feet the highest point so far. The walking may be plodding but these are four important miles. Halfway to St Bee's from Robin Hood's Bay was passed at Keld. Two miles from Raven Seat is 100 miles from the beginning, and two miles further on you cross the Yorkshire-Cumbria border. On the same line the path crosses the main watershed of England – spit on one side and it will go to the Irish, on the other to the North Sea. Best of all, though, hazy to the west you get the first sight of the Lake District Fells. Here is the crossing of England reduced to a single moment.

Half a mile beyond this crucial, boggy and quite unmarked place are the nine large cairns which give Nine Standards Rigg its name. They appear on the first good maps in the eighteenth century, but no one knows how old they are. From here the Vale of Eden is laid out, with the distinctive conic hills above

An old buttery in Keld.

Dufton on its eastern boundary and Cross Fell beyond them. If the sun catches it the Tan Hill Inn stands out sharply in the drear of a Pennine moor to the east. Thank God your way is towards those good-shaped hills in the west and not on the heart-draining monotony of the Pennines.

Kirkby Stephen is clear as a greyish string of buildings well below, just on the southern edge of the Vale of Eden. Tomorrow's limestone hills move plainly westwards to Shap. It is four and a half miles to Kirkby Stephen from the top of the Rigg, some of it squashy where the gritstone outcrops, but otherwise firmly turfy on the limestone. The last two miles are on a tarmac lane between beautiful crinkly grey limestone walls, round an enormous quarry above Hartley, but after that over the fields to Kirkby Stephen. Three upright flagstones stop cows following you across the footbridge over the Eden. On the far bank a high-walled lane brings you out on to the one main street of the town, which is a market, with several hotels on either side.

Kirkby Stephen to Shap Abbey
20 miles

From Kirkby Stephen to Shap is the most obvious stage of all, a day of passage between the Pennines and the Lake District. It seems as much an interlude as the crossing of the Vale of Mowbray, but this one is not over flat agricultural land, although it is easy to think of it like that. In fact, at one point you climb as high as 1,300 feet, far above the top of any hill in southern England. Nevertheless, the impression that stays with you is of crossing on a limestone causeway scarcely lifted above the red sandstone of the Vale of Eden and leading directly to the volcanic mountains of the central Lake District.

You leave Kirkby Stephen by the back lane

which turns into a delicious country road to Green Riggs Farm, where great long fingers of roof slope out down from the barn. Beyond it is about three and a half miles of green walled fields. Here and there are lumps in the turf that show the site of an ancient and abandoned settlement. You cross Scandal Beck by Smardale Bridge, which is built of stone but has turf on the crossing, and then on the other side of a disused railway reach another large area of abandoned settlement. To a layman's eye it reveals almost nothing. The site is unexcavated but is thought to be prehistoric rather than medieval. More impressive than any of these protuberances in the earth are the relatively modern but equally undated limestone walls. These are high, solid, workmanlike constructions, blotched by a lichen only just paler than the grey of the rock itself. The stones that stick out beyond the vertical face about halfway up are called throughstones or tie-stones, and make the wall stronger. Along the top the stones are placed vertically to provide a layer

Raven Seat in Whitsundale, near Keld, one of the remotest farms in the Pennines. The good 'white' land surrounds the farmhouse; beyond it are the acid moors.

which is difficult to remove (as horizontal top stones would not be) and, it is said, to stop sheep scrambling over, although none of the sheep round here look capable of the necessary gymnastics. For the animal that is more proverbially gregarious than any other these sheep display a remarkable independence of mind, distributing themselves with an almost mathematical efficiency over the available space.

The hills begin to rise a little over Ravenstonedale Moor, and the heather and bilberry take over from the grass. In four miles from Smardale Bridge you come to Sunbiggin Tarn, a large reedy pond which is famous for its birdlife. The far side of it the turf reappears and climbing to the top of a ridge you find yourself on the edge of a large area of limestone pavement. This calls for careful walking. If you happen to meet someone coming the other way you will get the usual hello, but no glimpse of his face, which will be kept staring fixedly downwards to avoid a disastrous slip. The pavement is cut by deep grykes that are worn into the stone by the mildly acid rainwater in which carbon dioxide has been dissolved.

*The barns or laithes of Upper Swaledale
regularly punctuate a swept landscape.
The hay from each field is stored on the
top floor of the laithe, and on the bottom
cattle are housed in winter.*

In the middle of this danger-fraught pavement is an island of green turf called Castle Folds, that was used by prehistoric men as a refuge. Your own painstaking progress towards and around it shows how effective a moat the broken limestone must have been. A high stile-less wall is the next obstacle. The secret of climbing a drystone wall without damage to you or it is to press *down* in every move you make. Gravity alone holds it together, and anything pulled or pushed in a direction different from gravity will come away. A wall costs five pounds a yard to repair for the labour costs alone. This is expensive for farmers, but if you compare the product with, say, the work of tailors or even carpet-layers the price seems rather a good one.

From Castle Folds to Shap Abbey is ten miles, over Beacon Hill and the Orton-Appleby road, then on to the thick heather of Crosby Ravensworth Fell. Large rounded boulders of the Shap granite have been left sitting on this moor by a glacier travelling east. One such boulder, after the glacier had

transported it along the Coast to Coast Walk, arrived in Robin Hood's Bay where it now sits. Limestone is far too brittle to boulder: it shatters first. Only a rock with the hardness of Shap granite could withstand and be rounded by the battering on the abrasive underside of a glacier.

You cross the dry stream-bed of the Lyvennet. At its source, a quarter of a mile away, a pillar says 'Here at Black Dub, the source of the Livennet, King Charles II regaled his army and drank the water on his march from Scotland, August 8 1651'. They were en route to the disaster at Worcester. You may wonder what they were doing up here on this desolate moor. The answer is at the top of the ridge to the west, along which a Roman road runs south from Carlisle and Brougham to the Lunedale gap, now occupied by the River Lune, the A685, the main west coast railway and the M6.

You cross the Roman road and head north to a bank of trees which shelters a little green-roofed shed called Potrigg, and then on past a pair of stone circles and the hamlet of Oddendale in trees, past an enormous quarry, to come to the banks of the M6. From fields

The landscape of a limestone wall.

Potrigg, near Shap.

full of Shap granite boulders, the path crosses the motorway by footbridge. Shap village is only two-thirds of a mile beyond it. It is on the A6, now superseded by the motorway and practically unused, leaving the village feeling empty and spare. There is an interesting seventeenth-century market hall in it. The abbey is less than a mile to the west, but instead of going straight there, walk through the fields to another Keld, where the National Trust own a small chapel, once dependent on Shap Abbey, and contemporary with it, but for centuries used as an ordinary cottage. This Keld is much less famous and a better place than the Swaledale one. A footpath leads from it above the River Lowther to Shap Abbey, of which only the tower stands above head height, but that is enormously tall, with two great arches in it, so that half the tower walls are open air. This of course was another centre of the monastic wool enterprise, and in the accounts of a fourteenth-century Italian wool merchant there is a reference to this West-morland abbey as 'Ciappi in Vestrebellanda'. Next to the ruins is the abbey farm, with two medieval stone faces set into its walls. The River Lowther forms the border of the National Park and the Abbey your first introduction to the Lake District.

Shap Abbey to St Bee's 62 miles

Over 50,000 books have been written about the Lake District. One hundred more are added every year. There is a paradox in this. Many – perhaps most – of them mention the 'unspoilt' nature of these Cumbrian mountains, often maintaining the alluring fiction that here is an uninvaded and self-sufficient nature which is better for you than the cultural and the urban. Of course this comes from Wordsworth, or at least from the long swell of Romanticism of which he for a time was the crest. In *Lyrical Ballads*, his first book, published in 1798, he inveighs:

> Books! 'tis a dull and endless strife:
> Come, hear the woodland linnet,
> How sweet his music! on my life
> There's more of wisdom in it.

> Enough of science and of art;
> Close up these barren leaves;
> Come forth and bring with you a heart
> That watches and receives.

That invitation to leave the barren for the fruitful leaves has been repeated 50,000 times since then, every book adding, like Wordsworth's own, to the sterile heap it claims to despise.

It is no exaggeration to say that the Lake District, because of all this, has become in a subtle but definite way an historical landscape as identifiable as the enclosure grid of the Midlands or the tiny Celtic fields of the West Country. These mountains have become a sump for romanticism, and that has shaped the landscape by ensuring, or at least trying to ensure, that nothing is done to 'spoil' it. This is landscaping by abstention. Of course the physical nature of the fells is highly suitable to the use we have put them to, but that is nothing more than the equivalent, say, of the fertility of the Leicestershire earth over which the enclosure grid was laid. Other things could have been done with the Lake District, but the whole push of at least one side of our civilisation now, enshrined in the 1949 National Parks and Access to the Countryside Act, is to preserve the aesthetic in nature. This is where romanticism has brought us. It is no longer revolutionary, but state policy. Ours is a naturally retrospective and conservative time, in which our vastly increased ability to strip the earth of its assets has made us aware – in a few highly selective areas – of the necessity of not doing so. The Lake District is one of them.

As you move off from Shap Abbey Bridge into a reputedly special landscape, you will be disappointed to find nothing odd about it at all. The path leads along the valley of the Lowther, over a pretty and narrow packhorse bridge across Swindale Beck, and then turns west at Rosgill Bridge towards the eastern end of Haweswater. But there is something different: looking up into Swindale (and this is exaggerated if a slight mist is hanging over it) there are verticals in the landscape, steep up and down edges which are not usual in England. Wordsworth was always a little peeved that his mountains were not the highest in Britain, but took comfort in the fact that they looked more like Switzerland than anywhere else.

The path comes to the bottom of Hawes-

*Stonethwaite Beck runs down through the fields of
Borrowdale, with the Derwent Fells beyond.*

Patterdale and the Helvellyn range beyond it.

water through an oakwood. For four miles you follow the northern shore of this reservoir, which is run by Manchester Corporation and supplies sixty million gallons a day to industrial Lancashire. The dam was built in 1919 and the water in what had been Mardale raised ninety-six feet. Lake-lovers were – and are – offended by what they see as a rape, and point to the stony shores of this and other lake-cum-reservoirs as symptomatic of the sterility the industrial intrusion has brought. Wastwater and Ennerdale Water are under the same threat, but there the intention is to raise the level by only a few feet. Recent schemes on Ullswater and Windermere have shown the subtlety with which modern waterworks can be built, but this has hardly quietened the complaints of the environmentalists. It is very typical that where reservoirs can be built with almost no complaint up in the Pennines, the attitude in Cumbria is that change is destruction.

The path through ferns along Haweswater is very good, crossing several becks falling steeply from your right. The best is the biggest, Measand Forces, where a large stream shatters itself on rocks, and is overspread by a thin veil of trees. This is a good combination – the heavily falling beneath the frailly held.

At the end of the lake you turn steeply up and in a two-mile climb through the rocky outcrops of Kidsty Howes – easily the steepest on the walk – you arrive at the top of Kidsty Pike, at 2,560 feet the highest point between Robin Hood's Bay and St Bee's. To the west you will look for Helvellyn and find it, but only in very clear air will Scafell Pike and Pillar stand out, fifteen and seventeen miles away respectively.

In the foreground is High Street, and you edge round Riggindale below to reach it. Incredibly there was a Roman road up here, not crossing from one valley to the next but keeping rigidly to the high ground on its way from Ambleside to the fort at Brougham. It was a considerable achievement to find as straight a line as they did through these mountains. Why not have kept to the valleys? The many Viking names in Cumbria ending in -thwaite, meaning clearing in the wood, show that even several centuries later the forest cover in the valleys was still thick. Perhaps it was safer for the Romans to run a road over the high fells.

From High Street quite a level but boggy path leads north-west for four miles past Angle Tarn to emerge at the pass called Boardale Hause above Patterdale. Especially if the walk up on Kidsty and High Street has been in fog, this can be a wonderful moment. The time to be there is when Patterdale is revealed through a luminous half-mist, no more than air made

visible, the kind of filtered sunlight you expect to find in Heaven. The tail of Ullswater you can see to the north, and to the south at the far end of Patterdale, the bright patch of Brothers Water. Between the two, digging deeply into the fells on the far side, are Deepdale, which rises quickly away, and Grisedale, the level floor of which is hardly visible at all. Like boats the cars move noiselessly on the road at the far side of the valley. The name Patterdale is a blurring of Patrick's Dale, which may record a Dublin Viking, or one of his descendents, who had taken an Irish name.

From Shap Abbey to Patterdale a high crossing had to be made over the High Street massif. On the next stage, to Grasmere, you can follow the well-worn route up Grisedale, and then over Grisedale Hause. This is an old road and although it reaches 1,929 feet at the top is a natural way through the mountains. Judging from Dorothy Wordsworth's Journal

do is take the most natural ways through it you can find, not go skipping off on to the nearest available summit. This may be an unnecessarily puritan view.

The Grisedale route is certainly straightforward enough. The track on the dale floor is plain and easy. After rain you can hear the heavy churning and clonking of the stones in the stream bed. The sharp white slash of the Nethermost Cove Beck coming down from Helvellyn is almost at the end of the dale on the right. The ground steepens and roughens, you pass a climbing hut, and in five miles from Patterdale reach Grisedale Tarn. Just below this grey lake is a place called Brothers' Parting. This is where in September 1800 William and Dorothy said goodbye to their brother John Wordsworth, who was going to join the ship of which he had just been made captain by the East India Company. This was not the last time they saw him – they all met in London in 1802 – but when Wordsworth heard of his brother's drowning off Portland Bill in February 1805 it was to this parting that his mind naturally turned. Some of the verses he wrote then have been carved – almost illegibly – on to the boulder here:

> Here did we stop; and here looked round
> While each into himself descends
> For that last thought of parting Friends
> That is not to be found.
>
> – Brother and friend, if verse of mine
> Have power to make thy virtues known,
> Here let a monumental stone
> Stand – sacred as a shrine.

Grasmere is just hidden from Grisedale Tarn, but once over the top of the hause the valley appears. It is about three and a half miles from the pass to the village, at first on a very rough track, which smooths out through National Trust land, and eventually emerges on to a proper road. Dove Cottage, the Wordsworths' home from 1799 to 1808, and de Quincey's for twenty-eight years after that, is beyond the village in a collection of houses almost on the lake edge. It is a very small, pale grey seventeenth-century cottage, a good place to live. The only jarring note is a small pair of scales with T. de Q. engraved on them. On these the opium eater weighed out his dosages. But the scales are from the later, more troubled years in Grasmere. One entry from Dorothy's Journal, written here, can encapsulate precisely the tone of Dove Cottage life in the happily productive years at the very beginning of the century. It comes in March 1802 when William was writing his most sublime poem, the 'Ode: Intimations of Immortality'. Dorothy simply enters: 'Saturday. A divine morning. At Breakfast Wm wrote part of an

Grasmere: 'the sun in heaven beheld not vales more beautiful than ours.'

this was a regular route in summer and, although dangerous in winter, still used. Her entry for 10 June 1802 is typical: 'Coleridge came in with a sack-full of books etc. and a branch of Mountain ash. He had been attacked by a cow. He came over by Grisedale. A furious wind.' Wainwright suggests you climb a mountain, Helvellyn or St Sunday Crag, on this section. By all means do, but one thing will suffer by it – the sense of crossing England. That idea will be looking quite fragile anyway by now. The Lake District is so much a thing of its own, that in it you seem to be wandering rather arbitrarily from one deep valley to the next. Cumbria, unlike the Pennines, is not a necessary obstacle. You could easily have gone south of it. The Lake District is an indulgence, and to counteract that feeling the only thing to ode. Mr Olliff sent the dung and Wm went to work in the garden. We sate all day in the orchard.'

Literary pilgrims of course crowd the cottage out, but it should also be a place of pilgrimage for walkers. Wordsworth, as de Quincey worked out, had walked 175,000 to 180,000 miles by the time he was thirty-five. On one occasion in 1799 he and Dorothy walked ten miles over a mountain road in two and a half hours, and then after quarter of an hour's rest in an inn, walked seven more in one hour thirty-five minutes. This is pretty heroic by any standards. What Wordsworth liked best was a public road at night:

A favourite pleasure hath it been with me
From time of earliest youth, to walk alone
Along the public way, when, for the night
Deserted, in its silence it assumes
A character of deeper quietness
Than pathless solitudes.

According to Hazlitt, he walked with 'a roll, a lounge in his gait'.

De Quincey, although no match for Wordsworth's athleticism, probably had the greater effect on the lives of subsequent walkers. We are all in his debt for the invention of backpacking. On a walking tour of Wales in 1802, when he was sixteen and playing truant from school, he found inns at 10/6 a night too expensive: 'I did for some weeks try the plan of carrying a canvas tent manufactured by myself, and not larger than an ordinary umbrella: but to pitch this securely I found difficult; and on windy nights it became a troublesome companion. As winter drew on, this bivouacking system became too dangerous to attempt. Still, one may bivouac decently, barring rain and wind, up to the end of October. And I counted, on the whole, that in a fortnight I spent nine nights abroad.' The one terror, and it has a familiar ring, was that cows would stand on his face during the night. How many of today's backpackers would guess that a drug-fiend was the father of them all?

From Grasmere to Rosthwaite in Borrowdale is nine miles, like the morning's walk from Patterdale, up a long valley to a pass and then down again to a dale and village. You leave

Sour Milk Gill in Easedale. The Wordsworths called this the Black Quarter.

Grasmere up Easedale, which the Words-worths called the Black Quarter. Helm Crag is a hunk of rock which stands at the mouth of the dale on its north side. You can climb it, if you want, and walk along the rim of the dale. Enormous areas of all this are owned by the National Trust. In the west the flash of Sour Milk Gill stands out from the darkness of the hills behind it. Easedale turns into Far Easedale. Rowan trees with bunches of red berries stand by the gill, harebells grow on islands in the middle of it, and in places on the damp ground you will find bog asphodel. The top of the dale is about four miles from Grasmere. To sit up there and look back down to the fields on the flat, which are an extraordinarily clear green, as if lit from inside, is one of the best experiences of a landscape in which high and austere country is so im-mediately available from the low and fertile. The Lake District is no Tibet, and the visual impression confirms the statistic that two-thirds of the National Park is below 1,000 feet.

The cutting sheds of the slate works occupy the top of the Honister Pass; no sense of intrusion or industrial rape.

You now cross the head of the Wyth Burn to Greenup Edge and there begin the slow descent to Borrowdale. This is lovely. In the glacier-scoured Greenup Dale are dumps of drumlins looking like the spooned-out help-ings they are. It is fast progress down past Lining Crag and along the swelling Greenup Gill. This is one of those places that make you marvel at the efficiency of natural water collection. An average of 1,700 million gallons of water pour off the Cumbrian mountains every day. As you enter more National Trust land the Langstrath Beck comes boiling in from the south-west. It is a gradual coast down the valley, now called Stonethwaite, through birch and rowan to Borrowdale. This pretty, flat, diamond-shaped dale is surrounded on all sides by high fells. Stonethwaite, Rosthwaite, Seatoller and Borrowdale itself all offer either Bed and Breakfast or places to camp.

At Borrowdale you feel almost inextricably stuck into the Lake District. Apart from the squeeze out northwards along the narrow ravine of the Derwent, you can only escape from Borrowdale by climbing. The Coast to Coast Walk goes west up the old toll road from Seatoller for a mile and a half to the top of the

Honister Pass. As you climb, Borrowdale is gradually hidden and yesterday's mountains gradually revealed. At the top are the cutting sheds of the famous slate quarries, which have hacked away at the crags round here. For once the stuff extracted seems worth the damage done. The rock already had a ravaged look about it, and the Honister slates are chips of a beautiful dark dull green.

The way beyond is up an incline to the quarries, and then steadily west, under Brandreth, and over an oddly un-Cumbrian landscape. Only in the distance are the expected sculptured mountains – the backsides of Great Gable, Kirk Fell and Pillar. In the foreground is a heathery and lumpy plateau of ice-mauled hills. It is not exactly a gentle landscape, it is just that the scale suddenly reduces. You come to a moment of decision. The obvious way to the sea – it is now only twenty miles walking away – is down the length of Ennerdale. The valley floor would be the quick way to get there, but for over four heavy miles in the dale it would be through Ennerdale Forest. This, unfortunately, is one of the classic early examples of the Forestry Commission's insensitive planting obliterating the character of a place. Instead, and this is a hard and difficult alternative, it is worth for once taking the high road, along the ridge that separates Buttermere from Ennerdale.

With this decision under your belt, it is exciting to make your way past Blackbeck Tarn, and another with no name, to the top of Haystacks, from where Ennerdale on one side, with the crags of Pillar beyond it, and Buttermere on the other, make you feel if not exactly on top of the world, at least within sight of it. One thing is new. For the first time no high ground closes the view westwards. These dales lead out of the mountains. If the day is clear you will see the sea.

A steep drop of over 450 feet to Scarth Gap is followed by a climb of nearly nine hundred feet, with bilberries en route, but once you are up you are up and a level two miles brings you via High Stile to Red Pike. Here you turn down to the valley of the Liza. It is absolutely crucial to make sure you are on Red Pike before you turn down. In mist it is extremely difficult to know just where you are on a ridge which is the same for its whole length. If you miss the right path you are in for a murderously slow, difficult and possibly dangerous descent over very rough ground, heavy boulder scree and eventually through back-breaking, prickly forest. After reaching the bottom at last, and the velvet luxury of a Forestry Commission Road, it is a five-mile tramp along either shore of the blustery grey Ennerdale Water to the village of Ennerdale Bridge, where there is a pub and a hotel.

Here the contours on the map, from being darkly concentrated since Shap, start to pool out towards the coast. The volcanic lavas and granites of the mountains are replaced by the newer and softer red sandstone, and then by the coal measures. The illusion at Ennerdale Bridge is that the walking is really over, and that all you have to do is relax and let the current waft you to St Bee's.

Not quite. You do not even leave the Lake District National Park at Ennerdale Bridge, and the lane you take from it, although lined with willowherb, ragwort and meadowsweet (with orchids here too) soon crosses again over open grassy fell. The Kinniside Stone Circle is here, a modern fake, but looking just as good as the real ones. Beyond it is Dent, a hill 1,131 feet high, which on a good day gives the last long look back at the Cumbrian mountains and the first proper sight looking forward of the sea. If the day is bad you will want to miss the hill, or at least climb only its shoulder. What you see below, although only the occasional chimney reveals it, is a deeply depressed ex-mining district. The long single street, facing the hill, of Cleator Moor, painted in exaggeratedly gay stripes, shows the kind of desperate effort being made to remedy some of the permanent psychological effects of economic depression. These are mining villages, mostly built from the new red sandstone, and now that the mines are closed almost without a reason for existence. The mills on the Ehen provide employment for some. From Dent you descend to Cleator. (Go by the farm called Row, made from large blocks of sandstone, with an enormous barn attached to the farmhouse, its walls leaning well out of true.) In Cleator almost all the sandstone is covered in roughcast or colourwash. A lane leads to Moor Row, another of these villages, in which a church has been converted to a garage. Only half a mile beyond it, after crossing a railway and the Whitehaven-Egremont road, you get the first sight, down the wide valley of the Pow Beck, of the tower of St Bee's Priory outlined against the sea. As the crow flies it is only two miles, but on the Coast to Coast path it is still about seven. The temptation may be enormous, but it is worth following the way round. You pass a series of substantial farms – Stanley, Bell House, Demesne – this last with paved courtyards and a line of water-troughs carved from single blocks of stone. The tubes and chimneys of the Marchon factory, the pride of West Cumbria, appear in front. On the basis of a mineral called anhydrite, sulphuric acid, cement, detergents and phosphates are produced here. The outer edge of Whitehaven spreads up from the sea shore.

You may be feeling impatient now. The pretty village of Sandwith will get short shrift

LEFT *Buttermere and Crummock Water from Honister Crag. The valley has been deepened and rounded by a glacier, gouging deep into slates which are softer than the volcanic rocks of the crag from which the photograph is taken. The two lakes were at one time joined, and soon, in geological terms, the valley will dry out entirely.*

BELOW *The last of the lakes: Ennerdale Water, with Pillar at the head of it.*

What seems to be the stub of England at St Bee's Head.

The west door of St Bee's Priory, built in the twelfth century from the same red sandstone of which St Bee's Head is made. The twisted decoration of the capitals shows Viking influence.

as you hurry coastwards. Of course the land makes no preparation for the sea. Its gentle agricultural rhythms ease up to the coast.

Then you arrive. The air is heavy with the smell of guano. It is still four miles to St Bee's, round the headland that Norman Nicholson has described, in prose as gritty as its subject, as 'a huge hull of rock, blunt-edged, rough as emery paper, shoving its rusty steel-plating straight into the sea'. You pass a lighthouse and on a path fringed with thrift make your way southwards above the 10,000 cormorants, fulmars, razorbills, guillemots, puffins, kitti-wakes and other gulls that all breed here. The towers of Calder Hall and Windscale come into view.

Where to end? With your feet in the sea is a possibility, but better is the west door of St Bee's Priory. This, the last, is one of the best man-made things on the Coast to Coast walk – a great, deeply-notched Norman arch in the red sandstone, blurred by the sea air, as if heavily scrubbed over centuries. Behind you as you look at it is the 'dragon stone', a door lintel of unknown age, with a sea monster and its looping tail carved on it. Surely this is a Viking

object? If you have been thinking of this walk as a Viking way then here is a reminder that this is the place to take ship for Dublin.

———

Buttermere. For the adventurous the Coast to Coast Walk can follow the horizon in the background, climbing High Crag and then keeping to the ridge between Buttermere and Ennerdale.

MAPS: OS 1:50,000 Numbers 89, 90, 91, 92, 93, 94, 98, 99

GUIDES:

A. Wainwright, *A Coast to Coast Walk*, Westmorland Gazette 1973

HMSO *Guides* to North York Moors, Yorkshire Dales, Lake District National Parks

BACKGROUND:

A. L. Binns, *The Viking Century in East Yorkshire*, E. Yorks Local History Soc. 1963

Hunter Davies, *A Walk around the Lakes*, Weidenfeld and Nicolson 1979

S. R. Eyre and J. Palmer, *The Face of North-East Yorkshire*, Dalesman 1973

C. J. Hunt, *The Lead Miners of the Northern Pennines*, Manchester University 1970

H. R. Loyn, *The Vikings in Britain*, Batsford 1977

Norman Nicholson, *Portrait of the Lakes*, Robert Hale 1963

Dorothy Wordsworth, *Journals*, edited by Mary Moorman, OUP 1971

Offa's Dyke Path

Prestatyn to Sedbury Cliff, Chepstow 176 miles

The Welsh Marches

The modern boundary between England and Wales does not drive a straight line from the mouth of the Dee to the mouth of the Severn. It meanders backwards and forwards in an attempt to reflect the geographical facts. A single line cannot properly define this frontier. Wales spreads its fingers of upland into the English plain and England in return pushes its valleys between the Welsh hills. Even where a wall of Wales seems to rise up, as in the Clwydian Hills and the Black Mountains, tucked in behind it are fertile valleys which reverse the expected relation of highland and lowland. The country through which the Offa's Dyke Path moves is in this way a borderland, a wide margin of geographical mixture.

There is a strange contradiction about this country. Everywhere – in the earthworks, the strings of castles, Offa's Dyke itself – there is evidence that this has been and is naturally a frontier zone; the remains of history tell you that you are walking down the hazy edge between two things in conflict. But the country itself has another quite different look to it. Here is agriculture and settlement, quiet and certainty. This is not an edge, but the heart of things. History's detritus is only a tide-mark, made irrelevant in 1282 when Edward I conquered Wales.

The Romans

Despite the presence of many Iron Age hillforts in the Marches, the history of the area as a border region properly begins only with the Romans. Although they were in Wales by as early as AD 79, it never became more than a military area. There are almost no Roman villas in Wales and the edge of Romanisation was along the Welsh borders, which were the real frontier. A band of roads and forts ran up from the legionary fortress at Isca (Caerleon) to that of Deva (Chester) in the north. This provided a broad base from which Wales could be policed.

Isca was partially abandoned at the beginning of the fourth century AD to provide garrisons for the new Forts of the Saxon Shore. A century later the Romans had left Britain entirely. The interval between their

The mattressy softness of a valley in the Black Mountains.

209

departure and the arrival of the English on the borders of Wales saw a flowering of Celtic culture in poetry and the decorative arts, which was accompanied by a growth in the strength and influence of the Celtic church. This Age of the Saints was brought to a symbolic end when in 615 twelve hundred monks were slaughtered at Chester by Aethelfrith of Northumbria.

Aethelfrith's arrival at Chester drove a wedge between the Britons of Cumbria and of Wales. His victory marks the beginning of a clearly defined Welsh nation. Northumbria had gained the leadership of the English, but the two great kingdoms of Mercia and Wessex stayed independent of its power. By the middle of the seventh century Mercia was on the ascendant, if only temporarily. By pushing his frontiers as far west as Oswestry, Penda, the first great king of Mercia, prepared the way for Offa, who, over a century after his death in 654, was to preside over the period of Mercia's greatness.

Offa

When Offa won the throne after a short civil war in 757, his work on Mercia's western border had been done for him. At Oswestry Penda had come to a natural frontier, the beginning of the Welsh hills. To the south and east, however, the midland kingdom of Mercia, based on the Lichfield–Tamworth area, had only arbitrary frontiers. The entire direction of Offa's reign was to make his kingdom on these sides more secure, in effect by extending his powers to the sea. The smaller kingdoms of East Anglia, Kent, Sussex, Essex and the Hwicce, at the mouth of the Severn, were all absorbed, more or less violently, into Mercia during his reign. Only Wessex and Northumbria remained independent. With such a coherent state at his back, Offa, newly styled *rex Anglorum*, could turn to Europe and negotiate on near-equal terms with both the Pope and the Emperor Charlemagne.

In this light Offa's Welsh problem takes on the appearance of a nuisance at his back door, and the Dyke an attempt to deal with it once and for all. The decision to build the Dyke may have been forced on him. English place-names west of it indicate that the Mercians had to withdraw in several areas. Near Llangollen stands the Pillar of Eliseg, a monument to Elise, the Prince of Powys contemporary with Offa. It may record the reasons which forced the Mercian retreat. 'It was Elise', the Pillar says, 'who united the inheritance of Powys, laid waste for nine years, from the hand of the English with fire and sword.' The building of Offa's Dyke, then, did not mark the high tide of victory, but may have followed defeat and perhaps humiliation.

If these were the circumstances of the construction of the Dyke, probably in the 780s, it is indicative of how adept a propagandist Offa was. For the Dyke, which must represent an end to ambition, a forced admittance of completion, has nothing of defeat about it. It is a great public statement of Offa's power. The idea of the Dyke, in Bishop Asser's phrase, was to draw a line *'de mari usque ad mari'*, 'from the sea right to the sea'. Nowhere is this idea clearer than where the Dyke crosses the central uplands of Clun Forest. Here all the rhythms of the land move from west to east, making the Dyke successively climb to the heights of the ridges and dip to the valleys between. Stand in the valley of the Unk or the Clun, the Teme or the Lugg. From the valley floor on either side the bank and ditch rise to the horizon in strong, lithe, easy strides. The Dyke's course is sensitive to the shape of the land, but not dictated by it. Here what the archaeologist Sir Cyril Fox called the 'intellectual quality' of the Dyke (a phrase almost unintelligible when not in its presence) is made obvious. In these valleys the Dyke becomes a work of art, beautiful for the strange reason that it disappears over two horizons in strength.

Offa intended his Dyke to have this effect. He was named after a previous Offa, his ancestor twelve generations earlier, king in Schleswig. In the poem *Widsith*, contemporary with our Offa, the heroic life of his semi-mythical ancestor is celebrated. One of the greatest of his acts was to draw the boundary between the Angles and the Swaefe, another German people, a boundary which following generations kept to *'swa hit Offa geslog'* – 'as Offa struck it out'. Our Dyke can be seen as a perfectly conscious re-enactment of this event in heroic poetry.

The course of the Dyke was probably from Prestatyn on the north Welsh coast, south through Ruabon to Chirk, and across Clun Forest to above Kington, where it turns west and makes for the Wye at Bridge Sollers. There is little evidence of the Dyke after Kington until it emerges at Redbrook on the Lower Wye, from where it is almost continuous to the Severn at Sedbury Cliff. The large gap in Herefordshire coincides with an outcrop of the fertile Old Red Sandstone. Sir Cyril Fox, in his great *Survey* of the Dyke (1955), produced evidence to show that this area was covered in thick forest in the eighth century. As this was impenetrable, an artificial frontier would have been both impossible and unecessary here. The Wye itself was the boundary.

No records remain of the construction but the Dyke is its own document. There were two stages: first, the choice and laying out of the alignment; and, second, the actual digging. The consistency of the skill in the alignment

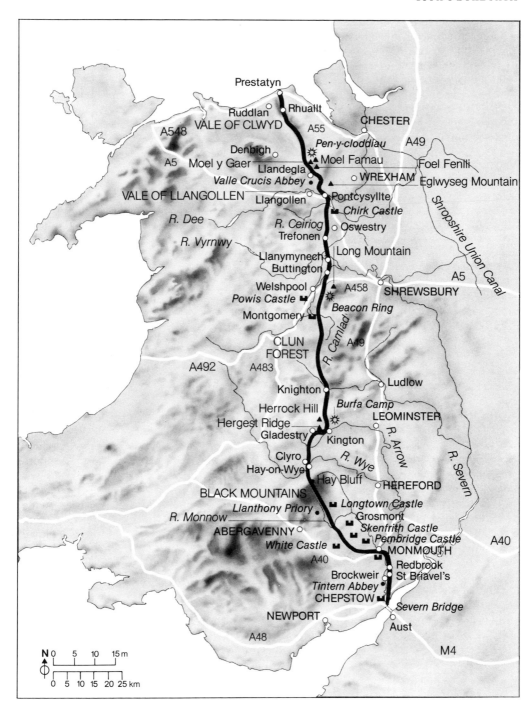

shows that the whole work was laid out by a central controlling intelligence – the royal engineers. Their skill was incredible. The natural slope of the country is to the east, but almost without exception the Dyke is aligned to command a view westwards. In the few places where this is not the case the west flank of the hill is so broken that the work needed to take the Dyke in and out of the side valleys would not have been justified by the benefit gained. On a map its line can look obvious, but the Mercian engineers probably had no maps, and that apparent obviousness is precisely their achievement.

The responsibility for the digging was delegated to the local thane, with, apparently, very little supervision. In almost every way the profile and actual construction of the Dyke vary. The standard is of a bank, with a ditch to the west, but it is sometimes to the east and sometimes not a proper ditch at all, but a series of disconnected spoil holes. On very steep slopes the bank itself disappears, the only mark being a slight shelf in the hillside. The Dyke is at its greatest at the heads of valleys and over ancient ridgeways, where the drop from the crown of the bank to the bottom of the ditch can be up to thirty feet. It is strange that a work on whose planning so much care was spent should be – in places – so carelessly executed. It may indicate an unexpected pressure of time, or perhaps an unwillingness to co-operate on the part of the local thanes in what they saw as their king's *folie de grandeur*.

How was it used? Its failure to make use of obvious tactical strongpoints rules out a primarily military use. From the scarcity of original crossing points, although it is of course difficult to decide how original a hole in a bank is, Fox concluded that the Dyke's purpose, similar to the Vallum behind Hadrian's Wall, was to control civilian traffic between Mercia and the Welsh kingdoms. It may be that both Offa and the Welsh realised that benefit would derive from such a plain demarcation of their respective powers. Perhaps in Offa's Dyke we have evidence of the first treaty to limit military ambition by mutual agreement.

It did not work. Neither the Romans, nor the earlier Mercians, nor the Normans attempted to define their Welsh border by a single line. Offa alone did so. The Short Dykes built by the Mercians during the century before Offa, in a wide band either side of Offa's line, deal more adequately with the demands made by broken country. Far less grand in conception, they plug holes. It is understandable that the first man to call himself *rex Anglorum* would want to do more than this. But the heroic gesture of the continuous earthwork was not good enough. Offa had based Mercia's power exclusively on his own strength – it was Offa's, not Mercia's, Dyke – and had not dealt diplomatically with the smaller English kingdoms. All Mercia's frontiers were vulnerable when Offa died in 796, and Alcuin, the great Northumbrian scholar, found the death of Ecgferth, Offa's son, five months later, an opportunity to moralise on the weakness that had lain behind Mercia's apparent strength: 'You know how much blood his father shed in order to establish the kingdom for his son, and this has been its destruction, not its establishment.' From now on no king of Mercia claimed to be king of the English. Coenwulf, Ecgferth's successor, was forced to campaign in North Wales to protect his western flank. The prestigious archbishopric at Lichfield, the Mercian capital, was abolished. English unity was not achieved under any Mercian, but under Egbert of Wessex. The end of the great midland kingdom came at its defeat by Wessex at the Battle of Ellendun in 825.

The Path

Offa's Dyke Path was opened in 1971. It does not always follow the line of the Dyke. Both begin at Prestatyn on the north Welsh coast, but from there the Dyke's course is through the industrial areas of Mold and Ruabon. The Path instead takes a route along the Clwydian Hills, a little to the west, as far as Llangollen on the Dee, thirty-seven miles from Prestatyn. South of the river the Path joins the Dyke over the low eastern edge of the Berwyn Hills, coming down at Llanymynech to the Vale of Montgomery, which it then crosses, only making a detour up on to the slopes of the Long Mountain, to arrive at Montgomery, forty-two miles walking from Llangollen. From here the best part of the walk begins over the bare central uplands of Clun Forest, where the remains of the Dyke are at their greatest. At Kington the Path leaves the Dyke again, crossing over to Hay-on-Wye, forty-five miles from Montgomery. On the far side of the Wye the route is up along the edge of the Black Mountains to Pandy, and then across to the valley of the Trothy into Monmouth. There is an alternative to this section, further east,

which follows a line of border castles. From Monmouth the way is down the Wye gorge, on the edge of which the Dyke reappears, both Path and Dyke ending at Sedbury Cliff on the Severn near Chepstow, fifty-two miles from Hay, and about 180 from Prestatyn.

Prestatyn to Llangollen 37 miles

Come To Sunny Prestatyn
Laughed the girl on the poster,
Kneeling up on the sand
In tautened white satin.
Behind her, a hunk of coast, a
Hotel with palms
Seemed to expand from her thighs and
Spread breast-lifting arms.

Prestatyn is just like its poster, an ordinary, sunny holiday place. The path climbs away

from it, up the High Street which soon turns into a suburban lane, possibly on the line of Offa's Dyke as it completed its course from Sedbury Cliff. If there was ever any evidence of the Dyke here, it has been obliterated now. The nearest indications are on Gop Hill to the south; but it is east of the path. The two short stretches of the Dyke there point in this direction; more than that it is impossible to say. Offa died in battle in 796 at Rhuddlan, three miles to the west. It is possible that he was fighting to establish the security in which his grand scheme could be completed.

The Path immediately climbs on to the western edge of the Clwyd hills. This will be the shape of things until the end of the range is reached and the Path descends to Llandegla, twenty-eight miles away. The Clwydian range is steeply scarped on the west, with many small side-valleys cutting back into the main edge; it is an easy agricultural landscape, with few proper villages, but quite a thick scatter of separate farms. For the next twenty-five miles the wide Vale of Clwyd, spotty with towns and spires, is the foreground of the view, on whose far edge are the mountains of Snowdonia. Defoe, arriving in this broad valley from the uncongenial wilderness of central Wales, described it as 'a most pleasant, fruitful, populous and delicious Vale, full of towns, the fields shining with corn, just ready for the reapers, green and flowery'. George Borrow learnt that cheese made here fetched a penny a pound more than cheese made in any other Welsh valley.

Throughout the length of the walk, especially when on the Dyke itself, the long view will be into the middle of Wales. This view westwards, of strategic importance for the Dyke builders, is for the walker a source of continual pleasure. For the men who farm here it seems to be rather irrelevant, since continually on this western side of the Clwyds you find farmhouses turned away from the valley, with their noses pushed right up against the hill.

Few have been as sensitive to landscape as Gerard Manley Hopkins, who when training to be a Jesuit priest lived at St Beuno's College, on the path just south of Rhuallt about four miles from Prestatyn. Here, after a break of seven years, he began to write poetry again, inspired at first by the death of some German nuns in the wreck of the *Deutschland*, and later by the 'pastoral forehead of Wales' itself on which St Beuno's rests. For him only one thing

Looking south along the Dyke at Carreg-y-Beg near Oswestry, with the ditch on the Welsh side and the bank on the English. The idea of the Dyke is more impressive than the object itself.

prevented this place from being God's perfect
creation – the Welsh:

> Lovely the woods, waters, meadows,
>   combes, vales
> All the air things wear that build this world
>   of Wales;
>   Only the inmate does not correspond.

From St Beuno's it is three easy miles, via
Sodom, to Bodfari in the valley of the Wheeler.
Here the high Clwyds begin. No flat top is
reached as in downland, but exhausting climbs
are followed by equally steep descents. The
hills are not enormously high, but they feel like
mountains. Each bump – called *moel* in Welsh –
is ringed by an Iron Age hill-fort. There are six
of them here in a line running south. This co-
ordination between hill-forts is rare. Usually
they were built without considering their
relationship to one another. This overall
control, together with the many-ditched
sophistication of their design, probably means
that they were built late in the Iron Age and all
at the same time. Only a major threat would
make such a vast building programme necessary. It may be that these Clwydian forts are the
defence line made by the British Deceangli
against the Roman invasion of Wales.

South of Moel Famau, large stretches of this
high wide walking are now under convenant
to the National Trust. It had in places already
been deformed by commercial forest, creeping
to the outer ditch of Pen-y-Cloddiau, the
largest of the forts, but where they are open
these hills stay covered in bracken and
bilberry, above which fly buzzards and
curlews. From the last fort of Foel Fenlli, it is
five miles before the path drops to the
meandering Alyn, whose valley it follows into
Llandegla.

Llandegla is separated from Llangollen by a
block of moorland, over which there are two
possible paths. One rather drearily plods
through a young forestry plantation to emerge
at the appropriately named World's End. It
then follows a road into the head of Llangollen
Vale, skirting the rocky frills which form the
great geological fault of Eglwyseg Mountain.

The other way, unsignposted but better,
follows field paths up a small tributary of the
Alyn – crammed in summer with flag irises –
and crosses over the moor to the head of the
Eglwyseg river. The next mile or two are
wonderful. Wooded valleys cut deep between
sheep-cropped hills, while, behind, layer on
layer of the Eglwyseg rocks look like giant
mille-feuilles. The main route can be joined
again here, or if you want to make a diversion

*The limestone frill of Eglwyseg Mountain dominates a
valley north of Llangollen. For travellers coming from
England this was the first taste of Wild Wales.*

you can follow the path down the river to the Pillar of Eliseg and Valle Crucis Abbey.

The Pillar is an ugly stunted stump, and even its famous inscription, about the defeat of the English, is all but illegible. It is a wreck of a monument and fails miserably where Offa's Dyke succeeds in triumph – to record the greatness of its builder. Two hundred yards away is the Abbey. The mainly thirteenth-century church is in great ruin, but the fascination of Valle Crucis is the evidence it still provides of the moral decline of its abbots in the fifteenth century. What had previously been a communal dormitory was at that time partitioned off to provide the abbot with a luxurious private suite, with large new fireplaces, elaborate carvings and every convenience provided. All this is still standing next to the dark, cool and inordinately large abbey fishpond.

It is a mile to Llangollen, a tourist town since the end of the eighteenth century, and a product of the picturesque boom. All the necessary ingredients are here – the abbey, the turbulent Dee, the ruined castle of Dinas Bran, the vale and the awe-inspiring Eglwyseg rocks. It seems to typify Wild Wales.

Two extra things increased the number of people coming here – Telford's Holyhead Road, and the growing fame of the Ladies of Llangollen. These two aristocratic intellectuals had eloped from Ireland in 1779 to live in Plas Newydd, their increasingly exaggerated Gothick cottage, until they died within

Valle Crucis Abbey, near Llangollen, and its fishpond, a vital source of food for the monastic diet.

eighteen months of each other fifty years later. Their way of life – 'very clever, very odd' a friend called it – attracted controversy and famous visitors. Passionate admirers of Rousseau, they lived out for the rest of the world the romantic ideal of friendship in a secluded vale. George Borrow thought Plas Newydd 'a small, gloomy mansion', but it still has the attraction and strangeness of being the complete realisation of the literary idea to which the Ladies devoted their lives.

Llangollen to Montgomery 42 miles

From Llangollen the official path goes high along the north side of the Dee valley. A shadier alternative is the towpath of Telford's canal which contours for four miles at a lower level. It brings the water of the Eglwyseg river to feed the main Shropshire Union Canal to the east, and a very slight current can be discerned flowing in that direction. It seems extraordinary that the extravagant engineering feats necessary to build this canal were justified by the small hydraulic or commercial benefits it produced. For at Pontcysyllte, four miles from Llangollen, the most spectacular work of the Canal Age bursts from the hillside directly across the valley of the Dee. Telford carried this mere water-feeder a thousand feet in an iron trough 126 feet above the river. Even at the moment of its completion in 1805 it was known that the canal could never be a commercial success. In the last decade it has become one for the first time, with the hired pleasure boats that now throng it nose to tail.

A mile the other side of the Dee comes the excitement of joining Offa's Dyke for the first time. It is a strong tree-crowned bank with a west-ditch. After three miles beside it you come to Chirk Castle (NT), which is precisely on the line of Offa's frontier. Chirk was first built as an Edwardian fortress in 1310 after the defeat of Llewellyn, the last Welsh Prince of Wales. Its bulky outside preserves that image, but inside every century from the sixteenth to the nineteenth has converted a wing or tower to its particular style. This can lead to contradictions. Carved from the solid middle of the medieval bastion on the north front is a staircase and next to it a dining-room both in the palest of Adam colours, decorated with the most intricate of gilt cornices and pilasters.

South of Chirk the Path descends into the deep valley of the Ceiriog which the castle was built to command, and for the next seven miles crosses a series of ridges separated by streams.

Telford's canal viaduct over the Dee at Pontcysyllte. The Ladies of Llangollen floated over it with 'a complete sense of security' at its triumphal opening in 1805.

On the Shropshire Union Canal high above the Valley of the Dee between Llangollen and Pontcysyllte.

RIGHT *The view north from the edge of the Black Mountains over the valley of the Wye.*

BELOW *Islands of flowers on the Wye near Hay.*

LEFT *The moorland comes down to the fields around Llanthony Priory in the Black Mountains, the favourite place of Gerald of Wales. 'Woe unto them,' he warned, quoting Isaiah, 'that join house to house, that lay field to field, till there be no place, that they may be placed alone in the midst of the earth.'*

BELOW *White Castle near Monmouth: originally it was coated in whitewash.*

Without hesitation the Dyke moves directly across the grain of the country, even where this means a loss of view to the west. It makes for steep walking, but the land is so well arranged that at exactly the right intervals the path reaches the next refreshing valley and its stream. The loveliest of all these small valleys is made by the River Morda, just north of Trefonen, which strangely has a lorry park in it.

From Trefonen the Dyke moves directly south, while the path curls to the west, to join it again at Llanymynech, where the Dyke makes use of the ramparts of an Iron Age fort on the heavily quarried hill, first worked by the Romans for its copper. The border between England and Wales runs down Llanymynech's main street. The sign at the cross-roads says it all. To the left, into England, it points to Knockin, to the right to Llansantffraid-ym-Mechain.

Llanymynech is on the Vyrnwy, which soon

Morning light catches the great bastions of Chirk Castle, built by Edward I to control the northern Marches.

runs into the Severn. Offa's engineers used the river as the frontier at this point, and the Dyke disappears for nine miles until it surfaces again on the far bank of the Severn at Buttington. The walk there is partly along roads, and partly beside an ugly, muddy river. It is a good opportunity to take the bus into Welshpool.

This brick town has kept its importance as a market (on Mondays), mainly for sheep and cattle, and consequently has none of the preciousness of those towns in the Marches whose economic function has fallen away. The park gates of Powis Castle, owned by the National Trust, are almost in the High Street of Welshpool itself, but this closeness of the mercantile and the aristocratic is more apparent than real. The tree-clumped park is the castle's buffer against the town, while in both fabric and association Powis, more than Chirk, has a grandeur that sets it apart. It has been continuously inhabited for seven centuries, each age moulding, adapting and, for the most part, enriching its inheritance from the past. The first stone castle was built here by the Princes of Powys, allies of the English crown, after Edward I's invasion of Wales. In the fourteenth century were added the great red

drums which guard the door to the Inner Bailey. Today the site and these towers are the only reminders that this was once a military stronghold. The slope down to the east, once the castle's protection, was smoothed in the early eighteenth century into four long terraces, decorated with lead shepherdesses and hung with bulbous yews. Inside not a hint of the castle remains. All is richer than at Chirk. The sixteenth-century Long Gallery, the Restoration State Bedroom, the staircase of a few decades later and the Blue Drawing Room of the early eighteenth century all exude an opulence which comes as a shock in this border country. A marriage into the family of Clive of India in 1784 further enriched the castle with furniture and paintings, bringing the most beautiful things there – the two Romneys in the Dining Room of Lord Clive's daughters.

Offa's Dyke Path climbs the other side of the valley from the ancient ford at Buttington to Beacon Ring, an Iron Age fort on the top of Long Mountain. Here enormous views stretch across the Severn valley into Wales and, for once, into England, over the Shropshire plain and to the Wrekin. The view makes it quite clear why the Welsh for Shropshire is Trees.

The Dyke itself keeps lower over the northern slopes of the hill, but in what is now the Leighton estate climbs higher than is necessary for the tactical westward view. Sir Cyril Fox performed here one of his most fascinating pieces of speculative archaeology. Overall the Dyke is laid out in straight alignments, but in detail it varies between an absolutely straight and a sinuous line. On the southern slopes of Long Mountain there is a particularly long section of entirely straight bank. Fox proved by excavation that the Dyke was not, as was previously thought, built on a Roman road; the straightness originated with the Dyke builders. He then examined the occurrence of straight and sinuous stretches in this part of Montgomeryshire. In what was or had been ancient forest the Dyke wove from side to side. Conversely, straight stretches identified what had been arable land in the late eighth century. The fertile lower slopes of Long Mountain, above which the Dyke is built and over which

The outer skeleton remains of the military castle at Powis, but internally it carries the improvements of centuries.

Monmouth from the Kymin and, beyond,
the mountains of Wales.

it finally descends to Forden, must have been such an arable area. The Dyke's alignment leaves this valuable land to the Welsh. Fox concluded that this represented part of Mercia's compromise with the Princes of Powys, the site of whose headquarters at Powis Castle can be seen quite clearly across the Severn. From the exact characteristics of an earthwork Fox was able to make a very detailed estimate of the political and economic circumstances of eleven centuries before.

From the bottom of Long Mountain the Dyke crosses the Camlad, making for the high ground of Clun Forest four miles away. On a high spur to the west are the ruins of Montgomery Castle, guarding the three corridors made into Wales by the Camlad, the Severn and the Rea Brook, which spread out from it in a wide crow's foot to the east. An Iron Age fort, a Roman camp and a Norman motte-and-bailey here all point to the permanent importance of the site. The earlier castle was abandoned in 1223 when Henry III, in reaction to the threat from Llewellyn the Great, began to build the present fortress. By the end of the decade both castle and the seeds of a market-town were established. With the Edwardian conquest of Wales the castle became insignificant and sank into ruin. The Herberts revived it in the sixteenth century, making of Montgomery a centre of aristocratic culture. Donne came here, and George Herbert was born in the castle in 1593. His brother, Lord Herbert of Chirbury, retired here from public life to write one of the first English autobiographies. After the Civil War the castle was 'slighted' and the house made uninhabitable. The Herberts moved away.

The great civic age of Montgomery was yet to come. The sheep-based prosperity which came about in the century after 1750 allowed many of the houses to be refronted. The characteristic air of the town is of this period. Its tiny urban centre feels like a kind of Ruritania in Wales. The real business of the region has moved to Welshpool, but this self-possessed borough seems unaware of that. It is slightly and charmingly ludicrous that Montgomery still has a Mayor and Corporation.

Montgomery to Hay-on-Wye
45 miles

Across the plain in the loop of the Camlad the Dyke slices with military directness. At its far edge, what Fox rather flatteringly called 'The Mountain Zone' begins. In this central section of upland the Dyke is at its clearest in profile and at its most complete. The path scarcely leaves the travelling earthwork for twenty-five miles until, on Rushock Hill above Kington,

Offa's engineers turned east to the Herefordshire plain.

There is a strategic reason why the Dyke is on such a scale here: the Mercian capital at Tamworth lay immediately to the east, towards which the upland ridgeways provided an easy invasion route for the Welsh. It is a marvellous chance that where the Dyke was originally built at its biggest it has most resisted the destructive effects of time and the intrusions of agriculture. As you walk from valley to valley you will have before you Offa's conception at its grandest.

At the top of the long climb from the plain

the Dyke crosses a metalled road on the line of the Kerry Hill Ridgeway. The county boundary between Powys and Shropshire follows this lane for miles, but at the Dyke the boundary is deflected a few yards to the south, through a hole which by its finished appearance and narrowness Fox concluded was original. This means that the ridgeway itself was originally deflected through the gap, only much later reverting to its straight course by cutting another hole through the Dyke. The deflection of the ridgeway is evidence of the psychology of the Dyke-builders. The Kerry Hill Ridgeway is undatably old. What could be more impressive to a Welshman, and what more epitomises the idea of the Dyke as a whole, than bending this ancient road so obviously out of its way? The diversion was in terms of yards, but yards make the point.

Looking north from Hergest Ridge into what used to be Radnorshire. The low land beyond the hills in the foreground was once occupied by the Mercians, but by the time the Dyke was built Welsh pressure had forced them to withdraw eastwards. The modern boundary between England and Wales runs just below the tree in the foreground.

Now follows a switchback course more exhausting than anything since the Clwyds, but the confidence of each plunge into successive valleys makes this the most exhilarating of rides. The completeness of the Dyke makes this sector rich in revealing features. On Hergan Hill, two miles from the Kerry Hill Ridgeway, and just north of Newcastle in the valley of the Clun, the work of two gangs building the Dyke meet in an awkward corner. The gang working north was building a massive bank and ditch, which had an additional bank on its western lip. Those working south were building on a far less monumental scale, but were keeping to an almost directly straight line, not deviating more than twenty yards from their exact course in the 900 yards before the slight dip in which the Hergan corner lies. At the col the junction of the two gangs is far from smooth. Those working from the south were forced to turn their bank in a sharp right angle to provide a point at which those working from the north could aim. The boundary is complete, but the lack of fluency in its line shows little planning or co-ordination.

The seven miles between Newcastle and Knighton on the Teme are as empty as any on the path. All you will find is Kerry Hill sheep cropping beside rusty ploughs. At 1408 feet Llanvair Hill is the highest point the Dyke reaches, and both along the earthwork and into Wales the views are long and wide.

Knighton has a hardness for which the last twenty miles cannot have prepared you. Although it is on the modern border with Wales, it is an almost aggressively English town. This movement from one cultural atmosphere to another is the inevitable result of tracing any single line down the Welsh Marches. The town is the centre of the Offa's Dyke Association, only due to the energy of whose members the path exists at all. They have set up an Information Centre for the Dyke and the Marches in an old school here.

South of Knighton Offa's Dyke represents a Mercian withdrawal. Evenjobb, Kinnerton, Walton and Harpton, places with very English names, are all west of the Dyke. The farms here wear a near industrial style. There is no hint of any self-conscious agrarian charm, except perhaps in the beautifully restored cottages, for example in the valley above Evenjobb, which are mostly English holiday homes.

After crossing Riddings Brook below the Iron Age Burfa Camp, the path climbs steeply to a saddle between Herrock and Rushock Hills. This is the last high ground the Dyke takes, and although the path does not follow the Dyke round Herrock Hill, you *can* climb to the top of the hill, from where the view is everywhere over the Vale of Radnor to the

west, while northwards the Dyke's course is clear even as far as Llanvair Hill twelve miles away. To the south Hergest Ridge and beyond it the Black Mountains close the view. The western horizon is formed by the mountains of Wales. The wind-hooked tree on this hill-top will itself be a landmark when the path to the south is taken.

From the saddle the Dyke turns on to Rushock Hill, where it takes an odd course. It passes directly through the highest point, but only by making a sharp detour from its line further down the slope, which has more visual control of enemy territory than a crest line would. Fox explained this by suggesting that the summit was one of a series of points through which it was agreed the Dyke should run. The English fulfilled the letter of their agreement, but no more than that. From here the walk down into Kington is over Bradnor Hill, owned by the National Trust, and invaded by golfers.

The town of Kington moved to where it now is in the thirteenth century. The older town, probably founded by Harold of Wessex, and named by him after Edward the Confessor, was further to the west along the valley of the Arrow, gathered round the church below Hergest Ridge. Consistently strange associations attach to the ridge and to the buildings at its feet. In Hergest Court lived Thomas (Black) Vaughan, a fifteenth century landowner, whose ghost could only be laid by enticing it into a silver snuff box, which was thrown, at the ghost's request, into Hergest Pool. His house had been the centre of Welsh culture throughout the fifteenth century. Here were preserved the *Red and White Books of Hergest*, semi-magical tales of Welsh heroes and a jumble of gnomic sayings in the form of Triads, such as:

Three things that enrich the poet:
Myths, poetic power and a store of ancient verse.

Only the *Red Book* now survives and is known as *The Mabinogion*.

The path leaves old Kington up the long convex spine of Hergest Ridge, whose summit moves away from you as you climb. The story which Conan Doyle made into *The Hound of the Baskervilles* originated in tales of a ghostly dog on this ridge. Even the rock near the crest known as the Whet-stone is said to go down to the Arrow each morning to drink; there can be no more numinous hill in the country. It is the most comfortable short-turf walking on the path.

Beyond Gladestry at the end of the Ridge hedged farmland closes in again, which from Newchurch begins to gather Kilvert associations. Francis Kilvert was from 1865 to

1872 curate in Clyro, a mile from Hay-on-Wye, and a great walker in his large parish. He recorded in his Diary every feature of the life around him. At Newchurch, where he was once greatly shocked to find the clergyman's daughters castrating lambs, he also rhapsodised on the landscape: 'On the Little Mountain above the village, the gorse that glowed and flamed fiery gold down the edge of the hill contrasted sharp and splendid with the blue world of mountain and valley which it touched.'

From here to the Wye the path follows steep lanes, past Bettws Chapel, where one day Kilvert found himself preaching to 'a red cow with a foolish white face that came up to the window by the desk and stared in'; and New Barn, the home of Mary Meredith, one of the several suicides who appear in the Diary. She conceived an illegitimate child, for which her brother, on whom she was dependent, despised and maltreated her. Kilvert describes how the intolerable conditions of her life

Graig near Grosmont: a picture of retraction and ruin familiar in the Welsh Borders.

finally led her to run from here to the Wye, into which she threw herself and drowned.

The last stretch into Hay is along the river, covered in summer with large pontoon floats of water plantain. Nothing is more delicious than a swim in the fast cold water between these floating islands of flowers. Hay is a mile up the river, a pretty market town cramped inside the line of its medieval walls. It has become the Town of Books, with second-hand bookshops at every corner, separated only by cafés selling wholemeal bread-and-honey sandwiches. On Tuesdays the older Hay revives, with the crowded agricultural market tucked behind Church Street above the Wye.

Hay-on-Wye to Sedbury Cliff, Chepstow 52 miles

From the valley of the Wye a steady climb of four miles brings the path out on to the first open moor since Hergest Ridge. This is the beginning of the Black Mountains, which have been part of the distant landscape since before Kington. Like the Clwydian Hills, they have a mountain atmosphere quite out of proportion to their actual height. After climbing to Hay

Bluff, there are two possible ways to Monmouth. The 'Castles Alternative' breaks off from the main route at the head of the Olchon valley and goes down the knife-edge ridge of the Cat's Back, making for the tower of Longtown Castle which is visible in trees below. To the east the view is of parallel ridges succeeding each other, separated by the Monnow, the Escley Brook, the Dore, and ten miles away by the Wye, now flowing south, above whose left bank the great wood on Garnon's Hill conceals the line of Offa's frontier. Longtown Castle may be the earliest round keep in England, built in the late twelfth or early thirteenth century on an earlier Norman mound.

From Longtown the Monnow makes a wide S-bend, its two curves stretching five miles through the hills. The path cuts straight across where the river must loop, meeting it again at Grosmont. Here is the second of the castles, the scene of Owen Glendower's first important setback, when he failed to capture it in 1405. At that moment, after three centuries of strategic importance as one of the castles of the Trilateral – the others were Skenfrith and White Castle – historical significance deserted Grosmont.

It is a further four miles south-east to Skenfrith, whose castle, owned by the Trust, is more complete than Grosmont, but seems even more emasculated. Its cosily diminutive village sits next to it across lawns, while the holiday traffic pours into Wales along the road the castle was built to control.

The path crosses the Monnow again here and climbs to the ridge on its east bank. Controlling this height is the last of the castles before Monmouth – Pembridge. In ruddy sandstone, it is the only one to have kept its strength in age. It is owned privately and walkers are allowed no nearer than three hundred yards. Where the castles of the Trilateral were almost entirely military in function, and were neglected once they became redundant, Pembridge was and is a public expression of private wealth and consequent power. This has ensured its preservation. The few miles left into Monmouth are good walking, on a path high above the Monnow, beneath hanging woods filled with foxgloves.

Where this Castles Alternative broke off, the official path kept to the west of the Olchon valley on a ridge between it and the Vale of Ewyas, below to the right. This valley is an Arcadia, although not by chance or the benevolence of nature: the golden landscape is the mature realisation of the schemes of Walter Savage Landor, the poet and author of *Imaginary Conversations*. He bought the valley in 1807 and in the next seven years spent almost £200,000 making it more beautiful, planting

Pembridge Castle: unlike White Castle, it is difficult to imagine Pembridge was ever built with serious fighting in mind.

the bare slopes with the trees we see today – cedars, beech trees and sweet chestnuts, and starting on the construction of a mansion which was never finished, and of which the stable block is the only surviving remnant. His conservative neighbours could not stomach such grandeur of conception, as he could not endure their pettiness, and in 1814 he left for the Continent in relative poverty and disillusionment.

The mansion was to have been above the ruins of Llanthony Abbey, which lies in the valley like the pupil in its eye. Everything is focused by its presence here. It was originally founded in the twelfth century after William de Lacy, a Marcher baron, strayed into the valley, which worked in him a sudden and deep spiritual transformation. He became an anchorite and founded an Augustinian abbey on the site. Gerald of Wales, who came here in 1188, plainly loved the place. Llanthony was attached to a daughter abbey in Gloucester, from where, Gerald says, 'the monks are brought back, afflicted and worn out with long labour, to Llanthony, to their mother's breasts, where they are soon restored to the health for which they yearn'.

From the mountains to Monmouth the way is broken by hedges and streams and lanes, and careful way-finding is needed along often very muddy paths. The high point is White Castle, five miles from Pandy at the foot of the Black Mountains, and in total isolation in fields. Its name originates in the whitewash with which the walls were once covered. It is an exclusively military structure, with a six-towered keep and a large outer ward. It is a ruin quite without charm, with a presumably intentional grimness.

From the castle the path sinks to the valley

of the Trothy at Llantilio Crosseny, where Sir David Gam, the Welsh hero knighted at Agincourt, lived at Hen Cwrt. It is now nothing but a lawn surrounded by its ring of moat. The Grace Dieu Abbey, in the meadows of the Trothy five miles nearer Monmouth, once a great Cistercian house, has also disappeared. The path now leaves the river for four miles of forestry plantation and soggy fields until it arrives in Over Monnow, the ancient suburb of Monmouth.

Monmouth is the finest town on the path. More vital than Montgomery, in detail more beautiful than the market towns of the central upland, it is busy and urbane. Over the unique fortified bridge, broad Monnow Street, lined with Georgian-fronted houses, leads to the middle of the old town, Agincourt Square and the castle. The keep has little left standing, but next to it Great Castle House, built by the Marquis of Worcester in 1673, encapsulates Monmouth's style. It is built from red sandstone of two colours – the pilasters and string-courses are slightly browner – which

has flaked unevenly with age. This softens the symmetry of the facade without taking away from the nobility of its design, which in three high storeys rises to a hipped roof with broad projecting eaves. The material of the house is local and technically bad building stone. The design is made according to Renaissance formulae of perfection and is quite alien to South Wales. These two work an inexplicable combination, expressing exactly the kind of meeting which has happened the length of the Marches, where distinct elements have reacted and fused to form strong new compounds.

This wonderful town has collected heroes, such as Geoffrey of Monmouth, the wildly imaginative historian of Cymbeline, Arthur and Leir, who in fact spent most of his life in Oxford. Henry V was born here. Nelson, to whom there is an excellent museum in the town, paid a visit with Emma when on a boating trip on the Wye, and nearby lived Rolls of Rolls-Royce, of whom there is a statue in Agincourt Square and an apocalyptic vision in the Local History Museum.

The final leg is down the Wye valley. As is right for the end of a walk, things begin to grow in scale. Where the way to Monmouth

At the top of the Vale of Ewyas.

seemed arbitrary at times, the great gorge of the Wye marks as decisive a geographical line as any in Britain. Offa's frontier joins the path again above Redbrook, and stays with it to the end. Chepstow Castle and the width of the Severn end the walk like two strong chords.

From Monmouth the path crosses the Wye and makes straight for the height of the Kymin, which was bought by the National Trust in 1902. For some reason views are always graded by the number of counties they command; the Kymin does well with nine. A round house for a dining club was built here in 1794, to which a naval temple, studded with commemorative plaques of recent victories, was added in 1800. The Trust have recently erected a statue of Britannia similar to the one that originally crowned this whimsical building.

The beginning again of Offa's Dyke at Redbrook, and its presence on the left bank of the Wye almost unbroken to the Severn, poses a problem. Surely the Wye below Redbrook, as it had been above, was good enough as the frontier? To explain the Dyke's presence here Fox suggested it was a tactful move by Offa to allow Welsh traders and fishermen full control of the river and both its banks. Redbrook is in a decisive position since it is the furthest point reached by the highest of high tides. Such a point would be easily agreed upon at negotiation. Above it on the Wye the presence of the great original forest of Herefordshire meant that there was little human activity on either bank, and consequently no Dyke was built, except in a clearing at English Bicknor. The river was the boundary as far as Bridge Sollers, thirty-seven miles away up the valley, where the Wye continues westwards and the Dyke strikes north. Even then it was built only in short, widely separated stretches – across English clearings made in the forest. Only when the fertile Old Red Sandstone gave way on Rushock Hill to Silurian strata – that is, when natural forest gave way to naturally open land – was a continuous earthwork necessary.

There might have been another reason for the building of the nine miles of Dyke from

Tintern Abbey: a point of Cistercian light in the darkness of a Welsh valley. The Devil preached at the monks from the woods opposite.

Redbrook to Sedbury. The great bank and ditch above the river are a dramatic statement of Offa's power. The propaganda value and heroic qualities of a Dyke from sea to sea diminish considerably if the final forty-five miles are absent and the only boundary is a river. The point of Offa's Dyke running parallel to the Wye is, at least in part, to show that the king of Mercia could parallel nature and himself define his territory to the sea.

At Bigsweir Bridge it is possible either to follow the river bank to Brockweir, or to go higher over St Briavel's Common in small lanes along the line of the Dyke. From Brockweir the necessary detour breaks off to Tintern Abbey, in meadows on the far bank. The thirteenth-century abbey church is remarkably whole, its transept arches standing to seventy feet, and the seven lights of the west window undamaged in any detail. Tintern's lack of ruination offended the picturesque traveller William Gilpin, who suggested: 'A mallet judiciously used (but who durst use it?) might be of service in fracturing some of the gable-ends, which hurt the eye with their regularity.' It is nevertheless, as the world knows, a place of great beauty.

Past the almost circular loop in the Wye at Lancaut, through oak and beechwood, the last miles into Chepstow begin to acquire the characteristics of suburbia, even on the rim of the Wye gorge. Into this Chepstow Castle comes as a show of strength. The form it has today, where ward after ward is strung out along a narrowing ledge, was given it almost entirely in the thirteenth century, when a Norman castle was remodelled. The most exciting moments of its history did not come until the seventeenth century, when it was besieged three times in the two Civil Wars and taken each time. After the Restoration Henry Marten, the regicide, was imprisoned in the comfortable tower to the left of the main gate for twenty years. He died there in 1680.

The path keeps to the other bank of the Wye. It is only a mile from Chepstow to Sedbury Cliff, through a housing estate (with names like 'Mercian Way' and 'Offa's Close') and by a sewage works. The final quarter-mile alone is clear, where the bank dips to a stream and rises the hundred yards or so to the cliff edge. The Severn is wide and grey, crossed to the south by the long motorway suspension bridge, which reaches the English shore at Aust. The name of this village records Augustine, who in 602 summoned the Bishops of the Celtic church to meet him here. They decided to watch how he behaved towards them before settling on their own attitude in the negotiations. If he rose as they entered, they would listen; if arrogantly he remained seated, they would have nothing to do with

The M4 bridge crossing the Severn to Aust. This triumph of graceful engineering can carry vehicles of up to 200 tons over its thousand-yard main span.

him. Augustine kept to his throne, and from that moment hostility closed off any hope of reconciliation of the Celtic and the Roman churches. It was, in its way, the same kind of proud separation as that which brought Offa to draw so clearly the western boundary of his kingdom, which we have followed from sea to sea.

MAPS: OS 1:50,000 Numbers 116, 117, 126, 137, 148, 161, 162

GUIDES:
John B. Jones, *Offa's Dyke Path*, HMSO 1976
C. J. Wright, *A Guide to Offa's Dyke Path*, Constable 1975

BACKGROUND:
Sir Cyril Fox, *Offa's Dyke – A Field Survey*, OUP and British Academy 1955
Francis Kilvert, *Diary*, edited by William Plomer, Cape 1944
Sir John Lloyd, *A History of Wales*, Longmans 1939
Elizabeth Mavor, *The Ladies of Llangollen*, Michael Joseph 1971
Roy Millward and Adrian Robinson, *The Welsh Marches*, Macmillan 1971
W. Rees, *An Historical Atlas of Wales*, Faber 1972
F. M. Stenton, *Anglo-Saxon England*, OUP 1943

INFORMATION:
Offa's Dyke Association,
Old Primary School,
Knighton, Powys

The Pennine Way

Edale in Derbyshire to Kirk Yetholm in Roxburghshire 270 miles

The Pennine Way is England's classic long walk. It was the first to be thought of (in the 1930s) and the first to be completed, in 1965. Apart from the South West Way it is the longest, and is certainly the hardest and most exposed. It became famous in the 1950s as a battleground between walkers and game-keepers, but that is all over now and thousands of people walk it every year. One man has run it in three days and an hour, and others bicycle up and down it, but most walk and most in the summer holidays. It is extraordinary, if you happen to be walking out of the usual season, to find herds of footprints in the peat of a desolate moor, which until thirty years ago can hardly have seen more than one or two men each year for centuries.

By great chance the emptiest hills in England separate the two areas of densest population, in the industrial cities on either side. The aim of the Pennine Way is to avoid people and even cultivation. There are inter-vals in it – along the Aire, the Tees and the Tyne – which are extremely gentle, but they are only intervals. For the most part the Way indulges in exposure, and for that one must be prepared. It would be lunacy to set off up Bleaklow without a sure knowledge of maps and compasses. The Pennine Way is genuinely dangerous, and that is part of the point of it.

Much of what is now empty was not always so bare. The Pennines were covered at one time in trees, but climatic change and the felling by the Romans of almost inconceivable amounts of timber for smelting means that there are none there now. The many ruined farms and the stone walls which are built over the hills in all except the most bleak places remind one that this is not quite untreated nature. It is as near as one can get to it in England, though, and the dominant im-pression of the Pennine Way is the uninter-ruptedness of it all, of days in which hour after hour one corduroy-clad leg swings against the other without break or hesitation.

The Pennine Way needs little introduction. By their nature the high Pennines have hardly been affected by history. There are pockets of it – the Roman Wall, lead-miners at Alston,

The monument commemorating Napoleon's defeat and surrender stands on Stoodley Pike above the Calder Valley. Here for a while the Pennine Way leaves the peat and grainy hardness of the gritstone moors.

monks on Malham Moor – and they are best described where they occur. What is left is the moor. It can be grim at times. 'You do nothing casual here,' Ted Hughes has written about these hills, and it is his conception that the sky and the Pennines are a pair of millstones which crush everything between them:

> The upper millstone heaven
> Grinds the heather's face hard and small.

But that is not half of it:

> Heather only toughens.
> And out of a mica sterility
> That nobody else wants
> Thickens a nectar
> Keen as adder venom.

There are whole days on the Pennine Way which consist of pure sterility, and others where one gets a taste of that bitter nectar.

Edale to the Calder 42 miles

Edale is a small, tightly gathered village in the valley of the Noe to the west of Sheffield. On either side the valley walls rise steeply from the fields at their foot. Above that, in all likelihood, mist will cover the tops. There is a strong sensation at the start of the Pennine Way of leaving the safe and comfortable for the unsafe and the uncomfortable.

There are two ways from the village. The official route is probably to be avoided, especially in bad weather. It starts up Grinds Brook and after a small climb arrives at the edge of Kinder Scout, which is fifteen square miles of acid peat hags, deeply riven by black winding drainage channels called groughs. On the map the main route strikes blandly northwest across this to the Kinder Downfall about two miles away, but the map-makers' obvious line bears little relation to reality. There are few landmarks, and you must try to head on a compass bearing towards the Downfall. The groughs will never comply with this intention, leading you invariably to black and wet dead ends. If lucky you will strike the headwaters of the Kinder, whose firm, grey, sandy bottom you can follow to where the river falls dramatically over the edge of the plateau.

It depends how much you like fierce introductions. The other way is much kinder, leading west up the vale of Edale through the regular grid of stone walls and coming occasionally to a stone farmhouse. The track itself is wide and firm as it leads up to Jacob's Ladder, a zig-zag rise at the head of the valley. At the top of it you meet the peat, which will stay with you uninterrupted till the Calder, after which it makes only occasional reappearances. Peat is the accumulation in areas of bad

drainage of centuries of vegetable matter which is semi-preserved in acid. The deeper levels of Pennine peat-mosses were formed in Neolithic times, partly of fallen birches, but the peat you walk on now is almost entirely made of cotton-grass, bog-moss and other small acid-loving plants. At the moment far more peat is being carried away by the streams each year than is being naturally built up.

The path soon reaches the edge of the plateau, which is made of millstone grit, windsculpted here along its horizontal faults. You follow this sharp and broken edge northwards, skirting the black centre of Kinder Scout. For Charles Cotton, writing in the late seventeenth century, this was

> A Country so deformed, the Traveller
> Would swear those parts Nature's pudenda were:
> Like Warts and Wens hills on the one side swell,
> To all but Natives inaccessible;
> Th'other a blue scrofulous scum defiles,
> Flowing from th'earths impostumated boyles.

In mist this is wonderfully strange country. The grit edge looms its shapes at you as you pass, while over towards the moor only the farmyard cluck of the grouse emerges from the grey into which the rough orange grass disappears. About six miles from Edale you reach the northern edge of Kinder Scout (the name is half Celtic, half Norse) and with it the end of firm going. The way now heads northeast over Mill Hill, Moss Castle and Featherbed Moss. All are identical, heavy, low, brown hills. 'Featherbed', which is quite a common Pennine name, may refer to the squashiness of the earth, or more probably to the look of the moor in June and July, when the cotton grass flecks the place with white feather-like tufts.

You trudge on. Your time will be spent unsuccessfully dodging holes filled with an acid Guinness. After some miles, though, you come to imagine yourself rather an expert on the consistency of peat. With a connoisseur's eye you detect the nuances of the terrain – there is some slightly flaky, light brown, almost fibrous stuff; some heavy-duty chocolaty stodge; and some in which the matter is powdered so fine and is so efficiently mixed with stagnant water that it has the feel underfoot of mayonnaise.

Two and a half miles from Mill Hill you cross the Snake Road, one of the Manchester–Sheffield roads across the Pennines. Beyond it, for a miraculous half-mile, the way has been laid with a track made of bunches of cut heather pegged to the earth and overlying horizontal stakes. This is exactly the kind of artificial track made by Neolithic people over

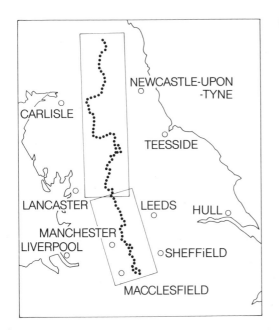

CARLISLE
NEWCASTLE-UPON-TYNE
TEESSIDE
LANCASTER
LEEDS
HULL
MANCHESTER
LIVERPOOL
SHEFFIELD
MACCLESFIELD

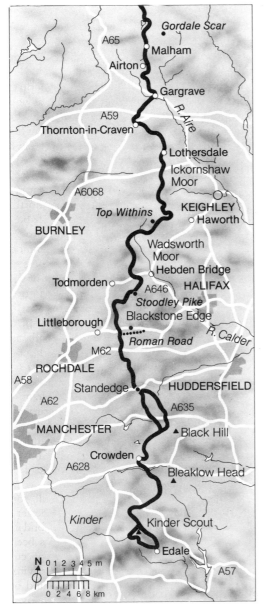

Gordale Scar
A65
Malham
Airton
Gargrave
R. Aire
A59
Thornton-in-Craven
Lothersdale
Ickornshaw Moor
A6068
Top Withins
KEIGHLEY
BURNLEY
Haworth
Wadsworth Moor
Hebden Bridge
Todmorden
HALIFAX
A646
Stoodley Pike
Blackstone Edge
Littleborough
R. Calder
Roman Road
M62
ROCHDALE
A58
Standedge
HUDDERSFIELD
A62
A635
MANCHESTER
▲ Black Hill
Crowden
A628
▲ Bleaklow Head
Kinder
Kinder Scout
Edale
N 0 1 2 3 4 5 m
0 2 4 6 8 km
A57

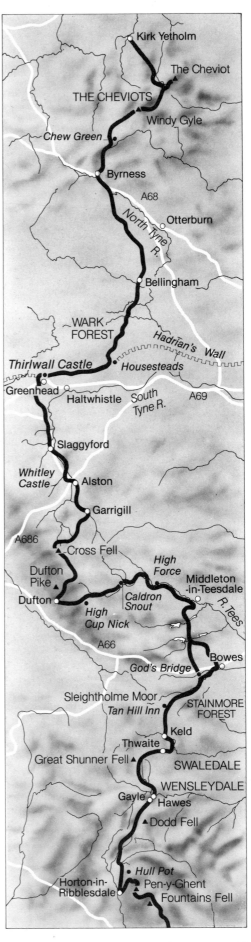

Kirk Yetholm
The Cheviot ▲
THE CHEVIOTS
Windy Gyle ▲
Chew Green
Byrness
A68
North Tyne R.
Otterburn
Bellingham
WARK FOREST
Hadrian's Wall
Thirlwall Castle
Housesteads
Greenhead
Haltwhistle
South Tyne R.
A69
Slaggyford
Whitley Castle
Alston
Garrigill
A686
▲ Cross Fell
High Force
Dufton Pike ▲
Middleton-in-Teesdale
Dufton
Caldron Snout
R. Tees
High Cup Nick
A66
Bowes
God's Bridge
STAINMORE FOREST
Sleightholme Moor
Tan Hill Inn
Keld
Thwaite
Great Shunner Fell ▲
SWALEDALE
WENSLEYDALE
Gayle
Hawes
▲ *Dodd Fell*
Hull Pot
Horton-in-Ribblesdale
Pen-y-Ghent ▲
Fountains Fell ▲

marshes in Somerset. There they laid an extensive network of such roads (the first known made roads in England); this soon comes to an end and you are back on the naked moor. The Way crosses a slight hollow stretching north-west and south-east. This is Doctor's Gate, a Roman road that joined a fort near Castleton with one near Glossop.

Again only names differentiate endlessly similar moor. You trace a ditch called Devil's Dyke up to Alport Low, from there making for Hern Clough, a stream which you follow via the Hern Stones (a lump or two of grit) to the top of Bleaklow. (There is pleasure at least in the consonantal hardness of these names.)

Bleaklow, 2,006 feet high, is the day's summit, and from there on firmer, drier ground you descend through heather towards Longdendale, a valley with two busy roads along it, either side of the ugly mess of a half-full reservoir. People have quite regularly seen ghosts of Roman soldiers in Longdendale. There is a campsite here, and a youth hostel a mile up the valley.

The next day starts marvellously. Crowden

The first climb on the Pennine Way, Jacob's Ladder, the easier alternative up to Kinder Scout from Edale.

Great Brook leads strongly and obviously north, a wide highway of a stream between tall brackeny hills. Soon these turn into rocky grit edges, called the Laddow Rocks, not as magnificent perhaps as the great parapets of Kinder Scout, but worlds better than the undefinition of Bleaklow. That low lump of a hill forms the southern horizon. The Laddow Rocks are the high point of the day. Crowden Great Brook breaks up into a welter of nameless streams, the earth starts to retain its water, and another Bleaklow, this one called Black Hill, rises gloomily ahead. The top of it is six miles from Longdendale, and the best moment to be there is when cloud is just touching its surface. Then this worse-than-lunar landscape is seen at its most intense. Hardly a blade of vegetation grows here. The low hummocks of peat are a naked and undiluted black. In the middle of them, revealed now and then by the cloud, is the sharply incongruous Ordnance Survey column. The Romantics' terror at wild places – which is easy to scoff at now – is quite understandable on Black Hill. This is not beneficent nature, nor luxuriant, but the image of a chemical, pre-vegetable, pre-animal world.

Black Hill is a visual horror, but the tingle it produces is soon dulled by the next two miles, an hour-long tramp over a yellow moor cut by deep groughs. At the end of it you arrive at the welcome firmness of the A635. A mile down it to the west police discovered the famous Bodies on the Moors in 1965. You cross the road and wade off into the unknown. Here is a succession of mosses – Featherbed, White, Broadhead and Black – into any of which you can sink up to your waist. But with the struggle on from one disaster to the next you begin to feel that if you can get through this, you can get through anything. Arrival at the Black Moss reservoir, about four miles from Black Hill, is significant. Not all the worst is over, but most of it is. An easy mile beyond it you cross the Oldham–Huddersfield road at the Standedge cutting, where there is a pub. This sounds better than it is. You will by now be caked with peat. On the door of the pub there is a polite notice about not bringing dirt inside. There used to be a café here too, but it has been demolished. Instead, have a picnic on the edge, looking out west over the reservoirs and spreading outskirts of Oldham.

It is eight miles from Standedge to the White House Inn above Littleborough, at first along a gritstone edge, and then across the moor, owned here by the National Trust. Ahead and behind, unchanging, are the endlessly unassertive Pennines, low-slung and stolid. Even their shape looks peaty. You head for the large aerial on Windy Hill, after that crossing the M62 on a narrow concrete bridge. Beyond the motorway is Redmires, once the worst mile of the Pennine Way, but recently improved with planks and bridges. At the far side of it are the flagstones and boulders of Blackstone Edge, called by Defoe the 'English Andes'. This is a great moment. Here you leave behind all the dreary slog and start to move through some of the best walking country in Britain.

The view from this edge above Rochdale is wonderful, from the towers of Manchester in the south-west to the heights of Rossendale in the north, and beyond them Pendle Hill. Between the end of the edge and the main road you come to and can descend a famous stretch of Roman road, sixteen foot wide and nobly paved in black slabs of the millstone grit. It is very steep for a road, but this is a recognition that a short sharp climb is preferable for both walkers and horses to a long slow one. Down the centre runs a broad groove, which may either have been for the brake-poles of carts or lined with turf, to make it easier for pack-animals coming up hill.

It may not be a Roman road. The line is certainly Roman – from Manchester to Ilkley – but the central groove on its own looks very like one of the several pack-horse tracks that cross the Pennines near here. This road may be a later widening for carts of a track which was laid, possibly, in the seventeenth or eighteenth century.

The White House Inn on the main road just beyond has no accommodation and dislikes dirty walkers. The thing to do is to descend to the excellent Lancashire town of Little-borough, once a booming textile place, but now only making PVC. It has a welcome and necessary launderette.

From the White House Inn to the Calder is six miles of good four-mile-an-hour walking along level gravel road, next to a succession of reservoirs and leats, some built to regulate drinking water, some to feed the canals, and some to provide a head of water for the industrial machinery in the valleys.

The great black obelisk of Stoodley Pike, commemorating Waterloo, comes into sight above the valley of the Calder, on whose far side it is balanced by the four sharp pinnacles of Heptonstall church. You cross a narrow paved track coming up from Mankinholes called the Long Drag. This may be what the Blackstone Edge road originally looked like. In a mile the Pennine Way arrives at the obelisk itself, which is a good place to stop and look at the Calder valley. This still beautiful place was the centre of Elmet, the last Celtic kingdom in Yorkshire, which stretched at least as far north as Craven, and as far south as Leeds (both Celtic names). During the Industrial Revolution the force of the Calder (yet another Celtic name, meaning 'violent water') was used to turn hundreds of looms. As elsewhere in England, this textile industry has been undercut by foreign competition.

As you descend towards the river the grid of blackened stone walls gets tighter and you come to some hard, nearly windowless farms. The blackness of the stone in the green fields makes the buildings here much more obviously an imposition on the land than in the south of England, where the colours of buildings – of brick and tile and a yellower stone – fit so much more easily with their surroundings. The impression of hardness intensifies when you find a line of crows gibbetted on a wire strung along the top of a wall. The last mile down to the river is through hazels, the first trees since Edale.

From the Calder to Malham
35 miles

The climb up out of the Calder valley is on narrow paved paths, round a small Baptist chapel and some cottages, one of which has an unexpected little Venetian window high up. This steep valleyside, with the farms not

The Pack Horse Inn near Hebden Bridge is often snowed in during the winter. The Pennine Way runs along the moor behind it.

grouped in a village, but spread around, each in the middle of its acreage, is a Scandinavian landscape. The names round here – Mytholm, Slack and Blackshaw – all come originally from Old Norse, while the shape of the farms themselves, with house, cow house and barn all on the same axis under one long roof, may have the same Scandinavian ancestry. To an eye unused to such long single houses they give the odd impression of being short lengths of street on the hillside, like drops of town in the fields.

As far as Colden, two miles from the river, the Way is through this walled grazing, but then the landscape opens out again on to wide, tawny moor. Ahead is the high Wadsworth Moor you must cross to reach Brontë country. The ground is firm and you can storm towards it while the plovers screech and dip around you. There are many ruined farms here, some of them once quite substantial, which have succumbed to various eroding forces – the movement of people to cities, the economies of size and the drowning of land by the new reservoirs. Since the Industrial Revolution the history of men on the high Pennines has been one of retreat. The only surviving building here now, apart from the reservoir keepers' cottages, is the whitewashed Pack Horse Inn, three miles from Colden. Another three miles,

most of it along the edge of a string of reservoirs, brings you to the top of Withins Height. Looking back from here Stoodley Pike is clear, and beyond it Blackstone Edge.

The way forward is into what, with parts of Dorset, is the most famous literary landscape in Britain. There is a crucial difference, though, between this, the Brontë country, and Hardy's Dorset. Where Hardy, with the architect's concern for precision, was always geographically exact in the settings for his novels, the Brontës manipulated their landscape for thematic ends. Within half a mile of cresting the rise you come to Top Withins, a very ruined and roofless farmhouse, whose walls have been harshly made good against further collapse. This is said to be Wuthering Heights, but there is nothing that can point to this rather than any of the other places on Haworth Moor. One aspect alone of the novel can be traced on the ground today. The limits of the book, both geographical and symbolical, are Thrushcross Grange, a well appointed and calm place set in a wide and comfortable park on the low ground below the moors; and Wuthering Heights, in its way no less of a house, its front covered with indecipherable carvings, and standing not in the ease of a park but almost inaccessibly high on a moor. The narrator explains the meaning of the house's name: '"Wuthering" is a significant provincial adjective, descriptive of the atmospheric tumult to which its station is exposed in stormy weather. Pure bracing ventilation they must have up there, at all times, indeed: one may guess the power of the north wind, blowing over the edge, by the excessive slant of a few stunted firs at the end of the house and by a range of gaunt thorns all stretching their limbs one way, as if craving alms of the sun.' The novel is strung between these two, between the harsh exposure of the moor and the welcome but at times suffocating quiet of the house in the valley. This psychological gap is easily recapturable on Haworth Moor today. From Top Withins most people will detour to Haworth itself, two miles to the east, but the Pennine Way goes on down north to the valley now filled with the Ponden reservoir. Here is Ponden Hall, much more Thrushcross Grange than Top Withins is Wuthering Heights.

The valley is just a thin insertion and the Way climbs again on to moorland. Five miles on a winding path over Ickornshaw Moor brings you to Ickornshaw itself, a black mill town, with three tall chimneys lining off down the dale to the east. Two and a half miles further through pastures is Lothersdale, a tiny village in a crack of a valley, with a silk and rayon mill hidden in it, which would be unnoticed but for its inevitable tall chimney.

Up on the hill is Stone Gappe, where Charlotte Brontë spent three unhappy months as governess in 1839. It became the Gateshead Hall of *Jane Eyre*.

To Thornton-in-Craven from Lothersdale is four and a half miles, green at first then in the blackness of a grouse moor. At Thornton the millstone grit which has been the basis of all the moors and mosses from Edale comes, mercifully, to an end. Much of the way to Scotland will now be on the carboniferous limestone, the rock which produces the best turf of all. But the first five miles of the new rock are not at all typical of the great bare shapes of all the limestone country to come. As far as Gargrave the Way is through a charming landscape-in-miniature, in which little hills, no more than fifty or sixty foot high, separate little streams in little valleys. It is an eiderdown of green, the kind of pet landscape that eighteenth-century designers laboured to build. If ever hills rolled or billowed these are they. No one is sure about their origins. They may have been islands in a limestone sea, or

Mill chimneys and black gritstone walls in fields near Lothersdale.

knots of harder stone which remained when their surroundings were eroded away.

The landscape sorts itself out into slightly less whimsical shapes; you climb the last hill above Gargrave and find before you the woods of Upper Airedale and in front of them the grey limestone town and church of Gargrave.

Things could not be more pastoral than on the seven-mile walk up the valley of the Aire from Gargrave to Malham. Here the fields are divided by beautiful pale grey limestone walls, giving the land a much cleaner look than walls made of the darker grit. Flocks of delicate-legged and heavy-fleeced blackface sheep can be found pastured next to the river in early spring. The Aire itself is bright and clear. There could be no better antidote to the moorlands you have left behind.

At Airton the Way enters the Yorkshire Dales National Park and in two miles comes to Aire-Head Springs, a wonderful place which can easily be passed unnoticed. The stream that comes south from Malham Tarn, high on the moor to the north, and which disappears at Water Sinks, reappears here after flowing underground in chambers it has gouged in the limestone. The stream emerges through the whole bed of a small pool, rippling up through the stones, a really magical effect. In half a mile you come to Malham village.

Malham to Keld 43 miles

Malham is lined up on either side of the falling stream that runs down to join the Aire at Aire-Head Springs. To the north is the sharp edge

TOP RIGHT *The low-slung dampness of a Pennine Moor, flecked here and there with a tuft of cottongrass.*

BOTTOM RIGHT *The fissured limestone pavement above Malham Cove, and Upper Airedale beyond. A 300-foot waterfall once plunged over this lip, but the water has now dissolved its own way underground.*

Limestone walls near Malham: most of these are from the eighteenth or nineteenth century, although some may be older. In the foreground on the left, where the wall steps regularly down a series of terraces, is evidence of a previous, possibly Anglian, field-system.

of the limestone uplands, marked here by the dramatic cliff called Malham Cove. This 300-foot-high wall of curving rock was once the site of a great waterfall, over which fell the outflow from Malham Tarn. The stream now goes underground and the cove is dry. The Pennine Way climbs up by the side of the cove and comes to a level surface of limestone at the top. This is quite bare and divided into curly-edged but squarish blocks, called clints, separated by deep ditches or grykes. This is the result of rainwater dissolving the stone along regular lines of weakness in its structure. In the dark cracks of the pavement are damp green ferns.

The Pennine Way officially moves on up the now-dry valley of the stream which once flowed over Malham Cove. But it is better to go back down to Malham, and then walk about a mile east below the limestone edge, as far as Gordale Scar. This is the best of all the limestone features here. A deep and rocky gorge cuts into the scarp, with a net of small streams running over its flat bottom. These repeatedly sink below ground and rise again a few yards later in pools filled with watercress. On the cliffs are a few spindly trees and dark patches of yew. One is led in and in, finally coming to a dark cold corner where the water falls from above through a hole in the rock. This hole is all that remains of the tunnel the stream cut through the limestone and which has now collapsed to form the scar. Thomas Gray, who spent most of his life cloistered in Pembroke College, Cambridge, came here to be deliciously terrified: 'It is to the right, under which you stand to see the fall that is the principal horror of the place ... one black and solid mass overshadows half the area with its dreadful canopy ... there are loose stones which hang in the air, and threaten visibly ... I stayed there (not without shuddering) a full quarter of an hour.'

You can climb up the waterfall and then follow the beck for about a mile northwards until you hit a walled lane running west and east. This is the Mastiles Lane, an ancient cross-country route, which is now associated with the time when the monks of Fountains Abbey had become the greatest sheep owners in England. This moor was part of their estates, and the lane came here all the way from Fountains twenty-seven miles to the east. To reach the Pennine Way again you can follow it westwards for about a mile until just south of Malham Tarn. The lane, now motorable, continues to the abbey's enormous sheep-walks in Crosthwaite, by Derwentwater and in Borrowdale. You must turn north, to skirt Malham Tarn and walk on over Fountains Fell, whose name of course records its medieval owners. Ahead is Pen-y-ghent,

whose Celtic name means Hill of the Winds. Like Fountains Fell, Ingleborough and Whernside, Pen-y-ghent is a block of limestone capped by millstone grit, but of them all Pen-y-ghent is the most beautiful, with a quite unEnglish profile given it by the double rock-step near the summit, the first made of limestone, the second of grit. It is the best and steepest climb on the Pennine Way, but not difficult. From the windy and snow-bound top the way is down a gradual track, getting very boggy in places until it turns down a walled lane to Horton-in-Ribblesdale. Before going down you must make a small detour to the Hull Pot. As Charles Cotton would have described it, this hole is 'a vast inanity', 300 feet long, 60 feet wide and 60 deep. The time to see it is in a heavy rainstorm, when the stream flowing in is too much for the outlet in the bottom and the whole thing fills with water until it floods off down the hill. From the Pot it is two miles down the rough lane to Horton, which has an inn and several B & Bs.

From Horton you climb steadily on an old pack-horse track above Ribblesdale. This is classic pot-hole country. All over the limestone one finds little sinks into which water dribbles, but this morning's walk from Horton passes some of the best holes there are. Just over a mile from the village the path crosses a natural bridge between the double entrance of Sell Gill Holes. Brown and white water churns down into these two gaps in the earth. There is a strange and irrational need to stare down into them to see where these thousands of gallons go, but of course they disappear into lightless tunnels. You pass more pots until four miles from Horton you arrive at the best of them, known as Dry Laith Cave, or Calf Holes. Here a heavy stream crashes underground, surely, one imagines, to fill a sunless sea, but actually emerging within half a mile to add its waters eventually to the Ribble.

Two miles further, after passing the small gorge of Ling Gill and crossing the sixteenth-century bridge over Cam Beck, you join the line of a Roman road heading straight for Bainbridge in Wensleydale. For an unwavering two and a half miles you keep to this line, which has no variation in gradient either. It is very dull. The winding beck, the lonely farm of Cam Houses and the spoonfuls of old snow like sorbet in the hollows are all there is to look at. At last the road comes to the top of the ridge. Here you leave the gathering grounds of the Ribble for those of the Ure. You leave the old West Riding for the old North Riding, and most important you leave uphill for down-hill. Now it is a lovely grassy descent to Wensleydale above Snaizeholme, a beautiful, round-headed valley, blotchy with bracken and veined with streams. The path moves

Duerley Beck, running down from Dodd Fell, pours through the village of Gayle in Wensleydale.

round the nose of Dodd Fell to lose sight of Whernside and the hills to the west, but to gain instead a view down Wensleydale, its stepped sides stretching to the east. Then follows the familiar slow descent from hill to valley, arriving at the bottom at Gayle, a village which has for its main street a noisy and wild river breaking over rocks between banks lined with prim cottages. From here it is quarter of a mile to Hawes, the market of Upper Wensleydale, with several hotels in the main street where it widens for the market place. There is a factory here which daily consumes 7,000 gallons of milk with which it churns out three tons of Wensleydale cheese.

North of Hawes you cross the Ure and climb one of the steps into which Wensleydale has been eroded as a result of the differing hardnesses of the rocks from which it is made. Hardrow Force is just to the north. At 100 foot high it is England's highest waterfall. Words-

worth, Turner and Ruskin all loved it. The way from here is up on to the broad back of Great Shunner Fell, a long five-mile tramp to the top. Some of it is on peat, which is fine if hardened by frost but otherwise hints at past horror. On the flanks of this hill is the best place name on the walk, which should, by rights, be plastered all over Bleaklow: Grimy Gutter Hags.

From the top there is an equally gradual descent into Swaledale, in its way a much finer and more delicate valley than Wensleydale, and without that look of a broad and fertile spread of fields. At the bottom is the tiny village of Thwaite – a purely Norse name, meaning 'clearing' – which has straw littering its streets, and beyond it a pattern of walled fields, each with its own barn or laithe into which the hay is swept in summer and where a few cattle are housed over the winter. From Thwaite it is only three miles to Keld, after a steep climb an easy walk high above upper Swaledale. Keld is another Norse name, meaning spring. The small village has a youth hostel and three different Nonconformist chapels. At Keld you cross the Coast to Coast Path.

Barns next to Widdop Reservoir, north of Hebden Bridge.

Keld to Dufton 42 miles

At Keld the limestone walking comes for a while to an end. It is twenty-one miles to Middleton in Teesdale, almost all of it on heavy wet moor. You must settle again into the Pennine trudge, the continuous rhythm that lets your legs do the walking and your mind drift off on to other things. The Tan Hill Inn, on the border of Yorkshire and County Durham, is the only incident for miles. It catered for the miners in the collieries that were once worked here. It is the highest inn in England, 1,732 feet above sea level, and is open only in the summer.

You walk on over Sleightholme Moor, at the far side of which an alternative path branches east to Bowes, an easier route which joins the main path in Baldersdale, four and a half miles away. It is probably better not to break your famous rhythm, and to keep on over the moor. If that is what you choose, you descend to the River Greta, which is spanned by a natural limestone bridge, called God's Bridge. This is less dramatic than it sounds because except in spate the Greta flows underground here, leaving only a still, whisky-coloured pool for the bridge to cross.

Beyond the river the moor continues, a little higher and less wet than before, but equally empty. This is a neglected part of England, which cannot be farmed or used in any way, and is not exciting or beautiful enough to attract the droves of people who go to the Yorkshire Dales. Instead it has become an area in which to store water for Teesside. Both Baldersdale and Lunedale are filled with reservoirs. Baldersdale, and this is the most interesting thing about it, is halfway from Edale to Kirk Yetholm.

It is six miles from Baldersdale to Middleton, crossing into Lunedale and then edging round Lune Moor on the boundary of the cultivated and the unworkable land. You pass a few ruined farms and a dark button of wood called Kirkcarrion and then drop gradually to Teesdale. This is the most dependably enjoyable part of the day. Middleton, on the river, was once the centre of lead-mining, but now has no hint of the industrial about it.

The way from Middleton is up the valley of the Tees on its right bank. The river runs over a bed of dolerite, an igneous rock. Upper Teesdale, High Cup above Dufton and the

Thwaite in Swaledale: the greatest pleasure is in crossing moorland to a valley and village with a shop in it, to get something to eat and then to set out up the hill again. From Thwaite, the Pennine Way climbs Kisdon, the block of moor in the background, and leads on to Keld.

*A farm below Pen-y-ghent. The Pennine Way climbs
the double step of the mountain here seen in profile; the
first is of limestone, the second of millstone grit.*

TOP *A peat-brown stream disappears down the sink-hole or swallet called Dry Laith Cave, which it has dissolved in the limestone below. It reappears in half a mile to flow down to the Ribble.*

ABOVE *God's Bridge over the River Greta on Stainmore.*

Whin Sill in Northumberland, along which the Romans built Hadrian's Wall, are all part of this same upsquirt of rock. It is hard and black, not easily eroded and even a river with the force and weight of the Tees has been unable to smooth down a bed over it. Four miles from Middleton is Low Force, a small waterfall over which the river tumbles rather than drops, and just over a mile further is High Force, a seventy-foot plunge for the Tees, which has already flowed seventeen miles and collected the water of over fifty tributaries.

The Way now passes a large quarry, and then moves on through twisted juniper bushes to cross a tributary of the Tees at Sayer Farm, where you turn west and make for the obvious gap in the hills. Widdibanks Farm, just over a mile to the west, is an isolated place that offers food and Bed & Breakfast at any time of the year, even when snow is thick around it. The

stone walls here are made from the rounded river boulders. Beyond Widdibanks the hills squeeze in, forcing the path to clamber over rocks fallen from the cliffs or clints above. All this is through one of the most famous botanical areas in England, where a small outcrop of 'sugar' limestone crumbles to make a special alkaline soil, in which rarities like Bog Sandwort and Spring Gentian can live, as well as many other common species, like violets, primroses and wild pansies. Acres of this precious land were drowned in 1971 when a new reservoir was built on the Tees. Just below the reservoir dam is Caldron Snout, yet another waterfall over the dolerite, a series of steps in the rock. The Way climbs up and crosses the river above the fall, so moving from County Durham to Cumbria.

Now follows a long but gradual ascent up the dip-slope of the Pennines, to their western edge, where a steep scarp walls the eastern side of the Vale of Eden. This is dreary at times, but it ends at the magnificent High Cup. This is a great steep hull of low land a mile long which has been driven into the Pennines, rimmed along its edges by the familiar dolerite. A small cleft at its very point is called High Cup Nick.

The River Tees at High Force, where it drops over the edge of a hard and brittle volcanic rock called dolerite, which also outcrops at High Cup Nick, and under Hadrian's Wall on the Whin Sill.

Dufton Pike on the edge of the Vale of Eden.

The cup may have been cut by a glacier or by the overflow water from a glacial lake on the moor above.

The drama of the four-mile descent to Dufton will be increased if the famous Helm Wind happens to be blowing. This cold and violent wind comes down off the Pennines into the Vale of Eden, creating two parallel banks of cloud, one along the foot of the fell, one a long whirling roll three or four miles to the west. It makes an extraordinary sky. Even odder is the way in which the fierce wind suddenly stops on the line of the river Eden, beyond which the air can be quite calm. All these effects are caused by cold air sinking down the sharp edge of the Pennines, being heated in the valley, then rising again to condense in the double bank of cloud. Dufton, a pretty village of red sandstone with a tree-filled green, is not lucky with its weather. In the middle of May 1979 it was cut off by a Pennine blizzard, while trees are often blown down and slates removed by the Helm Wind, of which the villagers are oddly proud. 'There is only one other wind in Europe like it,' they claim, but where or what they do not say.

Dufton to Thirlwall 38 miles

The footpath leads up from Dufton between Knock Pike and Dufton Pike, and on up to the top of Knock Fell, 2,604 feet above sea level. This is all high, bare ground, the highest in the Pennines and in England outside the Lake District. The Way heads for the various aerials and masts on Great Dun Fell, six miles from Dufton, and then continues north for another two miles to the boggy source of the Tees. A mile beyond it is the summit of Cross Fell, the highest Pennine, 2,930 feet above sea level.

Cross Fell is covered in the remains of lead mines. These were worked by the Romans, but what is now visible are the leavings of the industry in the eighteenth and nineteenth centuries, when it reached its peak. Most of the work involved was the digging of 'levels' – horizontal passages to the outside air – both to drain the mine and to improve ventilation. It was these levels that produced the tons of 'dead' (unprofitable stone) that now cover the surface. Despite these efforts and regular inspections, conditions for the miners were appalling, though not quite as hellish as in the Cornish mines. In the Pennines a single eight-hour day was worked, giving time for the mineral dust to settle during the night, where in Cornwall a continuous shift system meant the air was always filled with the lung-scarring particles. Equally, access to the mine here was relatively easy, along the horizontal levels, while in Cornwall the workings, which were well below sea-level, and almost impossible to drain, were accessible only down a long and exhausting series of ladders. Nevertheless the

Pennine miners had their share of suffering. In the mid-eighteenth century no man went down the mine before he was eighteen, but miners were lucky to live beyond 35. A century later life expectancy had increased a mere ten years. In 1858 a General Board of Health Inspection found that Alston, on the South Tyne a few miles to the north, had a higher proportion of widows than any other place in the kingdom, and that there was not a miner here whose spit was not a deep bluish black from the mineral dust he had inhaled. Two

TOP LEFT *Dropping down off Cross Fell to the valley of the South Tyne at Garrigill. The lower you come, the more enclosing the field walls. The stones which at two levels protrude beyond the line of the wall are known as tie-stones; they bind the two faces of the wall together.*

BOTTOM LEFT *Ashgill Head near Garrigill: the sheep is a Swaledale.*

The South Tyne at Garrigill – a lush and welcome interlude after the exposure of the highest Pennines.

things alone mitigated this: the vital spiritual life of the Nonconformist church and the fact that each miner was likely enough to have a smallholding of his own. From a day underground these men would emerge not to slum dwellings, but to houses attached to their own pieces of land, and a view of the empty Pennines much as they look today.

It is seven miles from the top of Cross Fell down to Garrigill in the valley of the South Tyne. The path is covered in the purple crystals of fluorspar, a waste product from lead-mining, which is now itself being mined for use in the steel-making process. Garrigill is a small village with a pub, the George and Dragon, around another tree-filled green. A comparatively lush four-mile walk along the river brings you to Alston, the town of widows, on a steep bank above the Tyne. It scarcely fits the image of a hard northern mining town.

From Alston to the Roman Wall is seventeen miles. You begin by continuing on down the Tyne (from whose far bank Alston looks its best, circled below the steeple of its nineteenth-century church), crossing into Northumberland in a couple of miles. Over the

walls here are some beautifully made oak stiles, with high curving handles. You move across these from farm to farm, passing the Roman fort at Whitley Castle, two and a half miles from Alston, which has on one side no less than six sharp rings of ditches. The Way winds on up the valley, crossing and recrossing the road and a defunct railway, both of which make their way north to the Tyne-Solway gap in which Hadrian's Wall lies and which marks the end of the Pennines proper.

There is a gathering sense of the approaching Roman wall. Past Slaggyford, six miles from Alston, you join the line of the Maiden Way heading directly north. This was one of the four great supply routes to the Roman frontier, joining it at Carvoran, by Thirlwall Castle. The Way is now overgrown in places with heather and is stiff going. It comes to a derelict colliery, beyond which a tarmac lane continues its line northwards. Unkindly, the Pennine Way ignores this and goes again for the wet and dreary moor slightly to the west.

Alston and the church of St Augustine, built between 1870 and 1886 in the centre of Pennine lead mining.

This is the northernmost nose of the Pennines, but they keep their cruelties until the very end. The consolation – and this is wonderful – is the sight to the north-east of the hump-backed spine of the Whin Sill, and on top of it the best part of Hadrian's Wall crawling along the ridge eastwards to Housesteads. From the Lambley colliery to the Wall is six miles, over which only your expectation of better things to come will keep you going.

Hadrian's Wall
Thirlwall Castle to Housesteads
11 miles

It would be impossible to arrive at Hadrian's Wall and simply walk on past. It is too important in our picture of Britain, and has always been so. Sir Cyril Fox decided that the many earthworks built by the Roman-Britons in the fifth century were almost certainly in imitation of it, and Offa may have had it in mind when he built his Dyke. On a fourteenth-century map of Britain in the Bodleian Library, a broad and impenetrable border of crenellations stretches across from the Solway to the

Hadrian's Wall near Housesteads: figuring more largely in our imaginations than it does in reality.

Tyne, and that is how we still think of it – it figures far more largely in our imaginations than it does in reality. One wants the border with Scotland to run along it; as it does not, the space between the two seems oddly superfluous.

In a way the Wall is quite un-Roman. The basis of the Empire was the mobile legion in the field. Until the end of the first century AD the Empire had no firm edge, and the limit of Roman rule at any one moment would be wherever the furthest Roman soldiers happened to be. If an area was to be permanently adopted into the Empire, a net of roads and forts would be laid, with no more emphasis on the outer strand of the net than on any other. There was no static outer edge to keep barbarians out. This was the system adopted in Wales.

At the end of the first century AD things changed. Military setbacks in Germany and in the East brought a loss of confidence. At the same time the Romans may have realised that their Empire could never cover the world. At this time the edge of Roman rule in Britain was just north of the Carlisle–Newcastle gap. A slight withdrawal established a line of forts along the road in the gap, known by its Saxon name, Stanegate. Twelve years later Hadrian came to power. He immediately made a tour through the whole Empire, rationalising its frontiers and putting a stop to expansion. Many natural boundaries – rivers, deserts, the sea – were available to him, but in Britain there were none, unless the whole island were to be conquered. It is just possible that Hadrian had heard of the Great Wall of China, built three hundred years before, and it may have been on that model that, after his return to Rome, he ordered a wall to be built just north of the existing frontier on Stanegate. (It was not the best place either geographically or politically. The Forth–Clyde isthmus, on which the Antonine Wall was later to be built, is far shorter, and efficiently separated the relatively friendly British tribes from the hostile Picts. Hadrian's Wall cut British territory in two.)

It was to be a massive obstacle. The enemy coming from the north would first meet a ditch, ten feet deep and twenty-seven feet

wide, twenty feet in front of the Wall itself, which was fifteen feet high and originally ten feet thick. Every Roman mile there was a gate with a small fort or mile-castle behind it. Between each of these were two observation turrets, a third of a mile apart. No one knows if there was a walkway along the top of the Wall or not.

The specifications from Rome were rigidly followed, and at the beginning the design was carried out without any attention to local topography. A gate and mile-castle were constructed once a mile for every one of the eighty miles from coast to coast, even where this meant a gate opening uselessly out on to a precipice. Within two or three years of this too-simple plan being started, it was radically changed. Twelve major forts were inserted into the Wall, at roughly seven-mile intervals; but significantly the distance between them was flexible to allow them to be placed at strategic points, such as river crossings. At the same time a broad ditch and two accompanying mounds – called collectively the Vallum – were constructed south of the Wall and roughly parallel to it. The Vallum was very important to the Romans. In places where the

On entering the great Border Forest: the trees on the edge of the rides are fluffy enough, but one look beneath them reveals the monotony of the Forest.

hardness of the rock forced them to abandon the construction of the ditch immediately in front of the wall, they made sure that the Vallum was completed. Its purpose was to prevent civilians straying into the military zone behind the Wall. Later, in the third and fourth centuries, the rule became lax and civilian access to the Wall easy.

Hadrian's Wall was much more a bureaucratic than a military phenomenon. The many gates through it show it was a barrier to control movement, not to prevent it. For most of its life forts were maintained well to the north of it. For a short time the Antonine Wall made it redundant, and regular patrols beyond it were probably the staple of a soldier's life there.

Although legionaries built the Wall, none of them ever manned it. Auxiliaries, drawn mostly from the local population, lived in the forts, with their families in the villages just outside. Except in the rare times of crisis, the atmosphere must have been something like a rather tedious customs post on the border between Belgium and France today.

Crises did occur, most famously in AD 180 when a Roman general was killed and his army massacred by barbarians who crossed the Wall and destroyed parts of it. It is important to note that the destruction of the Wall was the consequence of military defeat, not vice versa. The Wall was not a bulwark, but a line of gates from which to move out. Soldiers certainly never fought from the parapet-walk, if there ever was one, and almost certainly never encircled the enemy to pin them against the Wall, as was once thought. If enemy soldiers were allowed to get that close it probably meant that something had gone wrong further north.

Primed with all this, it is exciting to arrive at Thirlwall, which you know to be on the line of the Wall. Unfortunately, there is nothing Roman to be seen. Instead, rather disconcertingly, there is the crumbly ruin of a fourteenth-century pele-tower on a steep green hill above the Tipalt Burn. The castle explains the absence of Wall; it is mostly built from the squared Roman stones.

As you hurry east there is at least a ditch to follow along, but half a mile from Thirlwall both ditch and Wall have been destroyed by a large quarry into the rusty dolerite. Just beyond you find the Wall for the first time. The rim of the rocks is a switchback which the Wall keeps to in a dark, knobbly snake. William Camden came here in the 1580s and saw 'the tract of it over the high pitches and steepe descents of hilles, wonderfully rising and falling'. It is not continuous, but a modern farm wall made with Roman stones usually marks the supple Roman line. Three miles from the quarry you come to Great Chesters, a farm on the site of one of the twelve major forts, Aesica, where Roman masonry stands in one place ten courses deep. In the middle, half-underground, is the still-complete arch of the fort's strong-room.

Just beyond the farm yet another quarry interrupts the Wall. On the far side of it the best six miles, much of it owned by the National Trust, above the crags of the Whin Sill, and looking out over to the border forest, bring you to Housesteads. It is slow and arduous walking, especially in snow, but that is perhaps the best time to be there, when you might be alone, and the black line of the Wall stands out 'wonderfully rising and falling' as far as Sewingshields Crags.

Housesteads is the most famous place on the Wall, in the middle of the best preserved and most photogenic sections, and showing more clearly than any other the typical layout of a Roman fort. It escaped the stone-pilfering that destroyed so many of the others by becoming the headquarters in the seventeenth century of a band of moss-troopers who plundered the local farms. As a result you can now walk the well-ordered streets of the fort, with all the evidence around you of Rome's brilliant military efficiency.

It is impossible not to compare the confidence and open clarity of Housesteads with, say, a medieval castle, whose high walls and inaccessible site are the product of a culture which at heart was both anxious and weak. The comfort and efficiency which every corner of this Roman fort speak of – the latrines, the ventilated granary, the hypocaust, the plain rational shape – is a Mediterranean import. What Northumberland itself can produce the Pennine Way has already passed at Thirlwall.

The Way retraces its steps along the Wall for about a mile as far as Rapishaw Gap, and then turns to the north again.

The Wall to Kirk Yetholm 68 miles

It is three days' walk from Hadrian's Wall to the end of the Pennine Way at Kirk Yetholm. The danger of an anti-climax is prevented by two things only. The last day is an enormous walk of at least twenty-six miles, from one end of the Cheviots to the other, in all of which there is no place of shelter or refreshment. That is a final challenge to keep one going; and once the Roman Wall has been left behind the only possible place one can stop with satisfaction is after crossing into Scotland.

You leave the Wall and move across a series of ridges towards the dark green edge of an enormous spruce forest. This is the south-eastern corner of the largest man-planted forest in Europe, which covers 300 square miles on both sides of the border. The trees, planted in 1955, have brought prosperity to an area of extreme depression, and for that reason alone are a good thing. For the walker, though, forest rides are tiresome in the extreme. The first few trees are interesting and attractive enough, but mile after mile of them becomes tedious. Those bordering the rides at least look bushy with health, but one peer into the dark inside of the wood reveals what a pole factory this is.

The forest lasts for five miles, with occasional spaces for air, after which the Way emerges on to the kind of moorland which the forest has submerged. You cross the Warks Burn and continue through a landscape of small farms, each with their patch of good green land around them, sharply divided from the darker rough pasturage on the higher ground above. Lowstead is the prettiest of all of them, hung about with roses that seem foreign here. It is six miles through this kind of country to Bellingham, a market town on the North Tyne.

The next stage is from Bellingham to Byrness in Redesdale, sixteen miles, at first over rough tussocky moor, and then coming to a second plunge into the Border Forest. Two miles before the Way disappears again between the sitka spruces, it passes a tall stone monument on Padon Hill, vaguely in the shape of a pepper-pot. This marks the place where, far from any village and the danger of persecution, the Scottish Covenanter Alexander Padon preached to the faithful who had come over the moors to hear him.

Few people have ever lived in this empty part of Northumberland, but the sheep population of the county is over one million, and it is these silly Cheviots that you are bound to meet. Just to the east is Redesdale, which with Tynedale to the south enjoyed an odd status in the Middle Ages, when they were subject to the authority of neither Scotland nor England. From the fourteenth century onwards this area became famous as a den of thieves and outlaws. From 1296, when Edward I declared war on Scotland, until 1603 there was raiding and warring all over here. The most famous fight of all was in 1388 at Otterburn, a few miles to the east, when, according to the *Ballad of Chevy Chase*, the Douglases and the Percys met to contest the hunting in the Cheviot. The end of the day left the argument unresolved, with both captains and most of their armies dead:

> Teviotdale may talk of care,
>   Northumberland may make moan;
> For two such captains as slain were there
>   On the Border shall never be known.

The Way descends through the forest, which at least smells good, to reach the Rede at Blakehopeburnhaugh, where it turns along the banks to the tiny foresters' village of Byrness. Here there is a youth hostel, a hotel and some Bed and Breakfasts.

All that is left is the last day's long and tiring push over the Cheviots. The twenty-six miles have to be done in one go, unless a high and exposed bivouac is contemplated up on the hills. In an emergency, a descent can be made to one of the farms in the valleys that wind

The kirk at Kirk Yetholm, Scotland: the end.

their way in to the Cheviot massif, but this is not to be reckoned on. There are two great challenges on the Pennine Way: to finish it at all, and to walk from Byrness to Kirk Yetholm in a single day.

It is five miles to the first arrival, the border with Scotland, which is marked by a fence. You put one foot across for the record, and then turn east along the fence, coming at Chew Green to a complicated set of overlying earthworks. These are the remains of three Roman marching camps, and a later, smaller, more permanent fortlet, built as a staging post on the great Roman artery to the north called Dere Street.

You go on along Dere Street for a while, but soon turn off it and head for Lamb Hill. The topography of the Cheviots is complicated, and although the Way follows the main watershed between England and Scotland, it is far from plain on the ground. You are enclosed by the folds in these grumpy remains of volcanic hills. Seven miles steady trudging brings you to Windy Gyle, capped by an enormous stony tumulus called Russell's Cairn. This is half-way through the long day, if the detour to the Cheviot is left out, as it should be. The moment to decide whether to do this official detour through peat as bad as anything in the Peak comes five miles after Windy Gyle on Cairn Hill. It was brutish of the Countryside Commission to include it in the official route. Will you feel you have cheated if you give it a miss?

On returning from the Cheviot (its two extra miles have nothing new to offer) you turn north, past the craggy Hen Hole, making for the rocks on top of the Schil. To get here is a great moment. It is now downhill (almost) all the way. You step decisively into Scotland, having kept to the border from Chew Green, and arrive in three miles at Burnhead, the first building since Byrness. It is now two and a half miles to the end, on a good dry road. The village and the Kirk hide behind a slight rise until the last moment, when quite un-expectedly and almost unbelievably you find yourself strolling on to the village green, where you can sit down and know you have done it all.

MAPS: OS 1:50,000 Numbers 74, 80, 86, 91, 98, 103, 109, 110

GUIDES:
Tom Stephenson, *The Pennine Way*, HMSO 1969
A. Wainwright, *Pennine Way Companion*, Westmorland Gazette 1967
C. J. Wright, *A Guide to the Pennine Way*, Constable 1967

HMSO *Guides* to the Peak District, Yorkshire Dales and Northumberland National Parks

BACKGROUND:
D. J. Breeze and Brian Dobson, *Hadrian's Wall*, Penguin 1976
Emily Brontë, *Wuthering Heights* (1847), Penguin 1965
Ted Hughes and Fay Godwin, *Remains of Elmet*, Faber 1979
Arthur Raistrick, *Monks and Shepherds in the Yorkshire Dales*, Y.D. National Park 1976
Arthur Raistrick, *West Riding of Yorkshire*, Hodder and Stoughton 1970

INFORMATION:
Pennine Way Council,
14 St Barnabas Drive,
Littleborough,
Lancashire OL15 8E7

Peak District National Park,
Aldern House,
Baslow Road,
Derbyshire DE4 1AE

The West Highland Way

Glasgow to Fort William
100 miles

The original, highly imaginative, intention was for the West Highland Way to begin in the middle of Glasgow. Unfortunately the official beginning is now at Milngavie, on the northern edge of the city. To start here though, is to distort the excellent shape of the walk, which is one of gradual extraction – from the confines of the city and then of its suburbs; from the agricultural lowland which reaches as far as Loch Lomond, and then from the picturesque scenery of the lake into the full bareness of the Highlands. Beyond Tyndrum, fifty-six miles from Glasgow, the route is almost entirely on the old military roads, which are quite impossible for cars. The hills you thread between – never climbing one – get rougher and harder, while the passes you cross get higher and the prospects revealed as you crest them more and more striking. In this way the walk gets more intense with every mile, so that as you come to the end at Fort William, with the Great Glen stretching away north-eastwards and the mountains in Ardgour, Moidart and Arisaig making the north-western horizon, it is like arriving on the brink, not at the end, of something. Why on earth stop here? Perhaps there is a reason: to be carefully led this far, with signposts marked by the special yellow thistle, is very good, but from here you can fan out, and choose your own ways through the mountains that stand so enticingly to the north. The West Highland Way is only the launch vehicle for the higher stages that can take you beyond. The launch itself must happen in Glasgow.

Geology

Dr Johnson told a Scotsman: 'Your country consists of two things, stone and water. There is, indeed, a little earth above the stone in some places, but a very little; and the stone is always appearing. It is like a man in rags; the naked skin is still peeping out.' Scotland's ragged rocks are almost universally harder and older than those in England, and break down into soil far less easily. Where England crumbles, Scotland chips. Some of the most complicated geological structures in the world are here, and there is still a large area of the Highlands which the Geological Survey has not yet mapped in detail. But to the walker the more accessible aspects of the geology are fairly clear.

On the Old Military Road as it nears Fort William: looking back at Doire Ban.

Two periods have shaped Scotland more than any other. The most recent was the Ice Age, but the first, about 400 million years ago, was the Caledonian Orogeny, when a collision of continental plates, with the thrust coming from the south-east, folded the country into ridges and troughs running south-west and north-east. The pressure and the heat associated with it transformed the old sedimentary rocks into slaty schists and quartzes. In this geological heat the material of the Highlands was tempered and hardened.

The Highlands have a very definite edge, which crosses Scotland from the Isle of Arran to Stonehaven, south of Aberdeen. This is where in the Caledonian Orogeny the rocks that form the Highlands were down-folded into a trough which has been filled by the deposits of later seas, the Old Red Sandstone, and the limestone and Coal Measures on which Glasgow is built. Interrupting this productive land just north of Glasgow are the basalt Campsie Fells and Kilpatrick Hills, both the remains of volcanoes which erupted many times about 340 million years ago.

The Highlands have an equivalent, though different, insertion, around Glen Etive, Glencoe and in Rannoch Moor and Ben Nevis. Together these make up about one thousand square miles of granite, an igneous rock which differs from basalt in having been pushed up from below, only to be revealed by later erosion, rather than pouring out from a volcanic vent.

Much of the early landscape history of Scotland is the result of heat, but the country would look nothing like it does if it were not for the Ice Ages that have occurred within the last million years. During these Scotland was mauled beyond recognition. In the southern Highlands the metamorphic rocks differ widely in hardness, which meant that erosion by glaciers was highly selective. This produced sharp hills and steep valleys, compared with the north of Scotland, where more homogeneous rock underwent the ice-treatment and emerged with a long, low, heavy profile. The entire process was more one of redistribution than removal. As the ice contracted it left a smear of unconsolidated clay, gravel and boulders which geologists call drift. Time and again on this walk you see the two elements of the Ice Ages side by side – ice-cut rock rising out of ice-dumped drift.

Roads

You could argue that the execrable state of the Highland roads ensured the continued existence of the clan system into the eighteenth century, a medieval survival. A country in which communication between one glen and its neighbour is almost impossible will inevit-

ably see isolation and petty kingdoms. After the Jacobite revolt in 1715 a programme was begun to build a system of roads through the Highlands, primarily military in purpose. After 1724, when General Wade was put in charge, the programme was hotted up and, by 1736, 250 miles of road had been built. After the Jacobite rebellion in 1745 still more were constructed, often with commercial backing too, so that by the end of the century over 1,000 miles of road had been built in Scotland. It is on many of these, now disused and grassy, that the West Highland Way goes. This communication revolution in Scotland is impressive and has been compared to the Roman achievement in road-building in Britain. But the eighteenth century suffers by the comparison. The British army took over seventy years to build a road system which at bottom was badly designed and ill-constructed. The Romans, on the other hand, had taken an astonishing two years to lay a network of far better military roads over the north of England, many of which are still in use today.

Nevertheless, and not surprisingly, the engineer responsible was proud: 'The roads on these moors', he beamed, 'are now as smooth as Constitution Hill.' The Highlanders detested them: apart from the fact that they led to the wrong places, their surface was unpleasant for the Highlanders who 'were either barefooted or wore thin brogues of untanned skin, which the gravel pierced or frayed. . . . Besides, there was for the pedestrian mile after mile of elastic heather or dry velvet turf; and even the dangers and casualties of the passage presented that excitement and variety of incident, that contrast of ease with vigorous exertion, which could not be compensated to the mountaineer by the uniform drudgery of the dusty road.' Ironically, it is exactly to this state that many of the old military roads have reverted.

Even before the end of the eighteenth century they had become almost impassable. In the 1790s the Duke of Atholl regularly took twelve hours to go the twenty miles from Dunkeld to Blair on what was meant to be a new road. Thomas Telford changed all this in the first two decades of the nineteenth century, by building a further one thousand miles of beautifully graded new roads, the basis of Scotland's modern road system. As Alexander Youngson has written: 'Telford's roads were to the old ones what a Georgian mansion is to a bothy.'

Tourism

Telford's Highland roads gave a final kick to the dying clannishness and isolation of Scotland. They acted as drains along which the surplus population could flow to Glasgow and

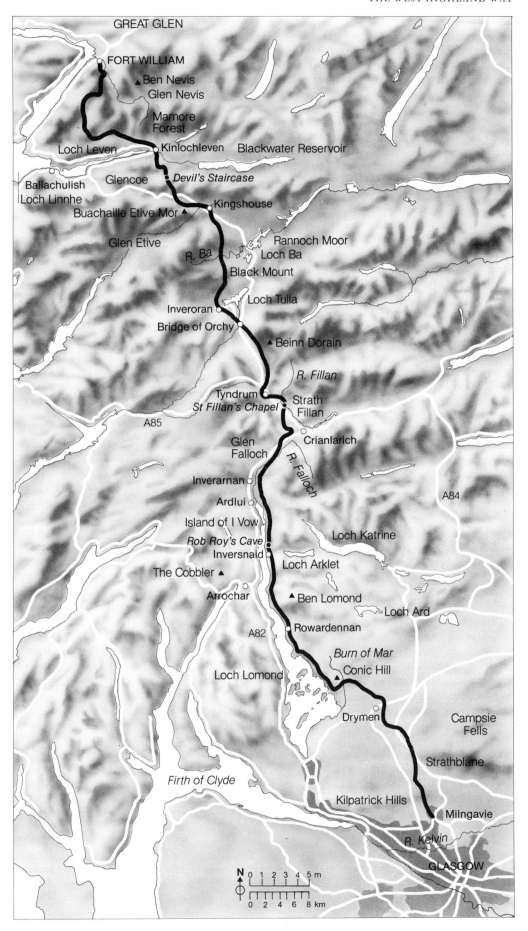

GREAT GLEN

FORT WILLIAM
▲ Ben Nevis
Glen Nevis

Mamore
Forest

Loch Leven — Kinlochleven — Blackwater Reservoir

Glencoe — *Devil's Staircase*

Ballachulish
Loch Linnhe

Kingshouse

Buachaille Etive Mor ▲

Glen Etive — Rannoch Moor

R. Ba — Loch Ba

Black Mount

Loch Tulla

Inveroran

Bridge of Orchy

▲ Beinn Dorain

R. Fillan

Tyndrum — Strath
St Fillan's Chapel — Fillan

A85 — Crianlarich

Glen
Falloch

R. Falloch

Inverarnan

Ardlui

Island of I Vow

Rob Roy's Cave — Loch Katrine
Inversnaid

The Cobbler ▲ — Loch Arklet

Arrochar — ▲ Ben Lomond — Loch Ard

A82 — Rowardennan

Burn of Mar
Conic Hill ▲

Loch Lomond — Drymen — Campsie
Fells

Strathblane

Firth of Clyde — Kilpatrick Hills — Milngavie

R. Kelvin

GLASGOW

A84

N
0 1 2 3 4 5 m

0 2 4 6 8 km

the emigration ports, and as conduits which brought visitors to see the picturesque, and rapidly emptying, scenes of the north. In the fifty years spanning the turn of the nineteenth century Scotland had a succession of famous and articulate visitors, and the way one sees Scotland now tends to be with the sharper, more selective and perhaps more superficial eye of these tourists. Between 1773 and 1818 Scottish tours were made by Johnson and Boswell, William and Dorothy Wordsworth (with Coleridge), and John Keats. They provide a spectrum of attitudes to the Highlands, all of which are relevant today.

Johnson did not make his journey to Scotland for the thrill of mountain scenery. To him mountains were a kind of negative: 'Before me, and on either side, were high hills, which by hindering the eye from ranging, forced the mind to find entertainment for itself ... The appearance is that of matter incapable of form or usefulness, dismissed by nature from her care, and disinherited of her favours, left in its original elemental state or quickened only with one sullen power of useless vegetation.' But Johnson did not dismiss Scotland as summarily as nature had: 'Regions mountainous and wild, thinly inhabited and little cultivated, make a great part of the earth, and he that has never seen them, must live unacquainted with much of the face of nature, and with one of the great scenes of human existence.' Johnson was in Scotland for information, not only about the country, but about himself: 'The phantoms which haunt a desert are want, and misery, and danger; the evils of dereliction rush in upon the thoughts; man is made unwillingly acquainted with his own weakness, and meditation shows him how little he can sustain, and how little he can perform.'

Boswell and Johnson toured on horseback. By 1803, when the Wordsworths travelled round Scotland, the roads had improved enough for them to go in a trap. Dorothy was depressed by the poverty of Highland life and by the contrast between the slovenly cottages here and the flowery gardens in Somerset. In Scotland she 'saw potatoes and cabbages, but never a honeysuckle'. To Loch Lomond, Walter Scott's 'noble lake, boasting innumerable beautiful islands, of every varying form and outline which fancy can frame', she reacted: 'I thought what a dreary waste must this lake be to such poor creatures, struggling with fatigue and poverty and unknown ways.'

But the Romantics' attitude to mountain scenery was quite different. Dorothy records in her journal that as she, her brother and Coleridge went along Loch Lomond, rather bored by the uniform appearance of its woody shores, 'at a sudden turning looking to the left,

we saw a very craggy topped mountain amongst other smooth ones; the rocks on the summit distinct in shape as if they were buildings raised up by man, or uncouth images of some strange creature. We called out with one voice, "That's what we wanted!"'

They got more and more of what they wanted the further they penetrated the Highlands. Glencoe was the high point. They actually climbed the Pap of Glencoe, an unimaginable lunacy for Johnson or Boswell, and then moved up the glen. 'Forward the greatness of the mountains overcame every other idea.' To her mind the glen was almost squeezed out of existence by the mountains on either side: 'The impression was, as we advanced to the head of this first reach, as if the glen were nothing, its loneliness and retirement – as if it made up no part of my feeling: the mountains were all in all. That which fronted us – I have forgotten its name – was exceedingly lofty, the surface stony, nay, the whole mountain was one mass of stone, wrinkled and puckered together.'

John Keats toured Scotland with his friend Charles Brown in the summer of 1818. The aim was to provide stimulating images from life, to improve his health and to escape from books. Glad to be away from the 'miasma of London' and 'hat-band ignorance' with which Windermere was tainted, Keats found he had 'an amazing partiality for mountains in clouds'. After a 'Monstrous Breakfast' every morning the two young men tramped 600 miles and rode 400 in a couple of months. Facetious letters were sent regularly back to London: 'Steam boats on Loch Lomond and Barouches on its sides take a little from the pleasure of such romantic chaps as Brown and I.' On climbing Ben Nevis: 'I have said nothing yet of getting on among the loose stones large and small sometimes on two sometimes three and stick, then four again, then two, then a jump, so that we kept on ringing changes on foot, hand, stick, jump boggle, Stumble, foot, hand, foot, (very gingerly) stick again, and then again a game at all fours.' Keats in fact was less interested in landscape than in people. 'Scenery is fine,' he had written that spring, 'but human nature is finer.'

But just as Keats was growing beyond the love of bare mountains and lochs, for most people the Scottish tourist boom was only beginning. In the same year as Keats' walking tour Sir Walter Scott published *Rob Roy*, some of which is set near Loch Lomond. This brought tourists in droves. Only four years later Dorothy Wordsworth made a second trip to Scotland, and found it changed. There were panes of glass where there had been only holes before, and carpets instead of mud floors. As she visited Rob Roy's cave, on the banks of

Loch Lomond, a piper started to play a lament. She writes: 'All crowd to Rob Roy's cave, as it is called, and pass under in uninterrupted succession, for the cave is too small to contain many at once. They stoop, yet come out all covered in dirt. We were wiser than this; for they seem to have no motive but to say they have been in Roy's cave, because Sir Walter has written about it.' This is the Scotland of the literary pilgrimage.

Midges

One practical thing must be said. Life can be made hell by midges on this walk. Everyone walking in the Highlands, from Bonnie Prince Charlie down, has been plagued by them, especially in late summer. To feel good on the West Highland Way you need a tube of anti-fly cream as much as a pair of boots.

The tower of Glasgow University rises above the trees of Kelvinside Park, a nineteenth-century improvement of the city's smart west end. The walk into the Highlands begins in the park, on the banks of the River Kelvin.

Glasgow to Drymen 18 miles

Glasgow is two cities. At the east end are the remains of some of the worst slums in Europe. Many factors combined to produce conditions of intolerable overcrowding and squalor in the nineteenth-century city. The introduction of the potato and the invention of smallpox vaccine brought a sudden and massive increase in the population of the Highlands. The disintegration of the clan structure and the conversion of many mountain square miles into sheep walks uprooted a large proportion of the Highlanders, for whom the old crofting system was becoming in any case impossible.

Glasgow, with coal and iron nearby, became the refuge for these pathetic hordes. In 1801 it contained five per cent of the population of Scotland. Fifty years later that figure had become twelve per cent. A parliamentary commissioner in 1839 commented: 'I have seen human degradation in some of the worst places, both in England and abroad, but I did not believe until I had visited the wynds of Glasgow that so large an amount of filth, crime, misery and disease existed in one spot in any civilised country.'

This is not all history. A report on Scotland's housing in 1967 commented: 'We have seen conditions in Glasgow that can be described only as appalling. Families are condemned to live in atrocious conditions which should shock the national conscience. ... We were particularly appalled at ... gutters choked with refuse of every description; burst and choked drains; heaps of uncollected garbage and rubbish; pools of stagnant and foul-smelling water – the catalogue could be extended almost indefinitely.' This is the price paid for the beautiful emptiness of the Highlands. In the 1960s there was a density in the Gorbals of about 64,000 people per square mile. The figure for an equivalent area of the Highlands was 11. The City Council has done an enormous amount to improve conditions here, and has moved many people out to tower blocks in the suburbs. The names have changed too, and officially there is no longer anywhere called the Gorbals.

The other Glasgow is west of the old city. It is here that the Way begins, on the banks of the Kelvin, as it runs through a park landscaped by Joseph Paxton in the 1850s. The streets around it, laid out in the two previous decades, are an excellent, Bath-like arrangement of crescents, circuses and terraces. The small hill around which they are wrapped is a drumlin of boulder clay, dropped by a glacier which advanced south-eastwards up the valley of the Clyde about a million years ago. The university, built on the far side of the Kelvin by Sir George Gilbert Scott between 1866 and 1870, stands on another.

The Kelvin Walkway is part of Glasgow's plan to clean up its image, a path along a riverside slip of countryside which winds into the middle of the city. It is a shame that it arrives at what has always been the smart and respectable quarter. It can hardly matter in the Gorbals that walkers or tourists are looking round the west end.

You start off along the tarmac path beside the river, which is milky with pollution and stinking. Willows hang out over it, and many bridges cross it, some grey, some red sandstone. The urban landscape becomes less genteel, and the spray-painted graffiti cover more of the walls. The well-cut lawns give way to less kempt grassy banks, and tall stone houses crowd in on either side. These too fall away and the riverside path runs through wasteland and by factories. Out here are the enormous white tower blocks of the new housing estates, into which people from the inner city were removed as part of the slum clearance programme. From the flats there is the first glimpse of the Campsie Fells away to the north.

The path leaves the river and after going

through Dawsholm Park comes out on to a dual-carriageway going north to Milngavie. This main road, lined by bungalows, but with wide grassy verges, is the Way for two miles. The only incident is after about a mile, where in a polite suburban road a notice points east to 'Roman Wall Section – 800 yards on left in cemetery'. This mile-long detour is rewarded only by the sight of two bits of the Antonine Wall's stone base. Above foundation-level it was made entirely of turf. Hadrian's Wall was abandoned almost as soon as it was completed, in 138, for this new Forth–Clyde line 100 miles to the north. Strategically the new line was much the better, stretching only thirty-seven miles from sea to sea. Nonetheless it is quite extraordinary that the enormous effort put into the first frontier should so casually have been wasted. The familiar subjection of foreign policy to domestic politics may have been behind it. Both Caesar and Claudius had authorised their invasions of Britain in order to make a good impression at home. The new emperor, Antoninus Pius, a philosopher rather

than a soldier, was Hadrian's adopted son but lacked the prestige that would make his place on the imperial throne secure. A short campaign in Britain, a slight stretching of the empire, and an extravagant celebration in Rome of the triumph, would be all that was needed. The Roman army moved north in enormous numbers in about AD 140. No mistakes were to be made, and the new wall was greatly overmanned, with almost no reduction in the size of the frontier garrison, even though it was only half the length of the old one.

In 163, only twenty years after it was built, the Antonine Wall was finally abandoned and the first frontier reoccupied. Rome was under no military pressure at the time, and it seems the abandonment of the northern wall, now almost entirely forgotten, was simply a recognition that its construction had been a political and not a military move in the first place. The whole short history of the Antonine Wall was one of irrelevance.

Houses are continuous all the way from

Glasgow to the far side of Milngavie, but the town still preserves an identity. Its centre has been recently, and very well, pedestrianised with neat cobbles. For those uninterested in the idea of walking out of a great industrial city into the Highlands, Milngavie (said Mulguy) will be the place to start the West Highland Way. Trains and buses come regularly from Glasgow.

Like the Kelvin out of Glasgow, the Allander Water leads out of Milngavie to the north, not milky but peat brown, past a middle-class suburb and its golf club. Beyond this you are into the rural lowlands, soon entering the broadleaves of Mugdock Wood, through which a good level ride takes you north. Just to the east is Mugdock Reservoir, the first monument to Glasgow's health, opened by Queen Victoria in 1859. Fifty million gallons of water a day flowed from here through thirty-four miles of tunnel to the centre of the city.

Beyond Mugdock Wood the Way follows the western shore of Craigallian Loch, beyond which the volcanic bottle-neck hill of Dumgoyne sticks above the trees. Skirting another small loch the path climbs a slight rise to a main road, just beyond which is the first major arrival of the walk. Looking north through the gap made by Strathblane in the lowland foreground hills you see the mountains around Loch Lomond, Conic Hill and Ben Lomond, which at last give a real promise of a Highland Way.

Past some Bronze Age standing stones and the woody knoll of Duntreath Hill, the Way drops to Blane Water, and turns up along a dismantled railway, whose course is now taken by a pipeline bringing water from Loch Lomond. A distillery on one side and an abandoned hospital on the other are inserted into this sheep-farming landscape. The Way leaves the old railway and crosses a branch of the Endrick Water, from where it is just over two miles to Drymen on country lanes. (This can all be safely be called countryside, a word which will sound quite wrong when you are in the Highlands themselves.)

As you come to Drymen the lane is on a high ridge and you get the first sight of Loch Lomond to the west, studded with islands and backed by blue mountains. Drymen itself is on lower ground and loses the view. It is a village of red sandstone, with some excellent and discreet modern buildings by the green, as well

Craigallian Loch, north of Milngavie. Behind are the Strathblane Hills, the accumulated lava of many ancient eruptions, and on the left the distinctive outline of Dumgoyne, a plug of solidified magma which once filled the neck of a volcano that has been eroded away.

as two pubs. The lights of Clydeside can be seen to the south at night.

Drymen to Inversnaid 20 miles

Drymen is the frontier post of the Lowlands. The Way climbs north from the village and into Garadhban Forest. It is about three miles through the larch and spruce, until you emerge at its north-west corner. A steeple of a stile crosses the ten-foot-high deer fence which separates the forest from the first Scottish moor. Here is the Highland edge, running down the far side of Conic Hill, whose peaked ridge is immediately in front of you. But the hill itself is not the first outcrop of the Highland rocks. It is where the red lowland sandstone and conglomerates have been pushed up by the fault into an unfamiliar peak themselves.

You come to the Burn of Mar across springy heather, where the water is clear and brown over the pale stone bed, with rowan and birch by it. This is the kind of place, on a sunny day, where simply to lie down and sleep seems so much better than the sweat and tramp of getting on with it. But then there is a choice.

The official Way climbs Conic Hill and drops on the far side to the shore of Loch Lomond, which it follows as much as possible to Rowardennan and Inversnaid. For quite long stretches, at least as far as Rowardennan, you are right next to the lochside road, if not actually on it. It has been reckoned that on a good summer day 40,000 people come to Loch Lomond, and the road is busy and unpleasant.

The other way is better, but harder. It keeps to the high ground, high above the loch and its woody islands, all through the heather and bilberry. If you are lucky, towards the end of the summer you will see the sheep being taken off these hillsides. This is always good to watch, the lithe, intelligent manoeuvres of the dogs, and the sheep's stupid blundering. The flock slowly moves down the hill, like a liquid, a white puddle pushed reluctantly along.

There is no good path along the top; on a hot day there is no shade and many flies. If this

Loch Lomond and the Luss Hills: Dorothy Wordsworth realised 'what a dreary waste must this lake be to such poor creatures, struggling with fatigue and poverty and unknown ways.'

all gets too much, you can easily drop off down the hill, exchanging the view of Ben Lomond to the north for the shade and fine grass of the oakwoods below. Loch Lomond is really two lakes joined together. There is the wide, relatively shallow and island-full lowland lake at the southern end, dammed up behind the leavings of a glacier that was here as recently as 12,000 years ago; and at the northern, Highland end is a narrow, deep trench – over 600 feet deep in one place – which was cut by an earlier glacier that came off a great ice-sheet on Rannoch Moor. Remnants of the pre-glacial pattern can be traced at the top of the loch, where water coming down what is now Inveruglas Water on the west once flowed straight across to Loch Arklet on the other side. This river would have been 500 feet above the present surface of Loch Lomond. Added to the loch depth of 600 feet, that makes 1,100 feet of rock excavated and removed by the glacier.

There is a good hotel and a youth hostel at Rowardennan, as well as an occasional ferry over to Inverbeg on the far side of the loch. A good track leads beyond it through woods for seven and a half miles to Inversnaid, climbing slightly and then dropping again to near the lake shore. In gaps in the trees are views over to the Arrochar Alps and the Cobbler.

You are walking through Rob Roy country. He was born in 1671, a member of the dispossessed Clan Gregor, who, after his cattle droving business had collapsed, turned protection racketeer at the expense of the Lowland farmers. Since the Macgregors were the people who had carried out most of the raids anyway, Rob Roy was collecting easy money. His home base was in the triangle of land between Loch Lomond, Loch Ard and Loch Katrine, rough Highland country, but conveniently near the lowland cattle. That this kind of lifestyle could exist at all is indicative of the breakdown of old Highland society, in which raiding of course was a way of life, but to which the whole idea of a cash-relationship between raider and raided was quite foreign. Rob Roy apparently looked rather odd. He was covered in red hair all over (Roy means red) and, according to a story the Wordsworths were told, his arms were so long he could pull up his socks without bending over. He died, after 'playing mony a daft reik', in his own bed in Balquhidder in 1734.

You come suddenly to Inversnaid, crossing above the waterfall for which it is famous, and which was produced when the Loch Lomond glacier cut through the Inveruglas-Arklet river, reversing its flow here. Three-quarters of a mile up the road is the Garrison of Inversnaid, an outpost built here in 1713, right in the middle of Macgregor country, in an attempt to control them. It became redundant after the 1750s when they were finally dealt with, and is now a ruin, used as a sheep-fold.

Inversnaid to Tyndrum 18 miles

Up the last half of Loch Lomond is very rough going, over boulders and slippery schists, but it is better than either the main road on the other side (which you can get to by ferry from Inversnaid) or the high route along the crags above, so this is the way to go. It is about six and a half miles to Inverarnan at the top of the loch, and might easily take you three hours to get there. For all this, it is good. Keats thought Loch Lomond 'grand in excess' at this end, and you have to be in the right mood to appreciate its almost Norwegian style. Soon after Inversnaid you reach Rob Roy's Cave (it has CAVE painted largely on it), which is in fact no more than a crack in the rock. It is also called Robert the Bruce's Cave. In the middle of the loch is the Island of I Vow, with the ruin of what might be a sixteenth-century castle on it. This probably belonged to the Macfarlanes, the clan on the far side of the loch, and enemies of the Macgregors on this. Dr Johnson, like everyone else, took to a boat to see the islands of Loch Lomond. This was a mistake: 'The islets which court the gazer at a distance, disgust him at his approach, when he finds, instead of soft lawns and shady thickets, nothing more than uncultivated ruggedness.' In fact, I Vow in spring is covered in daffodils, which do not grow wild round here. The flowers may have been planted by the monks of the monastery which is said once to have been here, and of which every other trace has disappeared.

Soon you come to the ruined farm of Doune, and beyond it a faint path leads on past the still-occupied Ardleish and the little loch Dubh Lochan, bringing you to the woods at the bottom of Glen Falloch. A railway, a very busy road and the River Falloch all crowd into this beautiful and noisy glen. The way is on the east bank of the river for three miles until you reach the farm of Derrydaroch, where you cross river, road and then railway to get on to the old military road, which, like all of those used by the West Highland Way, was built after Major William Caulfield had taken over from General Wade as the officer in charge of Scottish roads. On the damp remains of his road you head on up Glen Falloch, more open now that you are out of the trees by the river. On the far side of the glen, under Sron Gharbh, are a few scraggy Scots pines, remains of the old Caledonian Forest that covered the Highlands after the Ice Ages. Burning, felling and sheep can be blamed for the forest's failure to regenerate.

The old road comes to the top of Glen
Falloch just to the west of Crianlarich, where
three glens meet – Glen Dochart, Glen Falloch
and Strath Fillan. It is a skeletal place, with all
the necessary services – railway station, hotel,
post office, police station, mountain rescue
post, teas, youth hostel – but very little else to
flesh out those bones. This is typical of
Scotland. In England around such an array
there would be an immediate gathering of
people and their houses, which would turn the
place into a town. In Scotland the people have
moved off – or have been moved off – to
Canada, New Zealand or Glasgow. It is
shocking to realise that these bare hills and
valleys, although never crawling with people,
are now bare because of the nineteenth-century
clearances.

The Way is up Strath Fillan for about six
miles to Tyndrum, at first through a young
forestry plantation, then coming down to the
River Fillan, where on a shelf above are the
farm of Kirkton and the chapel of St Fillan, an
eighth-century wandering saint. Robert the
Bruce after being helped in battle by the relic of
Fillan's arm, built a priory here in the
fourteenth century, and the one or two bits of
masonry still standing are from this. Tyndrum
is two miles beyond it, a settlement with the
same spare and rather temporary atmosphere
as Crianlarich. Tyndrum was once a centre of
lead mining, in a particularly high quality vein
to the south-west of the town, where ore was
mined from 1741 to 1862 which yielded up to
half its weight in lead. Queen Victoria thought
it 'a wild, picturesque and desolate spot' when
she passed through in 1875.

Tyndrum to Glencoe 19 miles

At Tyndrum the West Highland Way at last
gets into its stride and you into yours. From
here to Fort William there is no twisting and
turning to avoid roads. The Way is clear on the
ground and firm underfoot, needs no navigation and is free of other travellers. You can
put the map away. A track leads up by the side
of the village shop, the last before Kinlochleven. This is the old road to Glencoe, made
redundant by the new A82. You climb to a
narrow pass, through which the railway and
the other road squeeze too, and then drop
down the eastern side of the glen to the square-
edged plantation in front. Ahead is the great

*The West Highland Railway climbs Glen Falloch from
the head of Loch Lomond. On the far side of the glen are
a few tattered remains of the Great Caledonian Forest
with which the Highlands were once blanketed, but which
human clearance and sheep have almost entirely destroyed.*

bare cone of Beinn Dorain. Beneath it the railway makes a wide horseshoe loop into Auch Gleann. A viaduct straight across would have been better, but more expensive. This railway was built as cheaply as possible in 1894, and the economies made these long, rather elegant diversions a necessity. To build the railway at all was an achievement – it crosses the worst horrors of Rannoch Moor, where all the materials had to be brought by pack-horse – but these sharp bends mean that trains can never go faster than forty miles an hour.

Where the railway loops you go straight across, over the Allt Chonoghais by the repaired eighteenth-century bridge built by Major Caulfield, and then on to the gravelly track which in three easy miles brings you to Bridge of Orchy. This too is scarcely half a place, little more than the railway station and a fishing hotel. It stands at the mouth of Glen Orchy, a long, dark and forest-filled valley, going south-west to the sea at Loch Awe.

Beinn Dorain. At Auch, hidden by the trees, the Kings of Scotland had a hunting lodge.

You go over the bridge at Bridge of Orchy and up into forestry on the now heathery and boggy military road, climbing with one zig-zag to a slight ridge. This barely discernible track has been scheduled as an ancient monument. As you near the top you get one of the best experiences that walking provides. The new prospect does not open smoothly, but as your naturally bobbing step brings you over the old horizon a new one is jerkily revealed. Immediately below in trees is the white Inveroran Hotel, and to the right the end of Loch Tulla. On the far shore is a spread of trees, some of them Scots pines left over from the Caledonian Forest. All this is foreground; over to the north and west is a stand of dark mountains, Stob Ghabhar, Stob a Bhruaich Leith, Stob Coir'an Albannaich, their bodies as craggy as their names, and a different world from the smoothness of Beinn Dorain and the hills above Crianlarich. To the north-west you are looking at the massive plutonic plug of the Glen Etive granite.

The Wordsworths called in for breakfast at the Inveroran Hotel on their way south from Glencoe and found 'the butter not eatable, the barley-cakes fusty, the oatbread so hard I could

not chew it, and there were only four eggs in the house, which they had boiled as hard as stones.' This was in the front room. Out at the back things were more homely: 'About seven or eight travellers, probably drovers, with as many dogs, were sitting in a complete circle round a large peat fire in the middle of the floor, each with a mess of porridge, in a wooden vessel, on his knee. ... There was nothing uncomfortable. ... Happy, busy, or vacant faces, all looked pleasant; and even the smoky air, being a sort of natural indoor atmosphere of Scotland, served only to give a softening, I may say harmony, to the whole.' The same house is still a hotel, for fishermen rather than drovers, and the breakfasts here now are the best in Scotland.

The ten-mile morning from Inveroran to the Kingshouse Hotel at the top of Glencoe is the best on the walk. You can go either on the old Glencoe road, a gravel track, or on the Military Road, which takes a slightly higher line and is just a thin sheep path now through thick rough grasses. Only the occasional culvert over a stream shows that this is a made road. In the nineteenth century 70,000 sheep a year would be driven south down this route.

As you climb up to Black Mount you can look back south along yesterday's glen to the Crianlarich Hills. It is good when cloud shuts the landscape in at the level of the mountain summits; it is like walking in an egg-box. But if the day is clear it can be even better. To bot south and north you are looking at hills wit hills behind them. In one direction you kno that all you can see you have been through, i the other you know that all of it is yet to b done. This is a powerful idea, focussing th entire landscape to the present step. At times can make you feel that it is you who a spinning the world with your feet.

At Ba Bridge, four miles from Inveroran, the river Ba, which comes from the Corrie I in the west and runs down over tilted jagge strata to Rannoch Moor. In *Kidnapped* Dav Balfour tells how he and Alan Breck, on tl run from English soldiers, arrive on the edg

Kirkton Farm by St Fillan's Chapel in Strath Fillan. Fillan was an eighth-century Irishman whose relics brought Robert the Bruce victory at Bannockburn. In th distance are the Crianlarich Hills.

of the moor: 'The mist rose and died away, and showed us that country lying as waste as the sea; only the moorfowls and peewees crying upon it, and far over to the east, a herd of deer moving like dots. Much of it was red with heather, much of the rest broken up with bogs and hags and peaty pools; some had been burnt black in a heath fire; and in another place there was quite a forest of dead firs, standing like skeletons. A wearier-looking desert man never saw; but at least it was clear of troops, which was our point.'

The track – rather stony now – continues after Ba Bridge, rising slightly to the top of a ridge, where the head of Glencoe is revealed, guarded on either side by the two solid gateposts of Beinn a Chrulaiste and the far greater mass of Buachaille Etive Mor – the Great Herdsman of Etive. This wrinkled block of granite divides the two glacial channels of Glencoe and Glen Etive, both smoothed and deepened by tongues of ice that slid out from the ice sheet on Rannoch Moor.

Looking east from Glencoe on to Rannoch Moor: it does not seem long since the Ice Age here.

From the top it is two miles past Blackrock Cottage and below a set of modern ski-lifts to the Kingshouse Hotel, another drover's stop-over. It has come up in the world since the Wordsworths stayed here, when 'The first thing we saw on entering the door was two sheep hung up, as if just killed from the barren moor, their bones hardly sheathed in flesh.' Dorothy and William, like everyone else coming to Glencoe, 'had been prepared for images of terror, had expected a deep, den-like valley with overhanging rocks'. But the valley is not like that. It is big, open to the sky, its superb mountains drawn back on either side. There is no 'giddy prospect of the raving stream' here. For all but one night of its history Glencoe has been the scene of pastoral farming, the conditions not particularly harsh as the Western Highlands go, and the inhabitants until the eighteenth century only a little more brutal and rapacious than most in their raiding and cattle-rustling. Like everywhere else in the Highlands, Glencoe became over-populated towards the end of the eighteenth century and was forcibly emptied in the nineteenth. The only real difference between the landscape now and immediately after the

evictions is the A82, built in 1933 despite screams of protest (it was called 'a million-pound racetrack') and now in summer incessantly busy.

But that one night, in fact the early morning of 13 February 1692, is what the name Glencoe means. At 5 a.m. – a blizzard was blowing – the officers and men of a company of Argyll's regiment, who had been billeted with the Macdonalds of Glencoe for twelve days, set about massacring their hosts. They were peculiarly inefficient; only thirty-eight were killed out of an adult male population of 150, although the same number may have died later of cold and starvation. The snow may have hindered the soldiers; their relative ignorance of the terrain certainly did. They failed to block off the passes going south over the mountains to Glen Etive and into Appin, and the Macdonalds escaped across them. There is evidence that the sense of shock felt by the world at the massacre – later whipped up by Jacobite propaganda – was felt by the soldiers

Glencoe is open to the sky, its mountains drawn back on either side.

themselves. They were all Campbells, the traditional feud-enemies of the Macdonalds, but were nonetheless Highlanders, and may have balked at breaking the hospitality laws of the clans. This taboo may have saved many of the Macdonalds' lives.

Why did the massacre happen? There was the inevitable legal excuse: MacIain, the chief of the Glencoe Macdonalds, had failed to deliver an oath of allegiance to William III by the time appointed, 1 January 1692. This was partly due to the purely practical difficulties of travelling in the Highlands in the middle of winter. He finally delivered it five days late. This technical rebellion, against a background, admittedly, of actual rebellion, was interpreted literally by the government, in the person of the Secretary of State for Scotland, the Master of Stair. (In the constitutional fiction of the time William III knew nothing about the massacre until after it was over.) Stair's intention may have been simply to kill the Macdonalds to encourage the others, but he was definitely in contact with the leaders of their enemies, the enormous Clan Campbell. They provided a reservoir of stored-up resentment which could be turned to ready

*Blackrock Cottage at the head of Glencoe, with the
pyramidal bulk of Buachaille Etive Mor behind.*

TOP RIGHT *Loch Leven winds out to sea between Beinn
na Caillich on the right, and on the left the still sharper
Pap of Glencoe.*

RIGHT *Bridge over the River Etive and the length of
Glen Etive behind it.*

use. The commander of the detachment sent to Glencoe was Robert Campbell of Glenlyon, a drunk and bankrupt dissolute, whose land had been heavily raided by the Glencoe Macdonalds only a few years before. This was the blunt tool the Master of Stair was prepared to use. It is Stair's words, though, in a letter sent to the commander of the garrison at Fort William, that are the most chilling of all. 'You cannot receive further directions,' he wrote from Kensington Palace on 30 January 1692. 'Be as earnest in the matter as you can; be secret and sudden, be quick.'

Glencoe to Fort William 25 miles

From the Kingshouse you cross the river on an arched iron bridge and start to move off down into Glencoe. The breadth of it, the sheer solid size of the mountains on either side, visibly hard and shaped with difficulty, means there is no sense of enclosure. If you share the Wordsworthian view of mountain nature as masculine and dominant, in Glencoe the real thing and the pre-conception for once coincide in a confident, bullish plainness. Two and a half miles from the Kingshouse, at a farm called Altnafeadh, a stony track, the same military road, leads up from the glen bottom, in a zigzagging climb of over 800 feet up the Devil's Staircase. This was the way that the 400 reinforcements came on the morning of the massacre, but hours too late, at about eleven o'clock. The snow may have delayed them, but it may have been a deliberate move by the commander of the contingent to keep all the blood on the hands of Robert Campbell of Glenlyon. The view from the top is wonderful: into Glencoe, and up a smooth, rounded gap in the mountains on the far side, called Lairig Gartain, that runs through to Glen Etive.

The way onwards, about 8 miles to Kinlochleven, is as high as the West Highland Way ever gets, over 1,800 feet at the pass. From there it is good, fast walking, with the Mamore Range opening in front at one moment, a clutch of mountains, their summits running into ridges and other summits. To the left is Ben Nevis, the last of this 'field of great, wild and houseless mountains'. In December 1644 the thirty-two-year-old Montrose shepherded an army over this pass on its way back from raiding the Campbells at Inveraray. In an amazing feat of generalship he took them on north over passes through the Mamores to Loch Ness, where he arrived at the end of January the next year. This was about 100 miles of midwinter marching.

The eight-mile long Blackwater reservoir, laid along the foot of the mountains in front, was built between 1905 and 1909 to produce a constant head of pressure for the hydroelectric turbines in Kinlochleven below. These produced the enormous amounts of electricity needed for the conversion of alumina into aluminium. The building of the reservoir took 3,000 navvies at sixpence an hour, thirty shillings a week. In all weathers they used to cross by this pass to the Kingshouse, where they would get drunk. Some would collapse on the way back, or get lost, and their bodies would be found only when the snow melted in the spring.

The way down to Kinlochleven is along a steep but roundabout service road, and then alongside the six fat black iron barrels, down which the water comes from the reservoir. For this last part the pipes drop nearly a thousand feet in less than a mile. You arrive at the long white sheds of the aluminium plant, with a row of fans spinning in the walls. The town of Kinlochleven is entirely dependent on this factory, and now that a bridge has been built across the mouth of Loch Leven no traffic comes all the way round through here, and it is a quiet place. With two thousand inhabitants, it is by far the largest concentration of people you have come to since the Lowlands.

From Kinlochleven to Fort William is fifteen miles. A steep climb from the head of Loch Leven is through birch and mountain ash, and reveals now and then the length of the loch, the water in it winding out to the sea past steep promontories. Above it is the sharp quartzite nipple of the Pap of Glencoe. At the top you arrive at another bald valley called Lairigmor, the great pass. The track rolls along it, rising and falling as a single grey ribbon over the brown-green nudity of it all. If you shout here you will get a five-times echo. You pass a couple of cottages, one complete, one ruined, where sheep stroll in and out of the rooms.

The glen turns a sharp corner about six miles from Kinlochleven, but even now the end – the Great Glen – is still hidden. The track goes through a patch of forestry, and then out on to a tarmac road. To the west here is the deeply scored hillside above Lochan Lunn da Bhra, where a water bull lives. It emerges from time to time to browse with real cows before enticing one of them back into the lake with him.

The West Highland Way now turns northeast through forestry to cross over into Glen Nevis, and make its way along the level floor of the glen to Fort William. This is about seven miles. A more direct, and easier, way is to

TOP RIGHT *A pair of Scottish Blackface crop beside Lochan Lunn da Bhra.*

RIGHT *A landscape of eviction: near Fort William.*

The Old Military Road begins to drop towards Glen Mor and the end of the walk at Fort William.

continue on the military road, now with a tarmac surface, for only four miles before it reaches the end. You drop gently into land that is more agricultural than any since Drymen. The view northwestwards is of big, pointed mountains. Over the fields to the east is Ben Nevis, a monstrously elephantine block of grey and red granite. On the lane there are some steep down and ups, and a short stretch along a valley desecrated by three separate wires and their attendant pylons, before you come over the top of a ridge – the last of those revealing moments which so characterise this walk – to find the wide shallow strath of the Great Glen going away to the north-east. This long valley has been dredged by ice to the depth of 2,000 feet along the line of a fault which may still be on the move. Scotland to the north-west of it has so far moved sixty-five miles in relation to the rest of Britain. The process is not easy. The earth rarely snaps, and the geologists' term for this kind of movement, a wrench-fault, gives an idea of the twisting and tearing involved. The shattering of the rock in a wide band on either side of the fault made the glacier's removal job easy.

You come down to Fort William, a bruisingly loud and trafficky place. This is as it should be: Fort William, since its foundation by General Monck in the 1650s, has always been foreign to the Highlands it was built to control. Traffic has always been its business, not least in the nineteenth century when it became the biggest of the ports from which the Highlanders emigrated to the New World.

MAPS: OS 1:50,000 Numbers 41, 50, 56, 57, 64

GUIDES:
Robert Aitken, *The West Highland Way*, HMSO 1980 (complete with a good map)
Tom Hunter, *A guide to the West Highland Way*, Constable 1979

BACKGROUND:
David Daiches, *Glasgow*, André Deutsch 1977
Frank Fraser Darling and J.M.Boyd, *The Highlands and Islands*, Collins 1964
Samuel Johnson, *A Journey to the Western Islands of Scotland* (1775), OUP 1924
John Keats, *Letters*, edited by M.B.Forman, OUP 1947
John Prebble, *The Highland Clearances*, Secker and Warburg 1963
John Prebble, *Glencoe: the Story of the Massacre*, Secker and Warburg 1966
Sir Walter Scott, *Rob Roy*, 1818
Robert Louis Stevenson, *Kidnapped*, 1886
John Thomas, *The West Highland Railway*, 2nd edition, Pan 1970
J.B.Whitlow, *Geology and Scenery in Scotland*, Penguin 1977
Dorothy Wordsworth, *Recollections of a Tour made in Scotland AD 1803*, James Thin 1974
Alexander Youngson, *After the Forty-Five*, Edinburgh University Press 1973

INFORMATION:
Scottish Tourist Board,
23 Ravelston Terrace,
Edinburgh EH4 3EU

TOP LEFT *Ben Nevis: elephantine granite.*

BOTTOM LEFT *Lochan Lunn da Bhra near Fort William.*

Bibliography

Classic English Travel Literature

William Camden, *Britannia*, 1586
William Cobbett, *Rural Rides*, 1830, Penguin 1967
Daniel Defoe, *A Tour through the Whole Island of Great Britain*, 1724–6, Penguin 1967
Celia Fiennes, *The Journeys of Celia Fiennes*, edited by C. Morris, The Cresset Press 1947
John Leland, *Itinerary*, 1534–43
J. B. Priestley, *English Journey*, Heinemann/Gollancz 1934

Modern Studies

William Addison, *Understanding English Place-names*, Batsford 1978
Alec Clifton-Taylor, *The Pattern of English Building*, 2nd edition, Faber 1972
David Daiches and John Flower, *Literary Landscapes of the British Isles*, Paddington Press 1979
H. C. Darby (editor), *A New Historical Geography of England*, Cambridge 1973
Margaret Drabble, *A Writer's Britain*, Thames and Hudson 1979
Dorothy Eagle and Hilary Carnell, *The Oxford Literary Guide to the British Isles*, OUP 1977
Eilert Ekwall, *The Concise Oxford Dictionary of English Place-names*, 4th edition, OUP 1960
J. G. Evans, *The Environment of Early Man in Britain*, Elek 1975
Richard Fitter (and others), *The Wild Flowers of Britain and Northern Europe*, Collins 1974
J. Forde-Johnson, *Hillforts of the Iron Age in England and Wales*, Liverpool 1976
Sir Cyril Fox, *Personality of Britain*, University of Wales 1943
Sir Cyril Fox, *Life and Death in the Bronze Age*, Routledge 1959
Jacquetta Hawkes, *A Land*, The Cresset Press 1951
Jacquetta Hawkes, *A Guide to the Prehistoric and Roman Monuments in England and Wales*, 2nd edition, Chatto and Windus 1973
Hermann Heinzel (and others), *The Birds of Britain and Europe*, Collins 1972
W. G. Hoskins, *The Making of the English Landscape*, Hodder and Stoughton 1955
H. R. Loyn, *The Vikings in Britain*, Batsford 1977
Gordon Manley, *Climate and the British Scene*, Collins 1952
Nikolaus Pevsner (and others), *The Buildings of England*, Penguin 1951–74
A. L. F. Rivet, *Town and Country in Roman Britain*, Hutchinson 1964
Trevor Rowley, *Villages in the Landscape*, Dent 1978
F. M. Stenton, *Anglo-Saxon England*, OUP 1943
Christopher Taylor, *Fields in the English Landscape*, Dent 1975
Christopher Taylor, *Roads and Tracks of Britain* Dent 1979
A. E. Trueman, *Geology and Scenery in England and Wales*, 2nd edition, Penguin 1971

Walking

John Hillaby, *Journey through Britain*, Constable 1968
Morris Marples, *Shanks's Pony*, Dent 1959
Edwin Valentine Mitchell (editor), *The Pleasures of Walking*, Loring and Mussey 1934 (includes essays by Leslie Stephen, Max Beerbohm, Dickens, Hazlitt, Belloc, Trevelyan, Thoreau, etc.)

Information

The Countryside Commission produces leaflets on all its designated paths. The Government Book-shops sell guides to all the National Parks, and to the Countryside Commission's paths, in addition to the twenty volumes of the *British Regional Geology* and many fascinating Forestry Commission Booklets. The Ramblers' Association publishes a series of *Fact Sheets* about equipment, maps and the paths themselves, as well as more technical ones about the legal and practical aspects of maintaining footpaths. Its most invaluable publication is the *Bed, Breakfast and Bus Guide*, which is updated every year.

Addresses

Commons, Open Spaces and Footpaths Preservation Society,
25A Bell Street,
Henley-on-Thames,
Oxfordshire

Countryside Commission,
John Dower House,
Crescent Place,
Cheltenham, Gloucestershire GL50 2RA
(Welsh office: 8 Broad Street, Newtown, Powys)

Countryside Commission for Scotland,
Battleby,
Redgorton,
Perth PH1 3EW

Long Distance Walkers' Association,
Beeches Hill House,
Bishops Waltham,
Hampshire

The National Trust,
42 Queen Anne's Gate,
London SW1H 9AS

The National Trust for Scotland,
5 Charlotte Square,
Edinburgh EH2 4DU

The Ramblers' Association,
1/5 Wandsworth Road,
London SW8

Government Bookshops:

258 Broad Street, Birmingham BM1 2HE
Southey House, Wine Street, Bristol BS1 2BQ
41 The Hayes, Cardiff CF1 1JW
13a Castle Street, Edinburgh EH2 3AR
49 High Holborn, London WC1V 6HB
Brazennose Street, Manchester M60 8AS

Index

Properties owned by the National Trusts, or areas where the Trusts have considerable holdings, are marked by an asterisk. Numbers in italics refer either to a picture or to a caption on those pages. Counties are abbreviated as follows:

Berkshire: *Berks.*
Borders: *Bord.*
Buckinghamshire: *Bucks.*
Central Highland: *Centr.*
Cornwall: *Corn.*
County Durham: *Dur.*
Cumbria: *Cumb.*
Derbyshire: *Derbs.*
Devon: *Dev.*
Dorset: *Dor.*
Gloucestershire: *Glos.*
Hampshire: *Hants.*
Hereford and Worcester: *Heref. & Worcs.*
Hertfordshire: *Herts.*
Highland: *Highl.*
Lancashire: *Lancs.*
Leicestershire: *Leics.*
Northumberland: *Northumb.*
Oxfordshire: *Ox.*
Pembrokeshire: *Pembs.*
Shropshire: *Salop.*
Somerset: *Som.*
Staffordshire: *Staffs.*
Strathclyde: *Strath.*
Surrey: *Sur.*
Sussex: *Suss.*
Wiltshire: *Wilts.*
Yorkshire: *Yorks.*

Other counties are not abbreviated.

283